Contents

Introduction

Citizenship education

■ About . . . this book

This book is primarily written for students studying for the OCR GCSE courses in Citizenship Studies; however, the materials provided are also suitable for inclusion in other citizenship courses. It covers the full content specification for OCR's Short and Full courses in Citizenship Studies, as well as the national Key Stage 4 Citizenship Programme of Study.

The numbers at the foot of each right-hand page identify those parts of the OCR specification covered in each double-page spread.

Content   The book contains twelve main chapters, each divided into a number of separate topics. The topics are self-standing, and may be taught or studied in any order. Each topic usually begins with a case study, followed by:

- questions for discussion and analysis
- explanations and background detail
- definitions of key words and concepts.

The questions are designed to encourage students to think about the issue concerned, to discuss it with others, to develop a viewpoint, and to be able to defend this view with reason and evidence. In some cases, it may be difficult to take one side or the other; often *both* sides have their own strengths and weaknesses. In this situation students will be given credit for explaining why an argument is finely balanced and for pointing out the key issues upon which the problem rests.

Most of the cases used in this book are based on real life events. Where possible, we have given details in the teacher's resource of the verdicts and outcomes. The teacher's resource also gives answers to the questions raised in each topic, along with detailed guidance on all aspects of the OCR Citizenship Studies course.

■ About . . . citizenship education

Citizenship education tries to give people the skills and knowledge to help them better understand what goes on in society. Good citizenship education provides people with an understanding of those areas of law, politics and economics that affect our everyday lives in a way that helps them make more sense of the complicated world in which we live. Good citizenship education takes place in a setting that provides opportunities for discussion, practical action and enquiry.

■ About . . . OCR GCSE Citizenship Studies

OCR GCSE Citizenship Studies is available as both Short and Full GCSE courses. The Short Course is equivalent to half a GCSE.

The Short Course The GCSE Short Course is made up of two units:

- Unit A341: *Rights and Responsibilities – Getting Started as an Active Citizen*
- Unit A342: *Identity, Democracy and Justice – Understanding our Role as Citizens.*

Unit A341 is assessed through a school-based assignment in which students are required to develop a *citizenship campaign*, designed to influence others, bring about change or to resist unwanted change.

The subject of the campaign will be either an issue provided by OCR or a topic chosen under guidance from the teacher. The themes will be drawn from the topics covered in Unit 341, and will generally be related to rights and responsibilities in the family, at school and in the wider society. Working with others, students will be expected to:

- identify a suitable issue
- collect and analyse evidence surrounding the issue
- outline the existing position and their own point of view
- explain why a campaign is needed
- plan their campaign
- run their campaign
- evaluate their campaign.

Students must provide evidence of how they planned and managed their campaign and a written report of their evaluation. The controlled assessment is worth 60 per cent of the Short Course marks and 30 per cent for the Full Course.

Unit A342 is assessed by examination, worth 40 per cent of the Short Course marks and 20 per cent for the Full Course. It is one hour long and is made up of 17 questions: a mixture of short answer questions, questions requiring a longer written response, questions asking students to analyse and evaluate case studies, and one piece of extended writing.

The Full Course The GCSE Full Course is made up of two further units, which are an extension of those making up the Short Course:

- Unit A343: *Rights and Responsibilities – Extending our Knowledge and Understanding*
- Unit A344: *Identity, Democracy and Justice – Leading the Way as an Active Citizen.*

Unit A343 is assessed by an examination worth 20 per cent of the Full Course marks. It is an hour long and made up of nine questions, requiring a mixture of short and long answers and analysis and interpretation of documents.

Unit A344 is assessed by a controlled assessment, worth 30 per cent of the total marks. This is a school-based assignment in two parts: a) *citizenship enquiry* based on a selection of source materials in a booklet supplied by OCR, drawn from the specification content for this unit, and b) *practical citizenship action* based around gender, race, ethnicity, culture, age or disability.

For their *citizenship enquiry*, students will be required to research the issues raised in the source book and to respond to one of three viewpoints given. For their *practical citizenship action*, students will need to:

- plan their action and provide evidence of this
- take action and provide evidence of their role in this
- submit a written evaluation of their action.

Students will be expected to work in groups to plan and take their action, but to evaluate it individually.

It's the rule

In this unit we look at some of the characteristics and features of law.

Home time

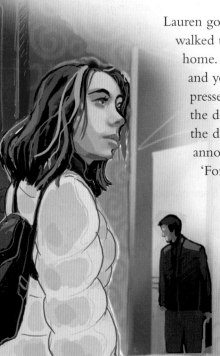

Lauren got off the school bus and walked the short distance to her home. She lives with her dad and younger brother. Lauren pressed the bell and waited on the doorstep. Her dad opened the door and, with a slightly annoyed expression, asked, 'Forgotten your key again?'

Lauren stepped inside and stood in the hall, still wearing her coat and holding her school bag. 'Hello,' she said.

'Aren't you going to take your coat off?' asked her dad.

'Oh, thank you,' said Lauren. 'Where shall I put it?'

'On the hook, of course,' her dad replied. 'Are you all right?'

'Yes, thank you,' said Lauren, still standing in the hallway.

Her dad walked through to the kitchen. 'Cup of tea?' he called.

'Thank you very much,' answered Lauren. 'No sugar, please.'

'Lauren,' said her dad, beginning to look worried. 'What's the matter? You don't usually behave like this.'

? Questions

1. How is Lauren behaving? Is she behaving like a daughter or like someone else? What kind of person does her behaviour remind you of?

Rules

Although we don't always realise it, most – if not all – of our behaviour with other people follows certain rules. These rules vary from one group of people to another.

It is sometimes easiest to see the rules that we follow when they are broken. Lauren was breaking certain unwritten rules. She wasn't behaving like a daughter. She was behaving like a guest.

▮ Relationships

One part of our lives closely controlled by rules is our relationships with other people. Take marriage, for example.

Here are some statements about marriage:

- **Age** Both partners must be aged 16 or over.
- **Faithful** A married person should not have a sexual relationship with someone else.
- **Sex** A couple should not have sex before they are married.
- **Support** When people are married they should behave reasonably towards each other and support each other.
- **Woman and man** The partners should be of the opposite sex.

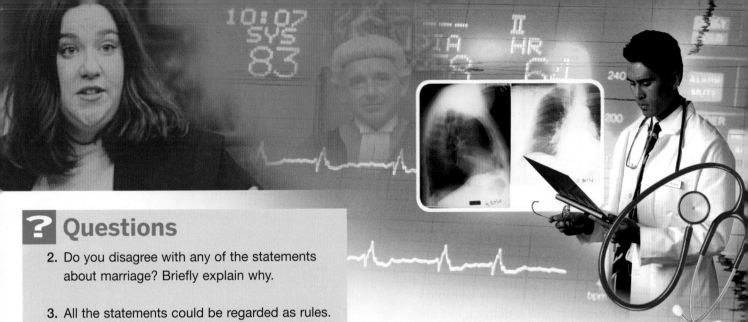

? Questions

2. Do you disagree with any of the statements about marriage? Briefly explain why.

3. All the statements could be regarded as rules. Some of them are laws, and some are not. Which do you think are laws? What are the others?

Right and wrong

Many of the rules that we have in society are about questions of morality. That is, about what people believe is fundamentally right or wrong.

There are certain rules that most people generally agree with. Most believe it is wrong for a person to steal from others. This is something that is regarded as being morally wrong, and is also against the law.

Morality v. the law

Usually laws reflect the moral beliefs of most people in society, but this isn't always the case.

Gay and lesbian relationships In 2008, the Advertising Standards Authority received nearly 200 complaints after a television advertisement for mayonnaise showed two men kissing. The advertisers said that the advertisement was intended to be humorous. Many of those who complained believed it was offensive.

Although gay and lesbian people have many more rights in law than they did in the past, measures to treat gay and heterosexual people in the same way remain controversial. In 1998, there was great opposition – particularly in the House of Lords – to lowering the gay age of consent from 18 to 16. It was not until 2000 that this finally passed into law.

In 2003, it became unlawful to discriminate against someone at work because of their sexual orientation. Soon after this the Government said that it wanted to extend this law to cover the sale of goods and services, making it illegal for someone to be refused things like medical treatment or a hotel booking because of their sexuality. Again, this measure was opposed on the basis that people should not be required to offer services or facilities to someone whose actions they believed were wrong.

Since 2005, same-sex couples have been able to have their relationship recognised in law (see page 37), giving them many of the same rights as people who marry. Although it is believed that most people support this law, there remains a certain amount of opposition. In 2008, a registrar in London asked to be excused from officiating at civil partnership ceremonies between same-sex couples, saying that she believed that gay marriage was sinful.

? Questions

4. Some people believe there are other things that people do that are morally wrong, and should be forbidden by law. Abortion and Sunday trading are examples of this.

Select one of these, or choose an example of your own, and try to find out the arguments that people give for changing the law from its present state.

It's the rule

Breaking the law

■ Money for nothing

In August 2002, a building society installed a new computer system in their cash machines in Coventry. It was designed to improve security, particularly for customers from other banks and building societies.

However, it wasn't long before a few customers realised that money they had withdrawn had not been taken from their account and, in effect, they were obtaining the money for free. Word of this began to spread; as long as there was money in the machine, people could return as many times as they wished and take out *any* amount of money, using *any* PIN number. The only limit was the fact that no more than £790 could be released through the slot in the cash dispenser at any one time.

The fault went undetected for five days, and during that time more than £1 million was withdrawn from the society's cash machines in the city. Some customers probably obtained extra cash without realising it, but a number of others did their best to get as much money as they could.

Eventually, arrests were made and twelve of the most serious offenders were charged with conspiracy to steal. Four of these were from one family, who stole £134,410 – spending the money on a brand new car, air tickets, electrical goods and furniture.

❓ Questions

1. Who was responsible for the building society's loss of more than £1 million?

2. How much blame do you attach to all those people who took money from the cash machines knowing that they were not entitled to it?

3. What kinds of reasons or excuses do you think people might give for taking this money?

4. How should the offenders be punished? Is the offence serious enough for them to be sent to jail?

■ Is it ever right to break the law?

As they learnt of the news of these thefts, many people probably wondered what they would have done in the same situation; and whether they would have been able to resist the temptation to steal. The case also raises questions of whether it is ever acceptable to break the law.

❓ Questions

5. Read the cases opposite and try to work out why each person claims it is right in their case to break the law:

   a) How acceptable do you find each argument? Explain why.
   b) In which, if any, of these cases should the courts show leniency?

Molly is a grandmother and lives in Glasgow. She strongly disagrees with the Government's decision to spend £40 million on a new system of nuclear defence. She believes that it is a criminal waste of resources and that weapons of this kind are immoral. For the past year, Molly and others have tried to prevent the nuclear base from functioning by causing as much disruption as possible. Most of their activities have been against the law.

Ricky, his brother and two sons have been involved in theft and burglary for most of their lives. They have tended to steal from the very rich, taking valuable furniture and works of art, and are believed to have taken millions of pounds' worth of goods. Ricky is now in prison, but before he received his latest sentence he said, 'I will only rob your house if I have to feed my children, and nobody is helping me achieve this. I really feel I have the right to rob the sirs, lords and ladies.'

Lee has been driving for several years, but does not have a driving licence, nor is his car insured. 'Lots of people drive around without tax or insurance,' he says. 'I don't see why I should bother.'

Maya selected three tops, a jacket and a pair of trousers. As she paid the bill at the cash desk, she was surprised that it was not for a larger amount, but said nothing. Outside the store she checked her receipt. The assistant had failed to charge her for the trousers, which cost £35. Maya decided to do nothing; it was the shop's mistake, she thought, and they can certainly afford it.

Ruth always thinks of herself as a law-abiding person, and tells her children how important it is to keep to the law. There are a few laws, however, that she does break. When she believes it's safe to do so, Ruth quite often exceeds the speed limit on the motorway. She also doesn't always declare her full income to the tax authorities. One day her daughter asked her why she did this. 'I have to pay far too much in tax,' she said. 'It's just not fair.'

Dan and his friends, for the last few years, have shared most of their music CDs and downloads. One evening in the pub, someone told him that this is against the law, and that it is an offence to copy CDs and download files without the permission of the copyright holder. Dan said that he didn't realise that they were doing anything wrong, but added that he has no intention of stopping. 'The law is crazy,' he said.

It's the rule

What is law?

On a wider scale

We have already seen that much of our life is affected by rules.

Rules made by our family or school usually just affect ourselves and the other people in these groups. If we come in late, don't put things away, or use the wrong entrance, we aren't normally breaking the law – just the rule of the group or organisation.

Laws are different. They are rules that apply in all situations, to everyone within the community – although there are some groups, such as children, who are not affected by some laws until they reach a certain age.

? Questions

1. Laws influence many aspects of our lives. Look at each of the pictures above and draw up a list of some of the laws that apply in each situation.

2. Your list probably includes many different laws. What purpose or function do you think they serve? In answering this, you may find it helpful to look at the text below.

The purpose or function of law   Many laws are designed to protect people's safety. The law forbidding murder is an example of this. Similarly, laws controlling drink-driving or health and safety at work also concern personal and public safety.

However, law is also used in a number of other ways. Laws like the *Human Rights Act* are designed to protect rights and liberties – such as privacy or free speech. Laws may also be used to give people political rights. Changes to the law in 1998 gave people in Wales and Scotland more political power than they had had previously.

Laws are also passed to create fairness and justice. Anti-discrimination laws, for example, are designed to ensure that people are treated more fairly than they were in the past. Laws like these are also developed in order to bring about a change in people's behaviour. Over the next few years we can probably expect a number of new laws designed to reduce people's consumption of energy.

Law is also used as a way of settling disagreements. One of the functions of a court is to decide who is right or wrong in a particular case, such as in a dispute over money, work, land or a relationship.

Civil and criminal law

One of the ways in which law can be divided up is into what is known as *civil* law and *criminal* law.

Civil law provides a way of settling disputes between individuals or groups of people. When you buy something that fails to work, or doesn't do what the shop assistant claimed, it is the civil law that you use to get your money back. It's a mechanism for settling the disagreement between you and the shop.

Criminal law covers behaviour that the State has decided must be discouraged or prevented – such as assault or theft. These actions then become crimes. They are also usually dealt with by the police, or some other authority – and not by the individuals concerned.

A year in the life

Dear Chloe

I just thought I'd put this note in with the Christmas card to let you know some of our news over the past year – although, by the time you've finished reading it, you may wish that I hadn't bothered!

In January, Dean, who is now 18, passed his driving test. He bought a car soon afterwards, but already has a speeding conviction and two parking fines.

In April, Madeleine was caught shoplifting while she was supposed to be in school. She was arrested and taken to the police station. I hope it has taught her a lesson.

In July, my brother, who works on a farm, seriously injured his hand. The farmer had failed to replace the guard on a cutting blade. His union is helping him to get compensation.

In August, after 19 years of marriage, my divorce from John was finalised.

In September I had problems with a neighbour, who is refusing to cut down a tree that blocks most of our light – and in October, I lost my job. They said I was no longer up to standard. I'd worked there for ten years, with a perfect record. I am making a claim for unfair dismissal.

Since then, it's been very peaceful, although there was a sign that things were getting back to normal when my car was broken into last week and my new phone stolen. The sales assistant had said it was the perfect mobile. How right he was.

Much love,
Anna

? Questions

3. Write down all the law-related events that Anna lists in her letter, and decide whether each one is part of the civil or criminal law.

It's the rule
Criminal responsibility

■ Picture this

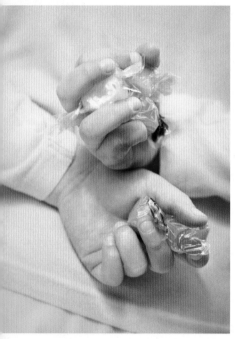

A little girl, aged two, is with her father in supermarket. Just as he is about to join the queue at the checkout, he sees an old friend and they stop for a chat. The little girl is soon bored. Without her father seeing, but still holding his hand, she picks a large bag of sweets off the shelf.
A few minutes later, the little girl's father says goodbye to his friend, pays for his goods, and walks towards the exit.
The sweets are in the little girl's hand. Just as he and his daughter have gone through the door, the man is stopped by the store detective who explains that he has not paid for the sweets.

? Questions

1. Has the little girl stolen the sweets? If not, why not?

2. Would it have made any difference if she was 5, 10 or 15 years of age?

■ The age of criminal responsibility

In England and Wales, the age of criminal responsibility is ten. This is based on the view that children below the age of ten are not old enough to understand the consequences of their actions and therefore cannot be taken to court for committing a crime.

England and Wales have one of the lowest ages of criminal responsibility in Europe. (It is 13 in France and 15 in Denmark, Norway and Sweden.) However, in some states of the USA, the age is as low as six.

Changes over time In the early nineteenth century, children who committed a crime were treated in the same way as adults. They were sent to adult prisons and some as young as 12 were hanged for their crimes.

Over the course of the century, the Government came to realise that children required different treatment from adults. New prisons were built for young people and special rules were introduced for children who were held with adults.

The age of criminal responsibility in England and Wales was first set in 1933 at the age of eight, and raised to ten in 1963. However, for a child aged between ten and 14 to be convicted of a crime, the prosecution had to prove that the child knew that their actions were wrong. This continued until 1998, when the present arrangements were introduced by the Government based on the view that the average ten- to 14-year-old *does* know the difference between right and wrong.

Young children and crime Today, young offenders from the age of ten are normally dealt with in the community, but may be sent to a secure children's home, a secure training centre, or a Young Offenders' Institution (YOI).

If a child below the age of ten does something that would otherwise be a crime, a court can make an order to place them under the supervision of a social worker or a youth offending team. The child will normally be required to go to school, be at home during certain hours, and not visit certain areas or be in touch with certain other children if they are thought to be a bad influence.

The child may also be required to attend sessions designed to stop them from repeating the same offences. The order can last for up to 12 months.

Young offender? Jamie is nine years old. He lives with his family in Newcastle. He's known by the police – and the firefighters – who often have to deal with his handiwork. His mum takes him to school, but he often slips away. Some days he goes riding on the back of buses, hanging on to the engine cover.`

In 2006, children under the age ten living in England and Wales were the main suspects in almost 3,000 crimes. Similar figures have been released in Scotland. Although most of the offences were relatively minor, almost half in England and Wales involved criminal damage or arson, and 66 children were suspected of committing a sexual offence.

❓ Questions

3. Some people believe that the age of criminal responsibility in England and Wales should be lowered, but the United Nations has said the Government should seriously think about *raising* it. Here are some views on the subject:

- 'All children, as young as four or five know that it's wrong to steal or damage things – and certainly to set fire to a building.'

- 'If we lowered the age of criminal responsibility many more young hooligans would be caught and punished – and crime would fall.'

- 'Children mature at different rates. It takes many children a lot longer to understand properly the consequences of their actions.'

- 'Children should be protected from the full force of the law. It is wrong to criminalise children as young as 10.'

The Government has three choices in this matter – to lower the age of criminal responsibility, to raise it, or to leave it as it is. Draw up a list of arguments to support one of these positions.

It's the rule
Legal rights and responsibilities

■ Time to change the law?

In the summer of 2004, eight people lost their lives in a road accident just outside Brighton. The crash occurred when a car carrying four passengers, aged between 17 and 20, lost control and crossed over the central reservation, landing upside down on top of an oncoming vehicle. The driver responsible was 19 years old.

The mother of two of those killed in the accident has since called for a change to the minimum driving age, suggesting that it should be raised from 17 to 18. She also supports proposals to extend the period over which a person learns to drive to at least a year, and to ban new drivers from carrying passengers aged between ten and 20 late at night.

Accident statistics

Each year, 50,000 17-year-olds pass their test in less than six months.

Twenty per cent of new drivers are involved in a crash in their first year.

One in three of all road deaths involves a car driven by someone aged 17–25.

❓ Questions

1. Put together a case either for or against raising the minimum driving age from 17 to 18 years of age or more. Whichever you attempt, indicate what steps you feel the Government should take to try to reduce the high accident rate of young drivers.

■ At what age?

The age from which young people are allowed to take part in certain activities is often, but not always, controlled by law. For example, young people below the age of 14 cannot generally undertake paid work. Similarly, it is unlawful for young people under 18 to buy alcohol.

Age limits are generally designed to protect the young person, and often the safety of the wider public. They may vary over time (the minimum age limit in England and Wales for buying a pet rose from 12 to 16 in 2006) and place. The minimum legal drinking age in the USA is 21.

❓ Questions

2. If you look at the information opposite, you will see some big differences in the legal ages of different activities. Some people have argued that this makes the process of becoming an adult more complicated, and suggest that there should be a single age at which a young person passes from being a child to an adult. What is your view of this?

3. From the information opposite, select one legal age that you would change, explaining why you would do so, and what you would put in its place.

Alcohol and bars Children may not be given alcohol, unless for medical reasons, below the age of five, and a young person may not buy alcohol until they are 18. From 16, a young person may drink beer or wine with a meal if it is bought by someone aged 18 or over and consumed in a restaurant or separate dining area of a pub.

Contraception A young person has the right to receive contraceptive treatment and advice at any age, as long as the nurse or doctor believes they understand what is involved.

Crime Children are legally responsible from the age of ten for any crimes they commit. A person may serve on a jury from the age of 18.

Leave home Parents have responsibility for their children's care until their child reaches 18. Young people don't have the right to leave home without their parents' permission until they are 18, but the police rarely order 16- or 17-year-olds home unless they are in danger or unable to look after themselves.

Leisure You do not have complete choice over what films, DVDs or computer games you watch, buy or rent until you are 18. This is also the minimum age for placing a bet and for buying fireworks.

Marriage You may marry or enter a civil partnership with your parents' agreement from the age of 16. If they won't agree, you must wait until you are 18.

Medical treatment You can agree to, or refuse, medical treatment at any age, as long as the doctor believes you understand the consequences of your decision. You can see your health (and school) records at any age as long as the doctor believes you can understand what you are looking for, and that neither you nor anyone else will suffer serious harm from what you read.

Money and property You can open a bank account from any age, as long as the bank believes that you understand what is involved. You cannot borrow money until you are 18. You are not able to own land until you are 18, but you may inherit money or goods from any age.

Politics You can vote in local, national and regional elections from the age of 18 (or 16 if you live on the Isle of Man or the Channel Islands). You may stand as a councillor or MP at 18, but currently need to be 21 to be a Member of the European Parliament.

Sex Men and women must be at least 16 years of age before they can legally agree to have sex.

Tattoos and piercings You have to be 18 to have a tattoo. There is no age limit for ear piercing, but some local authorities do not allow body piercing (with the exception of ear, nose and navel) below the age of 18.

Tobacco Cigarettes, tobacco and cigarette papers may not be sold to anyone below 18. It is not an offence to smoke below this age, but uniformed police officers and park keepers have the power to confiscate cigarettes from children under 18.

Work There is very little paid work a young person can do below 14. A person may join the army from the age of 16.

The law machine

This unit explains where our laws come from and the ways in which they are made and changed.

Law makers

▇ Development

The law in England and Wales is created and developed in three ways: by **Parliament**, by judges in court, and through our links with Europe. Laws in Northern Ireland and Scotland are sometimes different.

▇ Parliament

Governments are responsible for deciding the nature of most new law. During a general election, all political parties set out the policies they will follow if elected.

After the election, the winning party that forms the new government, puts its policies into practice and often introduces new laws, or changes in the existing law.

In its 2005 election manifesto, the Labour Party promised to improve education and training for 16- to 19-year-olds to give more people a better chance in life. After winning the election the Government began to draw up plans to extend the time that young people must stay in education or training from 16 to 17 (and later 18) years of age. *The Education and Skills Act* became law in 2008, and young people beginning secondary school in 2008 became the first to be directly affected by this, as they will have to continue their education until they are 18.

New laws may also be proposed by individual MPs through what is called Private Members' **Bills**. However, the time for debating these Bills is very limited and only a small number succeed in becoming law.

▇ Judge-made law

In the twelfth century, the King of England set up courts and appointed judges to travel around the country providing justice and sorting out disputes. Decisions made by these judges were written down and gradually built up to form a detailed record of English law. This is called 'common law'.

Today, when a judge hears a case in court, lawyers tell the judge about any other cases where similar facts have been heard before. If they have, the judge will follow the decision established by senior or equal ranking judges in the earlier case.

Sometimes, however, senior judges feel that decisions made in the past do not fit in with the present-day thinking and in these circumstances they may reinterpret and change judge-made law, in line with this.

For example, in 1991 a man was charged with rape after having sex with his wife against her will. His lawyers argued that he was not guilty because the law had said for many years that it was not rape if a husband forced his wife to have sex. Five senior judges disagreed. They said this was out of date and that the law should change. A man can now be found guilty of raping his wife.

■ Europe

Never again The Second World War, 1939–45, cost the lives of millions of people and caused huge destruction throughout Europe. In order to prevent the same thing from happening again, many people felt that it was important for European states to work much more closely together.

To try to achieve this, two important organisations were established: the European Union and the Council of Europe. Although many countries belong to both the Council of Europe and the European Union, the two organisations are quite different. Both have a major impact on law-making in Britain today.

The European Union The origins of the European Union (EU) go back to 1951, with a treaty between Belgium, France, Germany, Italy, Luxembourg and the Netherlands. Although the EU began (and continues to function) as a trading block, it has grown into a group of 27 nations, who now work together in many other spheres of life. These include employment, transport, farming, fisheries, environment, energy, and security.

When a country joins the European Union it agrees to allow EU law to become part of its own national law – and, if they differ, that EU law will take priority. Today much of our law on transport, employment, the environment, etc., comes from the European Union. (See also pages 156–7.)

The Council of Europe The Council of Europe is concerned mainly with protecting human rights and developing international understanding, and one of its most important achievements has been the creation of the European Convention on Human Rights. By signing the Convention in 1951, the British Government agreed that everyone in this country should enjoy the rights and freedoms set out in the Convention. In 2000, these rights became part of law throughout the UK when the *Human Rights Act* came into force. (See page 30 for further details.)

Key words

Bill
The name given to a proposed new law as it passes through Parliament. If it is approved by both Houses, it receives the royal assent and becomes statute law, known as an Act of Parliament.

Parliament
The main law-making body of the United Kingdom, consisting of the House of Commons, the House of Lords and the Crown.

The law machine
Parliamentary process

Government policy

The Government introduces most new Bills into Parliament in order to bring about changes in the law that it feels are important.

In the late 1990s, the Government believed much more should be done to reduce the damaging health effects of tobacco. Over the next ten years it introduced a number of new laws designed to help achieve this.

Consultation

A great deal of discussion and consultation normally takes place before the wording of a Bill is drawn up. The Government talks to people who have knowledge of the area covered by the new law and will often issue what is called a Green Paper, setting out its main ideas for change. This is followed by a White Paper, with firmer proposals, which becomes the basis of the Bill debated in Parliament.

Members of the public are also able to give their views by letter or email to their MP or to the government department concerned.

Pressure

Sometimes new laws are created as a result of public pressure.

In November 2000, the age of consent for male gay sex was lowered to 16, bringing it into line with the heterosexual age of consent. This was after a long campaign by many groups and individuals and a ruling by the **European Court of Human Rights**, which had said that discrimination of this kind broke the European Convention on Human Rights.

This meant that the British Government *had* to change the law in order to keep to the European Convention on Human Rights.

Getting down to detail Not all laws are discussed at great length. In order to save time, Parliament will sometimes give the relevant minister the power to determine the exact detail of the law. The law appears in what are known as *statutory instruments* or *regulations*. This process is known as secondary legislation.

Demonstration for gay rights, June 1998.

Stages of a Bill

A Bill normally starts its passage through Parliament in the **House of Commons**, where it is debated by Members of Parliament (MPs).

First Reading

The Bill is introduced to Parliament. The title is read out and a date fixed for the Second Reading.

Second Reading

This is a debate, not on the detail, but on the general principles of the Bill.

In 2007, the law was changed to ban smoking in public places. During the Second Reading of the Bill, MPs debated the strengths and weaknesses of this idea.

This is probably the most important stage of a Bill. Once a Bill has passed its Second Reading, there is a good chance that it will become law.

Committee Stage

A small group of MPs, or members of the House of Lords, now look at the Bill in close detail. They go through the wording line by line in order to check that it says exactly what is intended.

In theory this idea works well, but criticisms are made of the process.

After serving on a Committee one MP wrote that there was often very little discussion and a lot of pressure to work faster. 'We proposed our amendments,' he said, 'the Minister responded, and the amendment was usually voted down.

'Sometimes,' he went on, 'the Government actually agreed with the changes we were demanding, but couldn't be seen to be doing so. The answer was for us to drop our opposition and let the Government propose their own amendments, which were very similar to our own, and, hey presto, they're accepted.'

Report Stage and Third Reading

The Bill then moves back to the whole House where the Committee reports on the changes it has made.

The Report Stage is followed by the Third Reading, when the House of Commons takes a vote on the final version of the Bill.

The Bill is then passed to the **House of Lords**, where it is again discussed and examined in much the same way. Any changes that the House of Lords wishes to make are sent back the House of Commons for further consideration.

The Lords can delay a Bill for up to a year, but cannot prevent it becoming law.

Royal Assent

The Bill then goes to the Queen or King to be 'signed' – in practice this is just a formality. The Bill is then known as an Act of Parliament, and becomes law from whatever date it is laid down.

Key words

European Court of Human Rights
A court that decides on cases in which it is claimed there has been a breach of the European Convention on Human Rights. It is situated in Strasbourg, in northeastern France.

House of Commons
The section of Parliament made up of elected MPs.

House of Lords
The section of Parliament that consists mainly of people who have been specially appointed as peers. At the moment, certain judges, senior bishops and people who have inherited a title are also members.

The law machine
Judge-made law

WE HAVEN'T COME ACROSS **THIS** BEFORE!

■ Getting online

Almost every company in Britain now has a website. Usually their web address is closely based on the name that they trade under – such as Cadbury or Kellogg's.

Anyone who wants their own website address can, on payment of a fee, register their chosen name with one of a number of organisations.

Some people, however, have gone one stage further and registered names that are not their own, which they believe will be useful – and profitable – to sell to others.

In the late 1990s a number of well-known British companies, including Marks & Spencer, Sainsbury's and Virgin, learnt that a group of dealers in internet names had registered their companies' names without their agreement.

The dealers were hoping to sell the names back to the company or sell them on to someone else. Large sums of money could be involved. A chain of burger restaurants had been asked for £25,000 to buy back their name.

? Questions

1. Can you see anything wrong with this practice? Give reasons for your answer.

Offline?

Marks & Spencer, and the other companies involved, believed that the names of the internet addresses really belonged to them. They felt that it was wrong that they should have to pay a large amount of money for a name that they had used for many years. They also believed that their business and their reputation could be seriously damaged if the name was sold to someone else.

They decided to take their case to court to ask for their names to be handed back.

? Questions

2. Draw up a list of the points on either side of this argument. Who do you feel has the fairer case?

Problem We have already seen that, in reaching a verdict, judges must – where the facts are the same – follow the decisions made by senior judges in previous cases. This is known as a system of precedent.

The problem the judges faced on this occasion was that the internet was a new development and courts had never heard a case of this kind before. There was no exact precedent or guidance on how this case should be judged.

Solution The judges decided that the evidence in Court showed that the dealers were deliberately trying to extract as much money as they could from companies like Marks & Spencer by threatening to sell these names to other people if the company did not pay up.

The dealers were ordered to give back the names to the companies on which they were based.

Judge-made law In reaching this decision, the judges in court established a new piece of law that will stand until it is overruled either by the decision of a higher court or a new law passed by Parliament.

■ Precedent

The word *precede* means going before; and precedent is the name given to the system by which judges follow decisions made in previous cases, where the facts are the same.

If the decision of a court is challenged, the case is taken to a higher court, normally the Court of Appeal. Here judges will apply decisions already made by the Court of Appeal or the Supreme Court, which stands at the head of the court structure.

The Justices of the Supreme Court may follow a past decision (of their own or their predecessors, the Law Lords) or, when it appears right to do so, depart from this and create new law. This is called case law.

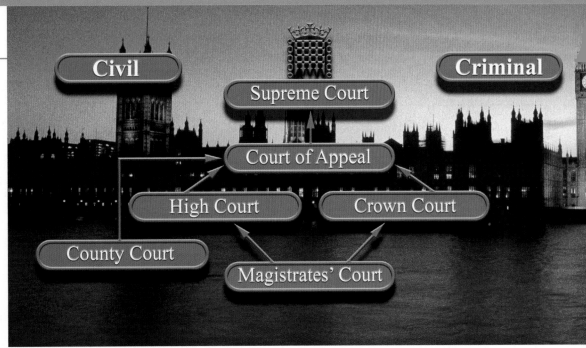

? Questions

3. Try to explain the advantages of developing the law through a system of case law. Can you think of any disadvantages? If so, what are they?

The appointment of judges Until recently, judges in England and Wales were appointed by the Queen or King on the advice of the Lord Chancellor – a senior lawyer appointed by the Prime Minister and a member of the Government. It was a relatively secret process with candidates being quietly invited to apply. Today, judges are selected in a more transparent way. Experienced lawyers may now apply to be judges and are sifted and selected by the Judicial Appointments Commission, an independent group of people, drawn mainly from the legal profession.

One reason for changing the selection procedure was to try to make sure that judges came from a wider section of society. This is a slow process. Today about 20 per cent of judges at all levels are women. (The figure for senior judges is half this.) Three to five per cent of judges come from ethnic minorities, and none of these serve at the most senior level (2008).

? Questions

4. A typical judge in England and Wales today is still male, white, privately educated and over 50. Does it matter if judges come from a relatively narrow section of society?

The law machine
European law

■ The big idea

One of the key ideas behind the formation of what is today known as the European Union was the creation of a common or single market, where goods, services, people and money could move freely between member states.

In order to achieve this, new rules and laws were required which would apply to everyone in the new 'market'. For example, countries could no longer have laws preventing entry by people from member states. If people were to be allowed to move around the EU, they needed to be given the same opportunities whoever they were and wherever they went; and, similarly, if trade between member states was to be encouraged, steps needed to be taken to make sure all goods and services met the same minimum quality and safety standards. Such measures, however, are not always popular. European law is often portrayed by the British press as clumsy and over-bureaucratic, and coming from an organisation outside Britain, not one that Britain joined voluntarily.

All change In 2008, a number of British newspapers reported that new European Regulations had come into force preventing bus drivers from driving more than 31 miles (50 km) without a rest. The consequences of this, they claimed, were that bus routes in country districts were being cut, or bus passengers now had to break their journey and change buses, so that drivers had enough rest.

However, those in favour of the Regulations pointed out that they were a very sensible measure that would improve safety and prevent drivers from falling asleep at the wheel. They also said that bus companies had had three years to make the required changes.

Treaties, laws and the European Court of Justice The nature of European law is often difficult to understand. This is possibly because EU law is determined by not one, but several organisations, whose nature and procedures are not always familiar to people in the UK. (For more information on European government see pages 156–7.)

European law is created in three broadly different ways: by Treaties; by laws known as Regulations, Directives and Decisions; and by rulings from the European Court of Justice. These are explained in more detail below.

Treaties Treaties are the building blocks of EU law. They are important agreements signed by EU member states about major programmes of action for the future. The Treaty of Rome, for example, signed in 1957 by a number of European countries (not initially including the UK), set out the intention for member states to let people move freely between countries for the purpose of work. It also stated that men and women should have equal pay for equal work. The Maastricht Treaty, signed in 1992, gave the European Parliament important new powers, created the idea of European citizenship, and set the way for a single European currency, the euro.

Regulations are the laws that put treaties into practice. They are binding on all member states, and do not require member states to pass their own laws. Regulations are created by the European Commission (see page 156) and must be based on a specific article in a Treaty.

As we have already seen, the Treaty of Rome allows people to move freely for work between member states. The Regulations that followed this Treaty were designed to put this aim into practice. As a result, all EU states must give visiting EU workers the same rights to education and housing as citizens of their own state.

Directives like regulations, are a way of putting EU policy into action. However, under a Directive, member states are allowed to decide for themselves exactly how this will be done.

For example, in 2006, the European Union passed the *Data Retention Directive* requiring member states to keep details of all mobile phone and landline calls for between six months and two years, a measure designed to help with the investigation and detection of serious crime. In 2007 the Directive became UK law, requiring details of all calls to be logged and stored for a year.

Decisions are judgements made by the Council of Ministers or European Commission which *must* be put into practice. Rather like a Regulation, no national laws are required to put Decisions into practice.

In 2008, the European Commission gave member states three months to put into practice a Decision requiring all toys containing small magnets to carry a warning about the particular risks magnets can pose if swallowed or inhaled.

The European Court of Justice (ECJ) The ECJ is at the head of the EU legal system. Two of its most important jobs are to consider claims that member states are not keeping to the terms of a treaty, and to clarify or interpret points of EU law (rather like the Supreme Court in Britain).

In 2007, the ECJ decided that a German law preventing the Volkswagen car company from being taken over was against EU law and must be changed. The law had been in place since the 1960s, largely to make sure that the company did not fall into foreign hands.

? Questions

1. The European Union today is an important source of UK law. What are some of the strengths and weaknesses of this?

2. To achieve its aims EU law today covers things like employment, business, transport, farming, fisheries, the environment, energy, and security matters. Think of two areas of UK life that are unlikely to be affected by EU law.

What are human rights?

This unit outlines the nature of human rights.

The abuse of power

■ Government control

When Adolf Hitler, head of the Nazi party, became Germany's leader in 1933, the country faced a severe economic crisis, with high unemployment and soaring **inflation**. Hitler's main priorities were to restore German prosperity, and to regain the power and influence that Germany had lost as a result of the First World War.

In the years that followed, Hitler put into practice a number of policies designed to achieve these aims. He rebuilt the nation's economy by boosting production and reducing unemployment, and began to reoccupy some of the land that had been under German control before the First World War. By September 1939 German forces occupied Austria, Czechoslovakia and western Poland.

One of the ways in which Hitler achieved these huge changes was to place people in Germany under much greater government control, something which he began within weeks of coming to power.

? Questions

1. Take two of the changes listed below and explain what impact each might have had on life in Germany at the time. (You might find it helpful to begin by listing their advantages and disadvantages.)

■ Persecution

Responsibility for Germany's problems, as far as the Nazis were concerned, lay with weak government and Jewish people – living both in Germany and elsewhere.

Although **anti-Semitism** had been a problem faced by Jewish people throughout Europe for hundreds of years, Jews living in Germany were, until this time, well integrated into local life. During the First World War they had joined the armed forces and fought and died alongside other German servicemen; yet after the war, found themselves being blamed by the Nazis for the German defeat.

In addition to placing German society as a whole under greater governmental control, Hitler also created laws that applied only to Jews. These were designed to reduce Jewish people's **civil liberties** and to exclude them as much as possible from society.

Rise of the Nazis 1933

30 January Adolf Hitler becomes Chancellor (leader) of Germany.

28 February An emergency decree is passed allowing any 'suspicious' person to be arrested.

24 March The normal procedure for creating law in Germany is abandoned. Hitler is given the power to create all laws on behalf of the Government.

2 May The Nazis seize control of the trade unions, arresting their leaders, and confiscating union property. German workers lose the right to strike.

10 May Under orders from the new Ministry of Propaganda, some of the very best German literary works are taken from the Berlin Library and burnt.

22 June The Social Democrat Party, the Nazis' main opposition, is outlawed. The Nazi Party becomes the only officially recognised political party in Germany.

Anti-Jewish laws in Nazi Germany

1933
- Jewish people could no longer serve on a jury in court.
- Anyone working for the Government who had at least one Jewish grandparent lost their job.
- All Jewish teachers were removed from schools and universities.

1934
- The public sale of Jewish newspapers was banned.

1935
- Marriage and sexual relationships between Jews and other German citizens were forbidden.
- Jews were no longer allowed to vote.

1937
- Jews were forbidden from obtaining passports and from travelling abroad, except in special cases.

1938
- Jewish children and young people could no longer go to school or university.
- All Jews were required to carry a special identity card.
- Jewish people were arrested in large numbers and forcibly taken to concentration camps.

Towards the end of the Second World War, the extent of the persecution faced by Jews and others under the Nazi regime became clear to people outside Germany. It is believed that about six million Jews died at the hands of the Nazis. Others who faced persecution included Gypsies, homosexuals and Jehovah's Witnesses.

Soviet citizens were either transported or killed under the rule of Joseph Stalin. More recently – until 1990 – the government of South Africa classified its citizens into different racial groups, and withheld important rights from those who were not white.

What are human rights? Human rights are fundamental rights, belonging to everyone, that should not be withheld or removed by governments or those in authority, unless for reasons that can be properly justified.

? Questions

2. Look at the list of some of the laws passed by the Nazi Government that applied to Jews. Draw up a list of the kinds of freedoms and liberties that were being denied.

3. What effect do you imagine these had on Jews in Germany?

? Questions

4. Draw up a list of the basic human rights that have been mentioned or referred to in the text on these two pages.

5. Why is it important to protect human rights?

■ Denying human rights

The atrocities faced by these groups are extreme examples of the abuse of power by a government. Although their actions are amongst the most cruel and inhumane, the Nazis are not the only group to have deprived people of their basic human rights. All those countries, including Britain, involved in the slave trade were responsible for millions of people losing fundamental freedoms, such as life and liberty. For much of the twentieth century people living in the Soviet Union had huge restrictions placed upon them by their government. During the 1930s and 1940s millions of

Key words

Anti-Semitism
Persecution and discrimination against Jewish people.

Civil liberties
Freedoms or rights that are thought to be especially important, such as free speech.

Inflation
A continual increase in the prices of the things that people have to buy.

Human rights law

This unit explains the place of human rights law in Britain.

Protecting human rights

■ The Council of Europe

During the 1930s and 1940s, millions of people throughout Europe suffered because of the failure of governments to uphold basic human rights. To try to prevent something similar from happening again, eight European nations, including Britain, came together not long after the end of the Second World War to create the Council of Europe.

Forty-seven countries have now joined the Council of Europe, with member states extending as far east as Russia and Armenia. The Council's main aim is to promote respect for human rights, **democracy** and the **rule of law**. All member states agree to follow the rights and freedoms set out in the European Convention on Human Rights.

■ The European Convention on Human Rights

In 1950, a year after the Council of Europe was formed, member states drew up the European Convention on Human Rights, setting out the rights and freedoms that people in Europe should be able to expect. A summary of the Convention is given on pages 28–9.

In many ways, the Convention is very similar to the United Nations Declaration of Human Rights (see page 34); however, unlike the UN Declaration, the European Convention gives citizens the power to enforce their rights – through the European Court of Human Rights in Strasbourg.

If the Court finds that the Convention has been broken, it can award damages to the person who brought the case, and the country involved will almost certainly be required to change its law to ensure that it no longer breaks the Convention – as happened to Britain over the question of corporal punishment in school.

Corporal punishment in school   One day in September 1976, Jeffrey Cosans, then aged 15, took a short cut through a cemetery on his way home from school. This was against the rules, and Jeffrey was reported to the head who decided to punish him with the strap. Jeffrey refused to be beaten and was backed up by his parents, who believed that corporal punishment was wrong. Jeffrey was excluded from school.

Eventually Jeffrey was let back into school – but the head would not guarantee that Jeffrey would not face the strap if he misbehaved again.

Jeffrey's mother thought that the school's actions broke the European Convention, and took the case to the European Court of Human Rights.

The Court agreed with Mrs Cosans, deciding that by allowing corporal punishment in schools the British Government was not respecting a parent's rights to have their child brought up according to their philosophical convictions (Protocol 1 Article 2).

This judgement made it clear that the British Government would be breaking the European Convention if it continued to allow pupils to be beaten in schools. As a result, corporal punishment was abolished in state schools in 1987 and in all private schools in 1999.

■ Absolute rights?

If you look through the list of Convention rights on page 28–9, you will see that most of them are not absolute rights, but have been restricted in some way. This is because it is felt that sometimes certain rights or freedoms either cannot apply or need to be limited.

Rights that are absolute and cannot be interfered with by the state are contained in Articles 2, 3, 4, 7 and 14. For example, torture (Article 3) is not acceptable under any circumstances.

Some rights, however, for example those contained in Articles 8, 9, 10 and 11, may at times be restricted.

Listening in Generally speaking, the police (and other officials) are not allowed to install secret cameras or listening devices in people's homes. However, this right to privacy can be removed if it is believed that the information that the police are likely to gain will be of substantial value in the prevention of serious crime.

? Questions

1. Describe a situation in which it might be reasonable to withhold certain rights or freedoms contained in Articles 8, 9, 10 or 11.

2. A political party that strongly opposes abortion wishes to make a party broadcast showing detailed images of the process of abortion. The BBC, who would transmit the broadcast, disagrees, claiming that images of this kind are too offensive. What right is under consideration here? Should it be restricted?

■ Competing rights

Both during and immediately after her time in prison, Maxine Carr, the former girlfriend of the Soham murderer, Ian Huntley, received many threats to her life. These were taken so seriously that in 2005 her lawyers asked the High Court to ban the publication of details of her whereabouts.

In reaching a decision, the Court had to decide whether the right of newspapers and others to publish this information (Article 10, freedom of expression) was greater than the threat to Maxine Carr's rights to life (Article 2) and to privacy (Article 8).

The Court decided that the evidence indicated that Ms Carr was likely to be in serious danger if her identity was ever revealed, and that this outweighed the right of newspapers to say where she was living or working. An order was therefore issued banning the publication of any information that could reveal her new identity.

This example shows how human rights cases can involve rights on both sides. It is the job of the Court to assess these competing rights and to decide which one should predominate.

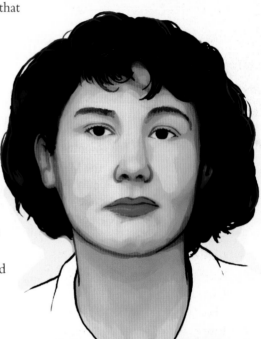

Key words

Democracy
Government by the people or by their elected representatives.

Rule of law
The idea that actions taken by the state (and those who work on its behalf) must be based on proper legal authority, as opposed to the whims or wishes of those in power.

Human rights law

The European Convention on Human Rights

This is a simplified summary of the European Convention on Human Rights.

The European Convention on Human Rights

Article 1
Introduction
This states that all countries signing up to the Convention have a duty to ensure that everyone within their borders has the following rights and freedoms.

Article 2
Right to life
Everyone has the right to have their life protected by law. Taking a life is acceptable only when it is absolutely necessary, for example in self-defence or to protect the life of someone else.

Article 3
Prohibition of torture
Everyone has the right not to be tortured or suffer inhuman or degrading punishment.

Article 4
Prohibition of slavery and forced labour
No one shall be held in slavery or be required to perform forced labour. This right does not apply to work related to military, prison or community service.

Article 5
Right to liberty and security
Everyone has the right not to be detained and deprived of their liberty, unless it is within the law and the correct legal procedures followed. Everyone who is arrested shall be informed of the reason for their arrest in a language they can understand.

Article 6
Right to a fair trial
Everyone has the right to a fair trial and a public hearing within a reasonable period of time. Everyone charged with a criminal offence shall be presumed innocent until proved guilty.

Article 7
No punishment without law
No one should be found guilty of an offence that was not a crime at the time it took place; nor should they receive a heavier punishment than was applicable when the offence was committed.

The European Convention on Human Rights

Article 8
Right to respect for a person's private and family life

Everyone has the right to respect for their private and family life, their home, and their correspondence; although this right may be interfered with in certain circumstances, for example in the prevention of crime.

Article 9
Freedom of thought, conscience and religion

Everyone is free to hold whatever views and beliefs they wish – but their right to express or display these beliefs can be restricted in certain circumstances.

Article 10
Freedom of expression

Everyone has the freedom to express their opinion –

but this may be limited for certain reasons, such as for the protection of public safety or the rights of others.

Article 11
Freedom of assembly and association

Everyone has the right to get together with other people in a peaceful way; this includes the right to form and join a trade union. No restrictions can be placed on this, unless it is for reasons laid down in law – such as national security or public safety.

Article 12
Right to marry

Men and women have the right to marry and have a family – but are bound by the laws covering whom people may or may not

marry and where a marriage may take place.

Article 13
A legal remedy

All states signing this Convention must provide an effective way for people to challenge public bodies or officials whom they believe have unlawfully deprived them of their rights or freedoms under this Convention.

Article 14
Prohibition of discrimination

Everyone is entitled to the rights and freedoms set out in the Convention without discrimination on any grounds, such as their sex, race, colour, language, religion, political opinion, national or social origin, birth or other status.

Convention on Human Rights

Article 2
Right to education

No one shall be denied the right to education. The State must respect the right of parents to ensure that their child's education follows their own religious and philosophical beliefs.

Article 3
Right to free elections

Elections for government must be free and fair and must take place by secret ballot.

Rights to the freedoms in Articles 8–11 may be restricted, where necessary, for reasons such as public safety, protecting the rights of others or preventing crime.

Protocol 1 Article 1
Protection of property

No one shall be deprived of their possessions, except in very limited circumstances. These allow, for example, the State to take money for the payment of taxes or confiscate goods which are unlawful or pose some kind of danger.

Protocol 6 Articles 1 & 2
Abolition of the death penalty

No one shall be condemned to death or executed. However, a state may make provision for the death penalty in its law at times of war or imminent threat of war.

A protocol in this context is a later addition to the Convention.

Human rights law
Rights and freedoms in Britain

■ Ancient and modern

People's rights in Britain are currently protected in three ways:
- by certain legal principles, established by the courts over many years
- by specific pieces of legislation, and
- in more recent times by the *Human Rights Act*.

The Magna Carta signed in 1215 by the barons (wealthy and powerful landowners) and King John, established the right of people not to be unlawfully arrested or to have their property seized by the King. It also established the right of those accused of a crime to be tried by a jury of fellow citizens.

The 1689 Bill of Rights was a very important step in settling the conflict between the monarch and Parliament, by firmly establishing the principle that the King or Queen could not dissolve Parliament and govern as they wish. The Bill also said that taxes could not be raised without Parliament's approval, and that excessive punishment could not be given for minor crimes.

Rights to vote and a ban on unfair discrimination are examples of rights and freedoms that have been created by law over the last 150 years.

■ The long route

Although Britain helped to write the European Convention on Human Rights in 1953, and was the first country to sign it, it did not – unlike many other European countries – give British citizens the right to enforce the Convention through the courts in their own country. As a result, anyone in Britain like Mrs Cosans (page 26) who wanted to try to enforce a right under the Convention, faced a long and difficult process by taking their case first through the British court system and then to the European Court of Human Rights in Strasbourg. One case took nine years to progress through the system.

All change Before the 1997 general election, the Labour and Liberal Democrat parties promised that, if either came to power, they would incorporate the Convention into UK law, enabling most cases to be dealt with by UK courts and tribunals. Labour was elected, and in 1998, the *Human Rights Act* was passed by Parliament. It became law in 2000.

■ The Human Rights Act 1998

Almost all the rights in the European Convention are now part of UK law (the rights are listed on pages 28–9). The Act has had a significant effect on the British legal system.

All laws Under the *Human Rights Act* all UK law must, so far as is possible, be compatible with the Act. This means that any laws we have that are not in line with the Convention must be changed, and that all new law must follow the terms of the Convention. The only time when this is not necessary is in very special circumstances, such as war or other national emergencies, or when Parliament agrees.

Courts When a judge in a British court makes a decision about a case, he or she must follow the principles of the Convention and take into account decisions already made by the European Court of Human Rights.

Public authorities All public bodies – such as local authorities, hospitals, schools and the police – must carry out their work in a way that follows the rights of the Convention. If they don't, then that body may be challenged in court.

Terrorism Article 15 of the Convention allows countries to release themselves from their duties under the Convention in times of emergency – if it is felt to be absolutely essential. This is called derogation. The UK has taken up this option, enabling it to hold or to deport people whom it regards as a terrorist threat.

Headlines On 13 May 2008, a headline in the *Daily Mail* read, 'Human Rights Act has "helped rapists and murders escape justice" for 10 years', alongside a

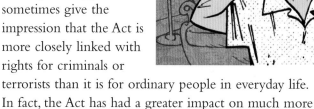

picture of a Middle Eastern terrorist suspect.

This reflects the way in which the *Human Rights Act* is sometimes reported in the press. Opponents sometimes give the impression that the Act is more closely linked with rights for criminals or terrorists than it is for ordinary people in everyday life. In fact, the Act has had a greater impact on much more normal aspects of people's lives.

When Reading Borough Council decided to re-route traffic in the town centre, there was a significant increase in the amount of traffic outside Mr Andrews' house. When the Council rejected his request for help with soundproofing he turned to the courts for help, claiming that the increased noise of the traffic was damaging the quality of his private and family life. The court decided that, although the Council was entitled to make the changes, it had ignored the effects they would have on local residents. Mr Andrews won the case and was awarded compensation.

Controversy The *Human Rights Act* is still an issue of some controversy in Britain today. Some people believe that the Act provides an important way of protecting basic individual freedoms. Others say that it sometimes protects the wrong people, such as criminals or suspected terrorists, and a third group say that our civil liberties need more, not less, protection.

? Questions

1. Should the *Human Rights Act* be changed or dropped? What is your instinct? Would you a) leave it as it is, b) give less protection, c) give more protection or deal with rights in a different way?

You may find the three views below useful in helping you make up your mind.

The *Human Rights Act* …
… protects people against the full force of the state machinery.

… was designed to protect us from over-powerful governments, but is of little use today from other people such as terrorists and violent criminals.

… has failed to protect our human rights: the freedom to protest has been reduced; the police have greater powers of arrest; and government agencies now potentially have access to details (though not including the content) of our phone, email and internet access records, and even our car journeys on motorways and through city centres.

Human rights law

Held in detention

■ The long view

DETENTION ORDER
. . . .

I have reasonable cause to
believe Jack Perlzweig alias
Robert Liversidge to be a
person of hostile associations
and because of this it is
necessary to exercise control
over him.

Under the powers available
to me under reg. 18b of the
Defence of the Realm
Regulations 1939, I direct
that the above-mentioned
Jack Perlzweig alias Robert
Liversidge be detained.

Signed:

John Anderson.
Home Secretary

Date: 26 May 1940

? Questions

1. Read through the note above and write down what you can deduce from its contents.

   a) What was the purpose of the note?
   b) Under what circumstances do you think it was written?
   c) What information is missing from the note?

Regulation 18b In September 1939, Britain declared war on Germany after German forces invaded Poland. By the following May, the occupation had extended to Denmark, Norway, the Netherlands, France and Belgium – and there were strong fears in Britain that it would be the next country to fall under German control.

The British Government's anxiety increased further when a group of British Nazi sympathisers was linked to the theft of top-secret documents. Within days of this discovery, the Cabinet amended existing regulations to allow the Home Secretary to lock up anyone indefinitely simply because it was believed that they might be of 'hostile origins or association'.

Robert Liversidge One of about 1,800 people to be detained in this way was a man called Robert Liversidge. Of Russian Jewish origin, he was arrested because of his business links with known Nazi sympathisers, although there is no reason today to suspect that Mr Liversidge shared these views.

After almost a year's detention, Robert Liversidge challenged the Government's right to hold him in this way, and began court action to require the Government to explain exactly why he was being held.

Mr Liversidge lost his case, with four of the five judges ruling that, in these circumstances, there was no requirement for the **Home Secretary** to give reasons for his detention. Eighteen months after his arrest, Robert Liversidge was released. No apology or explanation was ever given.

? Questions

2. Was Robert Liversidge's arrest reasonable in the circumstances of the time? Draw up a statement that is either in support of or criticises the Home Secretary's actions.

■ The law today

The *Defence of the Realm Regulations* were quietly dropped before the end of the war, and all detainees released.

Today a person cannot normally be detained for more than 24 hours without being charged, but if a serious offence is being investigated, this may be extended to 96 hours (four days) with the approval of a magistrates' court.

Terrorist offences Following IRA bombing campaigns in Britain in the early 1970s, the police were given extra time (up to seven days) to hold suspects before they were charged or released.

Police powers in investigating terrorist offences have since been further raised. In 2005, the maximum period that a suspect may be held without charge was raised from 14 days to its current level of 28 days.

If the suspect is from overseas and cannot be deported back to their own country, because of the risk of torture or death, the Home Secretary can order their indefinite detention under the *Anti-Terrorism and Security Act 2001*.

■ Greater powers?

Early in 2008, the Government announced further anti-terrorism measures, including proposals to extend the time a suspect can be held without charge to 42 days. They said that this power would be used very rarely and would contain safeguards to make sure that it was not abused.

In favour . . . Those in favour of the change argued that the growing complexity and international nature of terrorist plots meant that the police now needed more time to question suspects and gather evidence. Although they agreed that there had not yet been any cases where more than 28 days was required, they said that it would

be only a matter of time before the need would arise – and it would be a good idea to have a law already available to deal with this.

Against . . . Those disagreeing with the proposal said that it was inhumane and unnecessary and that Britain already has the power to detain suspected terrorists longer than many other comparable countries. Many also argued that it was contrary to a right that people in Britain had enjoyed for hundreds of years – the right to be brought before a court to check the legality of the detention. In October 2008, the Bill to introduce this measure was defeated in the House of Lords, and the Government announced that – for the time being as least – the proposal would be dropped.

? Questions

3. Do you think the Government was right to try to be able to detain suspected terrorists for 42 days? How would you have voted in the debate?

Key words

Home Secretary
The Government minister with chief responsibility for the maintenance of law and order in the UK.

International human rights

This unit outlines the work of the United Nations and human rights.

The United Nations

■ Origins

Although the Second World War did not end until 1945, discussions between the Allied nations began as early as 1941 about ways of maintaining international peace when the fighting was over. These continued for the remainder of the war, and in 1945, shortly after peace was declared in Europe, an agreement was signed by 51 nations, including Britain, establishing the United Nations (UN).

Today, UN membership has risen to 192 member states, all of whom have signed the UN Charter. This is an international treaty under which members agree to keep the peace between nations, to respect human rights, and to work together to try to overcome other international problems.

The UN's main objectives are:

- to help maintain international peace and security
- to promote respect for human rights
- to provide food, shelter and other assistance to people affected by natural or man-made disasters
- to help overcome other world problems, including protection of the environment, poverty, drug-trafficking and terrorism.

■ The General Assembly

Today the UN is the largest and one of the most important international organisations in the world. Its main body is the General Assembly (a kind of parliament) where all member states are represented, and where each has one vote. Decisions over questions of international peace and security, however, are mainly dealt with in the UN by the Security Council – a small but powerful group of 15 nations, with China, France, Russia, the UK and the USA as the five permanent members.

The General Assembly meets for three months each year at the UN headquarters in New York, where a wide range of international issues are debated and voted upon.

Recommendations or decisions by the Assembly do not carry the force of law, but they are an important way of telling a member state what other countries think it should or should not be doing.

■ The Universal Declaration of Human Rights

In 1948, after intense debate and discussion by UN member states, a Universal Declaration of Human Rights was adopted.

The Declaration is made up of approximately 30 rights, which include the right to:

- be free from slavery, torture and arbitrary arrest
- a fair trial
- freedom of thought, conscience and religion
- freedom of expression

- peaceful assembly – the right to meet and form associations with other people
- education
- take part in and select their government.

It is important to note that the Universal Declaration of Human Rights does not have the force of law, unlike the European Convention on Human Rights (see pages 28–9), but it is nevertheless a very important measure by which the behaviour of states can be judged.

Protecting human rights Sometimes the UN becomes directly involved in protecting human rights, as it did in Liberia in 2003, where atrocities were being committed by both rebel and government forces, resulting in the injury and death of thousands of civilians, including children.

■ The Human Rights Council

The Human Rights Council (HRC) is the UN's main human rights body, with the job of assessing human rights violations throughout the world and making recommendations on what should be done. It is made up of representatives from 47 UN member states. Britain is currently one of these.

Problems The Human Rights Council was created in 2006. Its predecessor, the Human Rights Commission, was closed down after heavy criticism of its failure to deal properly with human rights abuses. One of the problems, its critics said, was that some of the countries who belonged to the Commission had very poor human rights records themselves. This was embarrassing for the United Nations but, more importantly, often led to a refusal to take action in countries where human rights abuses were occurring.

? Questions

1. The idea of an independent council seems very sensible, but how should members be selected? Here are three possible ways of doing this. Which do you think is the best? Can you suggest any better alternatives?

   Seats on the Council should be:

   a) given only to countries with a good human rights record, or

   b) chosen by each UN member state voting for the country of its choice; with seats going to the countries with most votes, or

   c) allocated by giving each major area in the world, e.g. Africa, Asia, etc., a fixed number of seats, according to its population, and then allowing the countries in each area to choose the states that they would like to represent them.

   If you choose:

   a) it means that most of the seats will be given to countries in Europe, North America, and Australasia.

   b) or c) it means that seats will almost certainly be given to countries with poor human rights records, and that states like Britain, with a relatively good record, will have much less influence.

   However, at the moment the five states with the greatest influence in the UN are China, France, Russia, the UK and the USA, so if you choose b) or c) you will be giving power to smaller or less powerful nations that are not normally well represented at the UN.

2. The leaders of some states believe that other countries have no right to interfere in their affairs and tell them what they should or should not do. What is your view on this?

3. 'Building a country's wealth and prosperity should come first – then we can worry about human rights.' What are the strengths and weaknesses of this argument?

Family

This unit looks at some of the different kinds of family arrangements that are now common in Britain today and asks to what degree governments should attempt to influence people's family life.

Changing times

▉ Yesterday

Sheila and Patrick Callanan were married in 1953 and settled in north London. They soon started a family and, over the next 18 years, had a total of 12 children. This was unusually large by the standards of the 1960s and 1970s, but had been common in some communities in previous generations. Sheila and Patrick had been married for just over 35 years when Patrick died in 1989.

▉ Today

Although they are all now in their forties and fifties and holding down good jobs, four of the Callanan clan still live in the family home and 11 of them gather weekly for Sunday lunch, cooked by their mother.

❓ Questions

1. What do you think are the advantages and disadvantages of this type of family arrangement?

▉ Marriage

Six of the family have partners, five have married and three have children. Through their own choice most have decided to remain single or not yet marry – reflecting current trends towards later marriage, smaller families and independent living.

❓ Questions

2. Why do you think many younger people today have, like some of the Callanans, chosen to stay independent or to live together and not marry?

▉ Traditional families: image or reality?

The Callanans are what is known as an extended family. More common is the nuclear family of two married parents living with their children at the same address, and often some distance from close relations. This is just one example of the different forms of family patterns that we have today.

Married couples	Cohabiting couples	Lone-parent families

1986: 12%, 5%, 83%

2008: 24%, 12%, 64%

❓ Questions

3. What changes do you notice in family arrangements between 1986 and 2006?

4. Suggest and explain one positive and one negative consequence of the move away from the traditional nuclear family.

Explaining family diversity

Family patterns today can vary a great deal. They may be led by a single adult, based on cohabitation (living together) rather than marriage, or be a step-family containing parents or children from more than one family. Some reasons for these changes are set out below.

Marriage   More people are deciding to delay marriage (particularly those who spend longer in education) or not to marry at all. People who marry later tend to have smaller families.

Contraception   Advances in contraception have granted women greater control over when, whether and with whom they have children.

Employment   Changes at work and in the home have led to women gaining more financial and social independence from men. This means that they may be less inclined to stay in an unhappy relationship.

Women who want a career tend to have fewer children and take less time out from work.

New law   Changing attitudes to homosexuality have seen the emergence of more families led by gay or lesbian couples. A new law came into force in 2005, the *Civil Partnership Act*, allowing same-sex couples to register as civil partners, giving them the same legal rights as couples who are married.

Divorce   Separation and divorce have become more commonplace and are no longer stigmatised in the way that they once were. As separation and divorce have grown, so has remarriage, making step-families increasingly common.

Family values

Some people regret the decline of the traditional family and are critical of other kinds of family arrangements. They believe that, where possible, children should live with two parents who are married to each other – an arrangement, they argue, which works for the benefit of the individual and for society as a whole.

In 2007, the leader of the Conservative Party, David Cameron, made a speech about the importance of family life, stressing the value of time spent by parents and children together and the importance of families in times of crisis.

Mr Cameron quoted statistics showing that married parents with children are less likely to split up than those who are not married, and argued that more should be done to encourage couples to marry. This he suggested, could be done by giving extra help to married couples through the tax and benefit systems.

ONE-THIRD OF MARRIAGES NOW END IN DIVORCE!

CON
R

NEW GOVERNM
shown that the fail
is still on the incr
The results of a
the divorce rate
risen to a poin
couples enter
themselves i

? Questions

5. How do responsibilities, roles and patterns of behaviour vary in families that you know?

6. Should a government use the tax and benefits system to encourage parents to marry, stay together and live their lives in a particular way – or are these personal matters which they should not attempt to control? Try to explain your answer.

Family

Parents' rights and responsibilities

Not in school

In 2008, a mother from Middlesbrough was sentenced to 28 days in prison for failing to ensure that her two daughters attended school.

Her 16-year-old daughter had not been to school at all between April and October, and the girl's younger sister, aged 14, had been in school for only seven days during the same period.

The mother's 18-year-old son said, 'It's the girls' fault, not hers. She shouldn't be put away for something like this.' But Middlesbrough Council were pleased with the sentence. A Council spokeswoman said, 'I hope this helps parents understand that it is their responsibility to ensure that their children not only set off to school, but reach their destination and actually remain there all day. We always work closely with parents to try to help them get their children to school, and sending a parent to prison is always a last resort.'

? Questions

1. Many people support the idea of jailing parents who allow their children to play truant. Others disagree, believing that young people can't be forced to learn and that forcing pupils to remain in school often makes life harder for others. Outline how you would deal with young people who play truant from school.

Bringing up children

The responsibility to make sure that their children have a proper full-time education is one of a number of legal duties given to parents. These duties, however, are not set out in one law, but in **case law** and a number of different **statutes**. For example, the duty of parents to make sure that their children have an efficient full-time education is set out in the *Education Act 1996*.

Other responsibilities of parents can be summarised in the following way:

Protection   Parents must not ill-treat, neglect or abandon their children, and have a duty to protect them from harm. A mother from Powys, who left her 14-year-old daughter at home for six weeks while she went on holiday, was given a suspended jail sentence and required to carry out 130 hours of unpaid work. Before travelling to Greece to visit her boyfriend, she had given her daughter £100 and left the freezer stocked with frozen meals.

Support and care   Parents have a duty to make sure that their children are properly fed, housed and clothed. They also have a duty to support their children's emotional needs. These duties apply to both parents, whether they are married, divorced, living together or living apart.

Guidance and discipline   Parents have a responsibility to guide and discipline their children – but today physical punishment must not extend beyond 'mild smacking', otherwise a parent may be guilty of a criminal offence (see page 11). If a child damages something, or injures someone, the injured party may be able to make a successful claim against the child's parents if it can be shown that, for example, their negligence led to the accident.

Healthcare   Parents who fail to provide or obtain adequate medical care for their child may face a charge of neglect.

Parental responsibility

All married couples automatically have parental responsibility for their child. This gives them the duty to care for their child and the power to make all the appropriate decisions over his or her upbringing.

When parents are not married, only the *mother* automatically has parental responsibility. An unmarried father can obtain parental responsibility only by signing the birth register jointly with the mother (if she agrees), by marrying her, or by registering for parental responsibility through a court.

Parental responsibility lasts until the child reaches 18 years of age.

If things go wrong

If parents are not providing their children with basic standards of care, support and guidance, the local authority may step in. As far as possible, it will try to keep the family unit together, working with the family and the children to give them the support that they need.

If the local authority suspects that a child is not receiving the care that is expected of a parent, and that this is causing, or is likely to cause, significant harm, it has a legal duty to investigate and to decide what action is appropriate.

If it decides that the child is being harmed because of a lack of parental care (or their behaviour is beyond parental control), the local authority will apply to a court for the child to be taken into their care. If this is granted, responsibility for looking after the child moves to the local authority.

Under the *Children Act 1989*, additional powers are available to the police to remove a child to a place of safety, for a limited period of time, if the officer believes that there is an immediate risk to the child's safety.

Children are not always taken into care permanently. Sometimes it may be a temporary measure, because their parent is ill or cannot provide them with proper accommodation.

The best interests of the child When a court makes any kind of decision about the care or welfare of a child, it must place the interests of the child above all other considerations. In reaching this decision, a court will take into account the child's wishes, their needs, their age and background, the capability of their parents and the likely effect on the child of a change in circumstances.

❓ Questions

2. Why do you think the law, where possible, tries to keep parents and children together? What are the difficulties associated with this?

3. What are some of the questions that magistrates need to consider in deciding whether to place a child in the care of the local authority?

Key words

Case law
Law that has been established by the decision of a judge or judges that is applied in later cases to similar situations.

Statute
A law that has been passed by both Houses of Parliament and received the royal assent; also known as an Act of Parliament.

Parents' rights and wrongs

No harm done?

It's lunchtime in a busy fast food restaurant. A mother sits down with her two children. One is a little girl aged three, the other a baby asleep in his pram. The mother opens a box of chicken nuggets, and places it in front of the little girl; then she unwraps a burger for herself.

A few minutes later, the little girl decides that she has had enough to eat and climbs down from her chair. Her mother is still eating her own meal and tells her daughter to finish everything she has been given. The girl refuses, and moves away from her mother, starting to run around the restaurant.

The mother calls her back, but the little girl takes no notice. The mother is tired but decides to try once more to get her daughter to finish her meal. She walks across the restaurant to where her daughter is standing, and tells the little girl not to be naughty, but, just as she reaches her, the little girl lies down on the floor and starts to scream. The mother grabs her daughter by her ear and hits her across the side of the face. Then she hits the girl twice on her bottom, telling her to behave properly and finish her food.

? Questions

1. At least 20 people in the restaurant are watching. What, if anything, should they do? Is there anything they should not do? Explain your answer.

2. Has the woman done anything wrong? Has she broken the law? You can check this by looking at the section the law, opposite.

Criminal behaviour?

The manager of the restaurant first noticed the family when he heard the little girl's mother telling her to finish her meal. He continued to watch as events unfolded. When he saw the girl being hit, he decided to call the police.

Two officers arrived at the restaurant just as the woman was leaving with her children. One of the officers began to question her, while the other spoke to the manager. A few minutes later the woman was arrested and taken with her children to the police station. Later she was charged with causing actual bodily harm.

In court, a witness said that the mother hit her daughter with great force, adding that he had never before seen anything like it. The manager said that he had called the police because the blow was so severe.

The mother stated that she loved her daughter and would never do anything to harm her. She said that she had slapped the little girl only once on her bottom.

? Questions

3. Does the evidence suggest that the mother used unreasonable force and therefore broke the law?

4. Was the restaurant manager right to phone the police?

State interference?

The *Prevention of Cruelty to Children Act 1889* was the first piece of legislation in England and Wales designed to protect children from cruel parents. The main reason why this was so late in coming (the first laws against cruelty to animals had been passed almost 70 years earlier) was the attitude of the time that kept

www.childline.org.uk   020 7730 3300   www.nspcc.org.uk

people's public and private lives completely separate. For many it was unthinkable that the state should interfere in people's private or domestic lives.

The right of the state to control the ways in which parents bring up and discipline their children is still an issue today. In 2004, in a Parliamentary debate on whether to impose a complete ban on smacking in England and Wales, Conservative MP Andrew Robothan argued, 'Most parents can look after their children much better without the interference of legislators, the police or social services.'

Although the *Children Act 2004* is quite recent, a parent's right to smack their child continues to be debated. In 2006, the Children's Commissioner for England wrote a very critical letter to the Government, calling for a total ban on smacking. In 2007, Members of the Welsh Assembly (see page 152) tried to ban smacking in Wales, but lacked the law-making powers to do so. In 2008, a group of MPs again called for a change in the law.

The law

Under the *Children Act 2004*, a parent is allowed to issue 'reasonable chastisement' (punishment), but may not punish a child in a way that leaves marks such as a bruise, graze, cut or swelling.

A parent who inflicts unreasonable punishment on their child may be charged with cruelty, common assault, or causing actual or grievous bodily harm.

'If a parent cannot slipper a child, the world is going potty.'
Judge Ian McLean

'This Labour Government believes in parental discipline. Smacking has a part in that. Our law will do nothing to outlaw smacking.'
Paul Boateng MP, when he was Minister for Health

'Smacking children is morally wrong. If people are smacked a lot it's bound to cause problems. But I don't think it should be a punishable offence. That would be an invasion of individual rights.'
Si Piwko, parent

'There's a big difference between smacking, hitting and beating. There's no harm in a little slap given at the right time for the right reason.'
Dannii Fortune, parent

? Questions

5. Should there be an outright ban on smacking in England and Wales? Here are some of the arguments in favour and against. Which do you find the most and least convincing?

In favour
- Children should have the same protection against physical assault as adults.
- Smacking is bad parenting; it's much harder not to smack.
- By failing to ban corporal punishment, the UK is breaking the UN Convention on the Rights of the Child.
- Allowing parents to hit their children is out of step with modern society.

Against
- There's no harm in a little slap at the right time for the right reason.
- It is not the job of the State to tell parents what they can and cannot do with their children.
- Parents who give their children a light smack should not be criminalised.
- The nanny-state disapproval of smacking has led to greater violence in society.

School

This unit looks at some questions of rights and responsibilities in education and at the way it is organised today in England and Wales.

A right to education?

▮ Lesson time

Chris is in Year 10. His behaviour in class is usually quite disruptive; he rarely pays attention, but complains loudly that he doesn't understand; he swears a lot, and distracts other students by moving around the class. Most teachers find him difficult to deal with. A group of students complain to their head of year over the amount of time teachers spend dealing with Chris in lessons.

❓ Questions

1. In what ways is Chris's behaviour likely to affect other students?

2. What kinds of action could the school take to try deal with this situation?

3. Why should the school try to help Chris, if he won't help himself?

A duty to educate   Under the *Education Act 1996*, parents have the responsibility to make sure that their children receive a suitable education between the ages of five and 16. For most children, this means regularly attending school, although parents can also choose to educate their children at home.

It is the local authority's responsibility to ensure that there are enough places and facilities in schools to provide all children in the area with an appropriate education. This might include the provision of special schools for children with special educational needs or gifted and talented programmes for the most able.

Schools are expected to provide a good standard of education for all pupils. All schools are inspected by Ofsted (the Office for Standards in Education, Children's

Services and Skills) to check that they are working to the required standards and to help them improve where necessary.

Next steps   At first, teachers tended to give Chris extra work or place him in detention, which he rarely completed or attended. He was then placed on report, and his parents were asked to come into school. The school agreed that Chris needed support in lessons, but said that a shortage of funding and the needs of other children meant that a learning support assistant could be provided for only three lessons a week.

Although Chris's behaviour improved, especially with support, he soon started to misbehave again. On two separate occasions, he was excluded from school for three days for being abusive to a member of staff.

One morning the head of year is called to deal with an incident in class in which Chris has allegedly been involved. In the argument that follows, he loses control, strikes the head of year, and smashes a chair onto a desk. Two other teachers are called. Chris leaves the room and is taken to the head, who considers whether the boy should be permanently excluded.

? Questions

4. The headteacher has a number of options: a) fixed-term exclusion b) permanent exclusion c) to try to transfer Chris to another school, or d) to make arrangements by which Chris remains in his present school. Which would you propose, and why?

5. What would you suggest are the benefits and drawbacks of permanent exclusion?

Exclusion

All schools must have a behaviour policy, informing students and parents of the standards of behaviour that are expected in school, along with the measures that will be taken if the policy is not followed.

Fixed-term exclusions should only be given when a student gets into serious trouble, such as a persistent refusal to follow school rules, or behaviour that is harming the education of others.

The decision to permanently exclude a student should be taken as a last resort, and should be used only when the school has done everything it can to improve a child's behaviour. Students who commit serious offences, such as bringing an offensive weapon to school, face immediate permanent exclusion.

Some schools operate a system of *internal* exclusion, by educating students separately from the remainder of the school. Under these arrangements, students may be out of some or all classes for a short or long period of time. In many areas, students facing permanent exclusion are transferred to another school. This is known as a 'managed move' and means that no reference is made to permanent exclusion on the student's record. Schools that transfer a child in this way are required to take another pupil in their place. If the school refuses, it faces a financial penalty.

Too many exclusions?

In recent years, the Government has become concerned about the rising number of students who are excluded from school on a fixed-term or permanent basis; and has been developing ways of keeping in school students who would otherwise be excluded.

Students, who are permanently excluded must, within six days, be provided with a full-time education by the local authority. In many cases this means attending a pupil referral unit or learning centre. A smaller number of children are educated at home on a one-to-one basis.

Although the exclusion of a child may benefit the school that he or she has left, research indicates that permanent exclusion tends to trigger changes in the young person's life leading to further exclusion from society.

Exclusion is likely to reduce a young person's chances of educational success, cut their ties with friends at school, and increase the likelihood of their involvement in criminal behaviour.

? Questions

6. Is it possible to keep disruption in school to a minimum and avoid permanently excluding disruptive students? If you believe it is, explain how you think this can be achieved. If not, explain why, and what you feel needs to be in place to support excluded students.

School
A matter of faith

◼ New beginnings

2008 marked the opening of the first state-funded Hindu school in Britain. It's a primary school, built on a five-acre site, and situated in an area of north London where almost a third of the residents are Hindu.

For many people who live nearby, the school is a statement of their identity. It aims to help children of Hindu parents understand Hindu traditions and to show the rest of the community some of the important things that the Hindu religion can offer wider society.

Children of all faiths may be admitted to the school, but priority is given to those from families who either practise or broadly follow the Hindu faith. If there are more applicants than places available, children from families outside the Hindu faith have the lowest priority. (This policy is common amongst faith schools of all types.)

The children at school are taught the National Curriculum, combined with faith teachings (primarily about Hinduism, but also other faiths), Sanskrit and other aspects of Indian life and culture.

? Questions

1. Put yourself in the positions of two different people – one a supporter of the school, and the other, a critic. What arguments do you think a supporter might give *in favour* of a school of this type? What points might be made by the critic?

◼ Church and State

There has always been a strong link between education and religion in England and Wales. In medieval times, it was the Church that tended to provide the small amount of education that was available to ordinary people – and this pattern continued well into the nineteenth century, as Britain began to industrialise.

It was during this period that the Government began to recognise the importance of an educated workforce, and started to take more interest in the provision and organisation of schools. However, the Church was reluctant to lose its position of power within the education system and fought a number of battles with the State to retain some influence and control over what was taught in schools. Legacies of this are seen today by the presence of more than 4,600 Church of England schools and in the legal requirement for state schools to hold religious assemblies and teach religious education.

Today There are over 7,000 state-maintained faith schools in England and Wales today. In England they constitute one in every three schools; in Wales, one in seven. Most faith schools are in the primary sector. The Church of England (and the Church of Wales, in Wales) has by far the largest number of schools, followed by the Roman Catholic Church. There are also 37 state-funded Jewish schools, seven Muslim schools, and two Sikh schools. The Hindu, Seventh-day Adventist and Greek Orthodox religions each have one school.

No admittance

Mrs Foley lives opposite one of the largest schools in the north-west. The facilities at the school are excellent and its examination results are well above the local and national averages. However, Mrs Foley's daughter, Jane, will not be going to the school next September because her parents do not follow the Christian faith.

'We don't go to church,' said Mrs Foley. 'I don't believe in God; but I do think my daughter ought to have the chance to go to her local school.'

The school in question is a Church of England faith school. Its grounds and buildings are owned by the Church, but almost all the funding is provided by the local authority. Like all faith schools, there is a strong emphasis on religious values, and the school will only accept pupils from families who can demonstrate that they follow the Christian faith. Amongst the factors the school takes into account in deciding whether to admit a pupil is how regularly the child and their parents attend weekly worship.

The headteacher of the school explained, 'We don't discriminate on the basis of sex or race, but we do discriminate on grounds of faith.'

Good and bad Those who support faith schools often claim that they provide a higher standard of education than other schools. In fact, some parents are so anxious to obtain a place for their child that they start attending worship simply to get their child into a particular school.

Faith schools enable parents to have their child educated in a way that follows their own beliefs; they may also limit the child's exposure to other values with which the parents may disagree.

Critics, however, state that separate schools of this kind are a not a good way of drawing people together, or of helping children to appreciate different ways of life. Faith schools, they argue, tend to educate children for a single vision of life, which is not healthy in today's diverse society.

? Questions

2. In most areas of life in Britain today, religious discrimination is against the law. Is it acceptable for a child to be refused entry to a school on the grounds of their religion or lack of it? Explain your views.

3. Many faith schools, particularly in the primary sector, take children from other religious or non-religious backgrounds. It has been suggested that all faith schools should be required to do this by law. Would you support this idea?

4. Since 2001, the Government has given strong support to all faiths to develop schools within the state education sector, particularly when they have the support of the local community. Do you agree with this policy, or would you suggest a different approach? Try to explain your views.

School

School choice

▮ Admission impossible

Priya Watson is ten years old, and in her last year in primary school. She likes school, and is good at most subjects. Her parents are deciding to which secondary schools she should apply.

They have several choices. Most of her friends will be going to the local community comprehensive school, about a mile away. Others have applied to a new academy, with excellent facilities, which opened last year on the other side of the city. Two are hoping to go to a Catholic school, which has a very good reputation, but involves a round trip of nearly 40 miles a day.

Priya's parents have two further choices. They can put their daughter's name down to take the entrance exam at a grammar school, in a different county, 12 miles away; or they can apply for a place at an independent school, where the school fees are just over £15,000 a year. Mr and Mrs Watson have a combined annual income of £30,000.

❓ Questions

1. How should Mr and Mrs Watson decide which school(s) Priya should apply for?

2. On the information you have been given, are there any options that you think they should reject straight away? Explain why.

The way we were

School attendance first became compulsory in England and Wales in 1880. School choice was limited and, for the next 60 years, most children went to their local school from the age of five, until they were 12 or 14. Some obtained a scholarship to go to a grammar school, and a smaller number were educated privately.

After the Second World War, the education system in England and Wales was fundamentally altered. From the late 1940s, all children in the state sector went to primary school between the ages of five and 11 before transferring to a secondary school. Their choice of secondary school was largely determined by their performance in the 11-plus exam. Those who did well went to a grammar school. Those with lower marks (the majority) went to either a technical or secondary modern school.

Children at grammar schools tended to have many more educational opportunities than those who went elsewhere. Because of this, some people began to criticise the 11-plus system for the way in which it separated children from their friends and favoured a fortunate minority (often – but not always – children from better-off families).

In the 1960s, the idea of abolishing the 11-plus gained increasing support, and the Government tried to replace grammar and secondary modern schools with a new system of comprehensive education.

Comprehensive schools had no entrance exam, and almost all children were admitted, regardless of ability. Each school had a designated catchment area, and most children went to their local school.

Some grammar schools, however, were retained, particularly in areas with a Conservative-controlled council. A smaller number of children continued to attend church schools, most commonly under the control of the Church of England (or Wales) or the Roman Catholic Church.

Schools today

During the late 1970s and 1980s, politicians became increasingly concerned about the quality of education provided in many comprehensive schools, stressing the need for higher standards and improved performance. Since then, both Conservative and Labour governments have introduced changes through which these aims might be achieved.

Choice In 1988, the Conservative Government introduced the *Education Reform Act*, which allowed parents to choose for their child any school (in theory) that they wished. One of the reasons for this was the wish to give parents more choice in their children's education. Another was a desire by the Government to introduce competition between schools, in the hope that standards would rise as schools tried to attract as many students as possible.

This policy was further developed by the next Labour Government, with the creation of a wider range of schools, including specialist schools, academies, foundation and trust schools.

However, the opportunity for parents to choose their child's school has meant that better-performing schools are generally over-subscribed. In some areas, parents may not get their first or even second choice. This sometimes leads to anger and frustration, and time-consuming appeals.

Elsewhere In Sweden, currently, parents are given an education voucher for each child, which they can 'spend' at any school, including those run privately. Places are allocated on a first-come-first-served basis. In Scotland, and many other parts of Europe, most children simply go to their local school.

? Questions

3. Should parents be given a choice over which school their children attend? Write a response – in support or criticism – of one of these views:

   a) 'All parents have a right to choose where their children are educated.'

   b) 'The more choice you give, the more you raise expectations, and the more you are disappointed.'

   c) 'Choice doesn't help me decide where my children go to school; public transport is poor where I live, and I can't drive. Choice benefits children from wealthier families.'

4. Imagine it is the 2030s and your own children will be starting secondary school next year. Which of the following situations would you most welcome? Explain why.

   - **Back to the 50s** All children take an examination like the 11-plus to determine which type of school they will attend.

   - **Free choice** Parents apply to whichever school they feel is best for their child.

   - **Local schools** Children automatically attend the school closest to their home.

   - **Home** More encouragement is given to parents to educate their children at home.

School

Student voice

Reservations

Bernard Jones is headteacher of a comprehensive school in Oxford. He is a good head, liked by the pupils and respected by the staff. When thinking about changes to the school, he always makes a point of consulting widely before doing anything. With just over 700 students the school is not particularly large. Mr Jones prides himself on knowing every student by name.

'I make myself available to students every lunchtime,' said Mr Jones. 'I am out and about in the school. Pupils can always come up to me and tell me what's on their minds.'

Although there is a school council in Mr Jones's school, he has some doubts about its value. He thinks that too often school councils do not work and can give pupils the wrong idea about democracy.

'The one thing adolescents can spot a mile off is hypocrisy and I reckon schools typically are full of hypocrisy. The words don't fit the music. They say one thing and immediately do another. There are limits to the powers of school councils. I and my deputies see all students personally once a year and I give them a chance to tell me if they would like to see anything changed.'

? Questions

1. How far do you agree with Mr Jones's views? Discuss the advantages and disadvantages of his system of giving students a direct voice.

School councils

Since December 2005, it has been compulsory for every primary, secondary and special school in Wales to have a school council. The law is quite detailed in this respect,

setting out how often meetings must be held and requiring heads and governors to respond to all matters raised by the council.

School councils are not compulsory in England (although they are present in almost every school), but schools are required by law to consult with students about matters of school organisation that may affect them.

Stile Way School in Cheshire has 1,900 students. The school is divided into six houses, each with a student council. Each house council sends one student to the main school council, which also includes the head, teaching and non-teaching staff, a parent and a governor.

Recent questions for discussion:
- What new lunchtime and after school clubs would you like to see in school?
- What kinds of healthy food should we stock in the school vending machines?
- What measures can you suggest for improving the state of the school toilets?
- The school council has £800 to spend. How should it be used?

Organisation   The schools council in many schools is made up of one representative from each form, elected by class members.

This arrangement can produce a council of as many as 50 students, which some headteachers feel is too large. An alternative is to introduce a two-tier council, with house or class councils reporting to a relatively small council of year reps.

Havenden Community College in Sussex has 2,000 students. Every form elects a representative who sits on the school council, which is made up of more than 60 students. Two teachers also attend.

Recent questions for discussion:
- What are your opinions of recent changes in the school day?
- How can students become more involved in selecting senior staff?
- Who will represent the school on the town's youth council?
- Where is the best place to locate the new Year 10 base?

Agenda   Today, school councils are typically involved in decisions about school policies, recycling, anti-bullying, uniforms, charity fundraising and the purchase of new equipment for the school.

Less common is consultation with students over the appointment of staff, changes in the curriculum and feedback to teachers on lessons and courses.

Governing body   Students cannot legally become school governors, but can become 'associate members', which allows them to attend meetings and take part in discussions, but not to vote.

? Questions

2. Compare and contrast these two school councils, including the way that they are made up and the business they deal with.

3. One student said of the council in her school, 'We can complain until we're blue in the face about our limited choice of options or the lack of good sex and drugs education, but we're not really taken seriously unless we're talking about things like locks on the toilet doors and toilet rolls.'

   Why is this student critical of the council? What steps might improve the situation?

4. Are there any issues that should never be discussed by a school council? If so, what are they, and why?

5. School councils are sometimes criticised for not being representative of the whole school. Can you suggest any ways in which this problem might be overcome? Explain your answer.

6. What aspects of school life do you consider worth reviewing in your own school?

Consumer rights

This unit outlines the law covering many of the things that we buy every day.

Contract

■ Not necessarily in writing

Almost every time we buy **goods** or **services** we enter into a contract.

This is a legal agreement in which a person, a company or some kind of organisation agrees to provide goods or services for someone else in return, usually for money.

Contracts, as everyone knows, can be long and complicated documents. But most of the contracts that we make are not written down at all. Every time we buy something from a shop, a contract is made between the shop owner and ourselves.

A contract can also be made, even if nothing is said between the people involved. Paying for parking in a ticket machine or buying goods on the internet are examples of this.

■ Failing to deliver

If the thing that you have paid for doesn't work properly or is not what you were promised, it means that the shop or person you were dealing with has failed to keep their side of the contract.

In this situation, the law says that you are entitled to your money back or **compensation** from the person or company with whom the contract was made.

? Questions

1. Look at the pictures above and decide, in each case, whether a contract has been broken and, if so, by whom.

What if ...?

A
- the customer complains that the coffee is cold?
- the customer decides she would rather have tea?

- the checkout assistant realises that a jar of drinking chocolate has been wrongly priced and tells the customer she will have to pay £2 more?

B
- the customer buys the PC, but later decides that she can't afford it?
- the customer has to wait much longer for the computer to be delivered that she expected?

C
- the customer wishes to change the carton of orange juice for a cheaper brand?

■ Disappointment

Elaine and Gary booked their honeymoon in the seaside resort of Sosua in the Dominican Republic. The tour operator's brochure promised that everything was included in the price.

'Every single gin and tonic, every single snack and nightcap has been paid for in advance,' claimed the brochure.

'All leisure facilities, like archery, scuba diving and the health suite are completely free of charge.'

But when Elaine and Gary reached the hotel, the service that they received was not what they had expected.

'Just after we arrived,' Elaine explained, 'we were given a photocopied list of everything that was free. The trouble was, it just didn't match the brochure.'

Gary explained that they both planned to learn how to scuba dive when they were out there. 'The first lesson, in the swimming pool, was free,' said Gary, 'but after that it cost £30 an hour and you had to take a bus further up the coast, because it was too dangerous to swim in the water where we were.'

'We really felt cheated,' said Elaine. 'Our choice of free alcoholic drinks was limited to four – and you had to pay for anything you wanted to drink after eleven o'clock at night.'

'Sosua itself was lovely,' said Gary, 'but we felt we had been misled. There were no archery facilities at all – and the health suite was little more than a couple of cycling machines and a sun lounger. We've got one of those at home.

'The fortnight's holiday cost £3,000 – and I reckon we had to pay another £600 just to do the things that we had planned.

'We weren't the only ones who were disappointed. Other people at the hotel felt the same way. In fact when we complained to the manager, he said that the holiday that we had booked had been withdrawn in December – but that the tour operator was still continuing to offer it.'

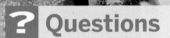

? Questions

2. Why were Elaine and Gary disappointed with their holiday?

3. Who was responsible for the holiday not being as they expected?

4. After their holiday Elaine and Gary wrote to the tour operator to complain about the problems that they had on their holiday.

   Look at the rest of the information on this double-page spread. What points would you suggest Elaine and Gary should make in their letter to the tour operator?

Key words

Compensation
A sum of money to make up for loss or damage a person suffers.

Goods
Items or possessions.

Services
Work that is done for payment, such as hairdressing, plumbing or repairs to a car.

Consumer rights
When things go wrong

■ As we were

For hundreds of years there have been laws designed to protect the quality and price of things that ordinary people buy. The sale of essential items, such as bread, beer, meat and fuel, has almost always been controlled by law.

However, anyone buying something else – like a horse or a cart – had very little protection in law. If the horse was sick or the cart fell to pieces, there was little a buyer could do, unless they could prove that they had been *deliberately* misled at the time of purchase. This is the origin of the legal expression *caveat emptor*, meaning *buyer beware*. It is still used today, and is particularly important when buying something privately, such as a car.

Best before   In 1350, Londoner Richard Quelhogge bought, for four pence, a pig that he found lying by the side of the Thames. Richard then apparently cut off the hind legs of the animal and tried to sell them.

Whether they were bought and eaten is not known, but Richard did find himself in court for selling *putride and stinking meat*. He was found guilty and sentenced to stand in the pillory, whilst the remainder of the animal was burnt at his feet.

Today, the sale of food continues to be heavily controlled by law.

■ Changing times

The end of the nineteenth century was a time of great change in Britain. Many people left the countryside and moved into towns and cities and more and more of the goods they used were made in factories. But when these items didn't work or failed in some way, it was very difficult for people to get their money back or obtain compensation.

One problem was the law. There were no neat rules, setting out people's rights and responsibilities. Instead, the law lay hidden in complicated documents, recording verdicts brought by judges in court.

In order to deal with this, Parliament in the late 1800s passed a whole new series of Acts. These tried to set out the law relating to goods and services in a much clearer and simpler way.

Today

During the twentieth century the law continued to change as shopping and buying things grew in importance in our society.

The law applying to most of the things that we buy today is the *Sale of Goods Act 1979*. This states that all goods sold by a trader must:

✔ *be of satisfactory quality* They must be free from faults and not scratched or damaged in any way

✔ *be fit for all their intended purposes* The goods must do what they are designed to do and, in particular, what the sales assistant or the packaging claims

✔ *match the description* They must be the same as they are described in an advertisement, on the packaging or by the sales assistant.

Goods bought privately, for example from a neighbour or through an advert in the local paper, must only match the description.

Problems Complaints about faulty goods should be made to the place from which they were bought. The contract is with the shop, not the manufacturer.

When faulty goods are returned, the customer has the right to have their money back in full.

Time There is no set time limit in which goods must be returned if they are faulty, but it is important to tell the seller about the problem as soon as possible.

For example, someone who buys an MP3 player, and finds when they get home that it doesn't work properly, has a right to reject the goods and get their money back.

If they use the player, knowing that it is faulty, or do not complain within a reasonable time, they are seen, in law, to have accepted the goods – and this makes it much harder to claim a refund.

IS IT TOO LATE TO **RETURN** THIS?

? Questions

1. Now apply the *Sale of Goods Act 1979* to each of the following situations:

Peter buys a CD over the internet. When it arrives he discovers that it is not the one that he asked for.

Chris buys a new battery for his watch. As he is trying to fit it he realises that the battery he has bought is the wrong size.

Lena buys a new television. She unpacks the set at home and notices that part of the casing is scratched. The television itself works perfectly well.

Jasmine buys a bed and wardrobe unit for her daughter. On the packaging it says that the unit is easy to assemble, but the instructions are difficult to follow. Jasmine is unable to complete the job.

Vicky buys a second-hand car from a colleague at work. A week later, a major fault appears, costing £480 to repair.

Consumer rights
Borrowing money

■ Fantastic plastic

Nicci is 25 years old and works as a journalist on a local newspaper, earning £17,000 a year. Until about a year ago she budgeted carefully, and had just about enough money to live on, pay her rent, council tax, water, gas and electricity bills, and cover the repayments on the loan for her car that she uses for work.

Nikki got her first credit card two years ago, intending to use it only occasionally, but she soon found it a very convenient way of paying for things like petrol and clothes and buying goods online.

Things started to get difficult, however, when she began to use the card to pay for her weekly shopping.

The trouble was that, unless Nikki paid off the money owing on the card in full each month, interest was added and the amount that she owed steadily increased. Soon she was finding it difficult to pay off even the minimum payment. It was at this point that she decided to apply for several more credit cards, hoping that this would help to spread her debts and enable her to pay off a small amount each month.

Today she has five credit cards and two store cards on which she owes £12,000, her car loan and a bank overdraft of £750.

? Questions

1. Nikki is thinking about borrowing more money to help pay off her debt. Do you think this is a good idea? What would you advise her to do?

2. Who do you think has responsibility for Nikki's debt? Explain your view.

■ The growth of debt

The level of personal debt in Britain today is more than twice the European average. In 2008, each adult in Britain owed, on average, £4,800 on loans, overdrafts, store and credit cards. (This figure does not include the money that people have borrowed for their mortgage.)

Credit cards first began to appear in Britain in the early 1960s. Originally a fee was charged for the use of the card, and holders were required to have a yearly income of just over £30,000 in today's money. Each month they also had to pay off the amount that was owed in full.

Today, credit cards are much more widely used and are available to people, such as students, who may have no income and little savings. Banks have been heavily criticised for making it far too easy for people to get credit cards and encouraging people to use their card to buy goods that they may not be able to afford.

■ Is borrowing bad?

Despite the widespread use of credit, there are still many people in Britain who believe that if you want something, you should wait until you have saved enough money to buy it. (They might also add that you will appreciate the thing you have bought all the more by having to wait for it.) But is borrowing *always* bad?

If people didn't borrow money to buy a flat or house,

home ownership would be limited mainly to those who inherit money. Other expensive items would be beyond the reach of many people. A lot of businesses would not exist today if their owners had not been able to borrow money to start up or develop. And if young people did not borrow money to go to university, the country would have a far less well-educated workforce.

Of course, not all borrowing brings advantages. People borrow money for goods that they do not need, or can't afford. Sometimes they borrow because of social pressures. Examples of this are the high level of credit that is taken out in the run-up to Christmas, and parents who buy things for their children so they won't miss out.

? Questions

3. What are the benefits and drawbacks of the widespread availability of credit? Is there such a thing as 'good borrowing'?

4. Some people borrow far more money than they can repay. What steps could be taken to reduce this risk?

■ The law

Under the *Consumer Credit Act 1974* a person who borrows money must be given a copy of the loan agreement outlining the amount of interest they will pay, the payments that must be made, and their right to cancel the agreement or to end it early. Borrowers are also entitled to an annual statement indicating how much money is still owed.

Customers who sign a credit deal at home (or away from the shop or business premises) have a 'cooling-off' period in which they are allowed to cancel the agreement, as long as they act quickly.

■ Borrowing money

A person must be 18 or over to borrow money. There are a number of ways in which this can be done:

Mortgages are loans for buying property, usually repaid over a long period, such as 25 years.

Personal loans might be used for buying a car or home improvements. They are obtained from banks and finance companies. Repayments are normally made each month over an agreed period of time.

Credit cards allow people to buy a wide range of goods and services in shops, over the phone or on the internet. The card holder receives a statement each month indicating where the card has been used, the amount of money owed and the minimum payment required.

Store cards offer credit when buying goods at a particular store. Interest is charged on the money that has not been paid, often at a higher rate of interest than credit cards.

An overdraft is an agreement between a bank and a customer allowing the customer to take out more money than they have in their account (i.e. go overdrawn) up to an agreed amount. A customer who exceeds this amount has to pay a higher rate of interest, and may be required to pay off their debt straight away.

Hire purchase (HP) is a form of credit used for buying expensive items like cars. Technically the goods are sold to a finance company and are 'hired' by the customer who pays off the cost over an agreed period. The goods become 'purchased' only when the final payment is made.

Interest is the price paid by the borrower to the lender for the use of the money. It is normally expressed as an annual percentage; the lower the figure, the lower the cost of borrowing.

Sometimes loans are interest-free, as are credit cards (but only if all the money owed is paid off each month).

Consumer rights
Selling old as new

Andrew thought he had just enough money to buy a new laptop. After checking prices locally, he found the model he was looking for at a computer superstore – and slightly cheaper than he had expected. The assistant explained that it had been used as a display model in the shop, but was completely new in every other respect.

Andrew bought the computer, but it wasn't long before he was beginning to have some regrets. The performance was slow and unreliable and not what he had come to expect.

He decided to contact the manufacturer, and to his surprise learnt that he was not the first person to own the computer. It had been bought by a local business a few months earlier and returned to the store with various faults.

Andrew decided to report the matter to the local **trading standards department**, who investigated the matter and decided to bring a prosecution against the superstore.

The laptop that Andrew bought was not as described and so, under the *Sale of Goods Act 1979*, he was entitled to his money back.

Criminal offence In falsely describing the laptop as a display model, the superstore had also committed a criminal offence. As a result, the company was taken to court, and charged under the *Trade Descriptions Act 1968* of supplying a computer with a false description. This was the company's second offence, and it was fined a total of £5,500.

? Questions

1. Why is falsely describing something for sale a *criminal* offence?

Dangerous goods

People have a right to expect that the things they buy are safe and are not dangerous to use. It's a criminal offence to sell something that is either dangerous or is not up to the safety standards required by law.

■ A tragic accident

Chloe, aged three, was playing on a children's slide in the garden at home when her head became trapped between the top of the slide and a metal support. Her mother found her hanging from the slide and, despite being rushed to hospital, Chloe died six days later.

An investigation into the accident was held, and the company that made and sold the slide was charged with selling an unsafe toy.

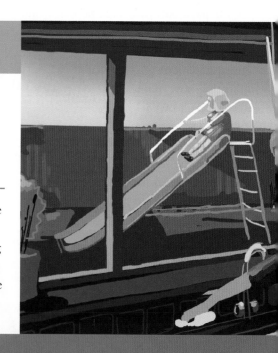

Evidence

Here are some of the facts and statements that were given at the trial.

A The company had made and sold 200,000 slides before this accident occurred.

B As soon as they heard about Chloe's accident the company withdrew the slide from sale. Sixteen days later it was on sale again with safety modifications.

C/ In the opinion of safety experts, the design of the slide meets current British safety standards.

D) A director of the company stated, 'This slide has an excellent safety record. We have never had a serious accident or a death with any of our products.'

(E) Chloe's mother explained, 'I had been with Chloe in the garden, watching her playing on the slide. I then went into the house. After a while I realised that I couldn't hear her. I looked out of the window and saw Chloe hanging from the slide'.

F - The company now offers a special safety kit for those people who bought the slide before the accident.

G - A safety expert said, 'It is not always possible to predict what young children will do.'

H - Another senior company director said, ' These slides are used in our stores. About two million children a year use them under staff supervision.'

? Questions

2. In court, the judge had to decide whether the company was guilty of selling an unsafe toy.

   Some of the evidence heard in the court is listed on the left. Which items would help the judge to decide whether the company had or had not broken the law?

3. Now choose the four or five pieces of evidence that you feel are most important in this case. Explain why you feel each one that you have selected is important.

4. Would you find the toy company guilty or not guilty of selling an unsafe toy?

5. If you feel the toy company is guilty, what punishment would you impose? The maximum fine for this offence is £5,000.

Key words

Trading standards department
People employed by the local authority to check that local shops and businesses are not breaking the law in the way that they trade. If they believe that an offence has been committed they can prosecute the trader.

Consumer complaints

This unit outlines ways of making a complaint and successfully dealing with problems of faulty goods and services.

Taking action

■ Washed up

Therese O'Dell bought an expensive new washing machine. But after six months' use it broke down. Mrs O'Dell rang the shop where she bought it and was told to call the manufacturer's helpline. This she did. They said an engineer would come to her house to look at her machine.

The engineer didn't arrive. Nor did he keep a second appointment. It took three weeks for someone to come. Then they left – saying that new parts were needed before the machine could be repaired.

A week later the parts were installed. But the washing machine soon broke down again.

Another call to the engineer, and another week passed before anyone appeared. The engineer told Mrs O'Dell that the same parts needed replacing and would take a further week to be delivered.

? Questions

1. Draw up a list of the difficulties that Mrs O'Dell is facing because of the problem with her washing machine.

2. What do you think is the greatest difficulty she faces in getting someone to deal with the problem?

3. What should Mrs O'Dell do next? Draw up a list of actions that she could take. Put them in order of effectiveness. Which would you recommend?

Problems

The difficulties that people face when the goods or services that they have bought go wrong are rarely straightforward.

? Questions

4. All the cases opposite are based on real life. Using the information on pages 60–61, put yourself in the position of someone who has been asked to give advice.

   In each case a) outline the person's position in law, and b) suggest what action they should take.

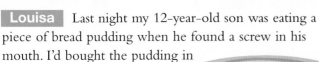

Louisa Last night my 12-year-old son was eating a piece of bread pudding when he found a screw in his mouth. I'd bought the pudding in the afternoon from the local supermarket. It cost me £1.79.

Adam I bought a new computer package, with a printer. The sales assistant said it would be able to print up to eight pages a minute. In fact it sometimes takes five minutes to do a single page.

I rang the company's helpline but got fed up waiting for someone to talk to, so I rang the printer manufacturer. They said that I'd been sold the wrong printer for my computer. The right one will cost me £140.

The company I bought the package from refuse to help. They won't take the old printer because it has been used and cannot be resold.

Clive I bought my car through an advert in the local paper. The man said it was a good runner and I paid him £4,200. It was fine for the first couple of weeks – now I've discovered it needs a new clutch and gearbox, which will cost about £1,000. I've written to ask him for £500 – which I thought was fair – but he's ignored my letter.

Yvonne I ordered a new bath. The shop said it would cost £340, which I agreed to. This week they called to say that the factory had put its prices up. If I want the bath I will have to pay another £120.

Tracy Last season I was one of 100 Wigan supporters whose tickets for a match against Manchester United failed to arrive in the post. Most of us, nevertheless, decided to travel to the match, hoping that we would still be admitted to the ground. However, despite having proof that we had paid for the tickets, we were still turned away, being told that the tickets had been dispatched and that duplicates could not be issued. It was terrible, we were so disappointed. There was nothing we could do.

Sairah Just over a year ago I bought a new flat screen television. It worked perfectly until a week ago, when the screen went blank. I checked the fuse and the aerial, and both were fine. The next day I went to the store where I had bought the set. The assistant explained that the television was now out of guarantee and, as I had not bought an extended warranty, there was nothing they could do. He agreed that there could be a production fault, and suggested I get in touch with the manufacturer. I don't think I should have to pay so soon for repairs to a very expensive television.

Lenny I bought an external disk drive for my computer at the weekend and then saw the same model for sale much cheaper elsewhere. I took the disk drive back to the shop where I bought it, explained the problem and asked if I could have my money back or a credit note. They turned me down even though I hadn't taken it out of the original packaging.

Consumer complaints
Problem solving – a guide

■ First things

Take it back Many shops will exchange faulty goods immediately, as long as the customer has a receipt or some other proof of purchase.

Ask to see the manager Sometimes it helps to ask to see a more senior person, such as the manager or supervisor.

Write a letter A letter to the company head office is often the next stage, with the customer explaining why they are dissatisfied with what they have bought.

Keep a record If the matter is not settled immediately, it's a good idea for the customer to keep a note of everything they have done, as well as copies of letters sent and received.

■ Finding help

Citizens Advice Bureaux These are advice centres, usually known as CABs, which give free help and guidance about all kinds of problems. There are offices in most towns and cities. The telephone number is in the local phone book.

Consumer Direct A Government-funded online and telephone consumer information service, www.consumerdirect.gov.uk.

Small claims procedure Anyone over 18 unable to get satisfaction over a problem with faulty goods or poor service can try to recover their money by putting their case to a judge in a county court.

The court is very informal and there is no need to employ a lawyer. It is a relatively simple and inexpensive way of settling a case, up to the value of £5,000.

Solicitors These are trained lawyers able to give advice and take action on behalf of their clients over a range of legal issues. With consumer problems, however, there is a danger that the cost of the solicitor's fees will be greater than the value of the goods concerned.

Trading standards departments Sometimes known as consumer protection departments, these give advice to the public about all kinds of consumer problems. However, their main job is to check that shops and traders keep within the law and they will prosecute if there is evidence that the trader has committed a criminal offence.

■ The law

Sale of Goods Act 1979   This states that all goods sold by a trader must be:

- *of satisfactory quality*: They must be free from faults and not scratched or damaged in any way.
- *fit for their purpose*: The goods must do what they are designed to do and, in particular, what the sales assistant or the packaging claims.
- *as described*: They must be the same as they are described in an advertisement, on the packaging or by the sales assistant.

Goods bought privately must be only *as described*.

OF SATISFACTORY QUALITY!

FIT FOR THEIR PURPOSE!

AS DESCRIBED!

Supply of Goods and Services Act 1982

This states that a service must be provided:

- with reasonable care and skill
- within a reasonable time, and
- at a reasonable cost, if no price has been agreed in advance.

Consumer Credit Act 1984   If there's a fault with something bought using a credit card, the customer may be able to claim from the credit card company as well as the firm from which the goods were bought.

This applies only to goods costing more than £100, but can be useful if the trader is being unhelpful or is no longer in business.

Unfair Contract Terms Act 1977   The wording or small print of a customer's contract must be fair. If it is not, the customer can ask a court to overturn it.

For example, a security firm that fitted alarms had a section in its contract that said they would not be responsible if their alarm failed and the customer's house was burgled. This, a court decided, was unfair. The customer was paid compensation and the company forced to change its contracts.

Trade Descriptions Act 1968

It is a criminal offence for a trader to make a deliberately misleading or false claim about what they are selling.

STIFF QUIFF — *hair styles in a can*

IT DOES **WHAT** IT SAYS ON THE TIN!

Consumer Safety Act 1987

It is a criminal offence for a trader to sell goods that are not safe. The law applies to both new and second-hand goods, unless the buyer was specifically told that they were faulty or in need of repair.

Anyone suffering injury or damage from unsafe or dangerous goods can claim damages from the manufacturer.

in:tro **credit card**

electronic use only

5562 9873 0892 6165

valid from 06/08   expires end 06/12

S JONES

835687   49761203   02
sort code   account number   issue

plug

electronic use

7468 9867

valid from> 04/07 expir

J SMITH

785442   87354429   02
account number   issue

Looking for work

This unit looks at the main ways in which the law deals with unfair discrimination at work.

Equal opportunities

■ Car crazy

Karen had liked cars for as long as she could remember, and whenever anyone asked her what she wanted to do as a job, she always replied, 'be a mechanic'.

In her final year at school, she saw an advertisement in the paper for two apprentice mechanics at a local garage. The apprenticeship would last five years, at a starting salary of £6,000 a year. Karen thought she stood a reasonable chance of getting the job. She had the required GCSEs in maths and science and had been to the garage earlier in the year on two days' work experience.

When Karen was called for interview, the manager asked her why she wanted the job and if she thought she would fit in. He also asked Karen if she minded getting her hands dirty.

During the interview Karen learnt that she was the best qualified of all the applicants and was told that she stood a good chance of getting one of the jobs.

Two days later, Karen received a letter telling her that her application had been rejected. She later learnt that the apprenticeships had been given to two 16-year-old boys.

Karen suspected that she was a victim of **sex discrimination**. She made some enquiries and decided to take her case to an **employment tribunal**.

? Questions

1. Karen claimed that she had suffered sex discrimination. One test of sex discrimination at a job interview is whether a person is asked questions that would not be asked of someone of the opposite sex. Can you find any examples of this in Karen's interview?

2. On the evidence that you have been given, do you think Karen suffered unlawful discrimination?

3. If you decide that Karen did suffer unlawful discrimination, how should she be compensated? How would you decide on a fair and reasonable figure?

■ Boys too

Sarat Sharma applied for a job as an office junior with a company making textiles. He had all the right qualifications, including English and maths GCSE.

The letter inviting Sarat for interview began 'Dear Miss Sharma', and when Sarat rang to confirm that he would attend, the person he spoke to said that they were looking for a young female – and that Sarat would not be suitable.

When Sarat's careers officer learnt about what had happened, he suggested that Sarat report the company for sex discrimination. With the help of the **Equality and Human Rights Commission**, Sarat was successful, and received £4,000 in compensation. 'I think it is a lot easier for women to get typing and clerical work,' said Sarat.

Stereotypes

Karen and Sarat were looking for jobs that people of their sex do not usually do. In doing so they were breaking the conventional image – or stereotype – that we have of women's and men's work.

Engineering apprenticeships

97% men

3% women

Health and social care

11% men

89% women

IT services

88% men

12% women

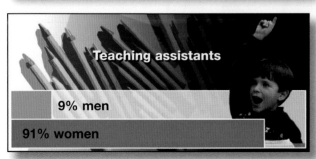

Teaching assistants

9% men

91% women

Source: Directory of Apprenticeships 2007/8

? Questions

4. How do you explain why there are so many more men working in IT servcies or as engineers, and so many more women in health care and as teaching assistants?

5. Does it matter if most mechanics are men or most nurses are women? What are some of the consequences of these stereotypes?

6. Are there any jobs that women can't do? Are there any jobs that men can't do?

The law

Under the *Sex Discrimination Act 1975* it is against the law for an employer to discriminate against job applicants because of their sex or marital status.

It is also almost always against the law to publish a job advert that discriminates in favour of, or against, either sex. This means that words like waitress or salesman cannot normally be used.

However, the law does allow employers to discriminate in favour of women or men for reasons of decency, privacy or authenticity, for example, by choosing a male actor for a male role in a play.

Hi I'm your waitress

Key words

Employment tribunal
A court of law that decides on employment disputes, such as discrimination and unfair dismissal.

Equality and Human Rights Commission
An organisation working to eliminate discrimination, reduce inequality and protect human rights. It is able to help people who feel they have been unlawfully discriminated against.

Sex discrimination
Treating someone less favourably because of their sex.

Looking for work

■ Train departure

There aren't many women train drivers in Britain – and when Gemma Haxey left London Underground, there was one less.

Gemma quit her job when the train company decided to change drivers' working hours. The new shift patterns required Gemma to work at any time and on any day of the week. This meant that she could no longer be certain of being at home with her nine-year-old daughter in the evening or at weekends.

Gemma felt that this was unfair because it made life particularly difficult for single parents, who did not have a partner to look after their children while they were at work. As most single parents were women, Gemma felt that London Underground's action amounted to sex discrimination. She took her case to an employment tribunal.

The tribunal agreed with Gemma. They said that London Underground's new working arrangements unfairly discriminated against women – because more women than men were single parents.

This is known in law as *indirect* discrimination.

■ Direct and indirect discrimination

Direct discrimination takes place when someone is treated less favourably because of their sex, race, disability, religion or sexuality.

The discrimination suffered by Karen and Sarat, outlined on the previous pages is an example of this.

Indirect discrimination occurs when a situation or condition is imposed that discriminates against a particular group of people.

In Gemma's case, the tribunal decided that the new work rotas particularly discriminated against women.

? Questions

1. Look at the following cases and decide whether they show *direct* or *indirect* sex discrimination.

Judy started her new job as a training manager. During her second week she arrived at the office in a trouser suit, but was asked to go home and change, as the company's dress code did not allow women to wear trousers at work.

Neil aged 21, was asked during his interview if he would be prepared to cut off his ponytail if he was given the job. He said that he would not. His interview came to an immediate end.

Linda who was in her thirties, with two children, was unable to apply for a job with the local council, because the advertisement indicated that only people aged between 18 and 28 would be considered.

Nathan wanted to spend as much time as possible with his daughter after she was born and asked the insurance company where he worked if he could be employed part-time – as some female employees were after having a baby. The company refused his request.

Rhianna became very uncomfortable at work, and eventually decided to leave, after her boss, Daniel, kept putting his arm round her and repeatedly commenting on her figure.

1971	Women's average full-time earnings = 69% of men's
2007	Women's average full-time earnings = 83% of men's

Equal pay

Top of the form   Recent studies show that girls generally get better results at school than boys. This pattern continues at college and university, but by the time they start full-time work, the position has begun to change.

Closing the gap?   In 1971, a year after equal pay laws were introduced, women's average full-time earnings were 69 per cent of those of men.

By 2007, the differences in pay had been reduced – but women's average full-time earnings were still 17 per cent less than those of men.

Who's the boss?
Almost certainly it is a man. In 2007, only 18 per cent of managers and directors were women.

Who's the **Daddy?**

? Questions

2. What suggestions can you offer to explain the continuing differences in men's and women's pay?

   Compare your answers with other people in your group, and identify what you think are the most significant reasons.

3. Imagine that we have moved on 20 years, to the 2030s. Which of the following situations would you most welcome? Explain why.

   As we were   Life has moved back to what it was in the 1930s – when most married women stayed at home looking after the house and family.

Women on top   The position of men and women have been reversed. Women's wages are now, on average, 20 per cent more than those of men.

All on merit   At work it makes no difference whether someone is a man or a woman. Their progress depends entirely on their qualifications and how well they do their job.

No change   The position of men and women is just as they were at the beginning of the twenty-first century. Some women do very well, but the earnings advantage remains with men.

The law

Under the *Equal Pay Act 1970*, women and men working for a company or organisation should receive the same wages and benefits (like holidays or pensions) – provided they are doing either *like work* or *work of equal value*.

Like work refers to work that is broadly similar in nature. For example, technicians who are working for a particular company and doing a similar type of job should receive the same wages and benefits – regardless of sex.

Work of equal value is work that may be different but is of equal skill or difficulty. For example, a court decided that carpenters, painters and cooks who worked for a shipyard all had work of equal value and were entitled to receive the same level of pay and benefits.

Looking for work
Race discrimination

■ Prejudice

Suzanne Jones, a black English woman, applied for a job as a clerical assistant at a firm of solicitors. She was 19 and well qualified for the post. But, after an interview with Mr Wheeler, the senior partner, she was not offered the job.

Six weeks later, Suzanne saw an advertisement for a similar job at the same firm. She phoned to say she was interested, and realised that she was speaking to the same Mr Wheeler whom she had previously met.

Suzanne was again invited for interview, but when she walked into Mr Wheeler's office he recognised her and became very upset. He did not even ask her to sit down, saying that there was no point in going ahead with the interview. He asked Suzanne to leave.

Suzanne believed that she was being rejected because of the colour of her skin. She told Mr Wheeler that she had no wish to work for him, called him a bigot – and left.

Later that day, Mr Wheeler interviewed another applicant, Deborah Cook, who was white. During the course of the interview Mr Wheeler said to Deborah, 'A coloured girl applied for the job – but why would I want to take her on, when English girls are available?'

Deborah was offered the job, but turned it down. Instead she decided to tell someone in the local race relations office what Mr Wheeler had said.

■ Advice

Suzanne knew that racial discrimination was against the law and went to see a solicitor to seek advice – but not one who worked for Mr Wheeler's firm. The solicitor told Suzanne that she believed that Mr Wheeler had broken the *Race Relations Act* and that Suzanne was entitled to take her case to an employment tribunal. If

the tribunal decided that Mr Wheeler had acted in an unlawful way, Suzanne would be entitled to compensation.

■ Tribunal

Mr Wheeler told the tribunal that he hadn't unfairly discriminated against Suzanne. She failed to get the job, he said, because she was rude and not sufficiently qualified.

❓ Questions

1. What are the key points of evidence in this case? Does the evidence show that Suzanne suffered race discrimination? Give reasons for your answer.

2. If you believe Suzanne was a victim of race discrimination, how do you think she should be compensated? Should the tribunal take any other action?

■ Yesterday and today

In the 1950s and 1960s some people feared that those coming from the Caribbean, India and Pakistan posed a threat to their jobs and housing. Although this was a period of full employment, with not enough people to

fill the jobs available, black people still faced considerable discrimination. It was not uncommon to see signs saying Rooms to let – no coloureds.

Racial discrimination of this kind, in employment and housing, became illegal in 1976.

■ No joke

Trevor McCauley, from Antrim in Northern Ireland, had worked in England for 20 years. During this time he heard more than his fair share of jokes about the Irish. Over the last two years, however, working at a firm in Derbyshire, he was on the receiving end of critical comments almost continuously.

'Every day,' he said, 'they were saying things like "typical thick Paddy" and "what else can you expect from an Irishman?".

'I decided that I had had enough. When I started to complain, they told me I had an attitude problem.

'I was harassed every day. You feel absolutely useless. Eventually I got the sack for being a troublemaker.'

An employment tribunal decided that anti-Irish remarks amounted to racial discrimination and that Mr McCauley had been unfairly dismissed from work. He received an award of £6,000 in compensation.

? Questions

3. Mr Wheeler rejected Suzanne because of her colour or ethnic background. What possible explanations can you suggest for his **prejudice**?

4. Is it right to have a law banning racial discrimination at work? Give reasons for your answer.

■ The law

Under the *Race Relations Act 1976* it is against the law for an employer to treat a person less favourably because of their race, colour, nationality or ethnic origin.

However, race discrimination is not always against the law. It is not unlawful if the employment is in a private household, nor if a person's race is regarded as a genuine occupational requirement. For example, the owner of a Chinese restaurant looking for a new waiter is entitled to advertise for Chinese applicants only and, similarly, a local council seeking someone to work with the Bengali community can insist on applicants coming from a similar background.

Key words

Prejudice
Disliking people from a particular group or category, based on their race, gender or sexuality etc.

Fairness at work

This unit outlines further ways in which people can be protected from unfair discrimination at work.

Religious discrimination

No right

In 1991, a textile factory in Dewsbury in Yorkshire, was not doing well and needed to increase efficiency. One way of doing this, the management decided, was to say that workers could no longer take their holidays in May, June or July, which were the factory's busiest months.

When this decision was made, the managing directors had not realised that, in the coming year, it would be in this period that the festival of Eid would take place. Eid is one of the most important days in the Muslim calendar, when Muslims celebrate with family and friends after a period of fasting and prayer. Like the Christian festival of Easter, the day of Eid is determined by the phases of the moon, and Muslims in Britain do not know the exact day of Eid until shortly beforehand. Almost half the workforce at the factory were Muslims, who had originally moved to Britain from India and Pakistan.

In June 1992, the Muslim workers informed the management that Eid would fall on 11 June. They explained that they wished to take the day off, but would be prepared to work extra hours to make up for lost time. The management refused, stating that anyone who was absent would face disciplinary action. On 11 June, the Muslim workers stayed at home, and when they returned the following day, they all received an official warning.

A small group of workers challenged this decision. They took their case to an employment tribunal – and won. However, their victory was not because of religious, but racial discrimination. There was no law at the time forbidding religious discrimination. The workers had succeeded not because they were Muslim, but because they belonged to an ethnic group that had suffered indirect discrimination (see page 64). Had the textile workers been white Muslims, they would not have won their case.

Protection in law

Laws protecting people in England and Wales from religious discrimination at work were not passed until 2003, although religious discrimination had been against the law in Northern Ireland since 1976.

Until 2003, members of the Jewish and Sikh faiths were the only groups in England and Wales protected against religious discrimination. This was because the law makers decided that Jews and Sikhs were distinct ethnic groups and therefore came under the protection of race discrimination laws. Buddhists, Christians, Hindus and Muslims did not, and it took many years for the situation to change.

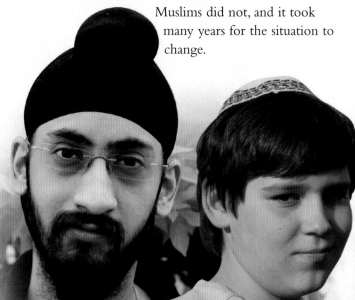

The law Today, under the *Employment Equality (Religion or Belief) Regulations 2003*, it is against the law for an employer to treat a person less favourably because of their religion or beliefs.

This covers *direct* discrimination, such as refusing to employ someone or offer them training because they are Jewish or Muslim, and *indirect* discrimination. This occurs if an employer has working practices that put people at a disadvantage because of their religious beliefs (or lack of them). Employers need to make sure that their working arrangements, such as uniform or dress code, do not put people at a disadvantage as a result of their religious faith.

As with legislation designed to prevent race and sex discrimination, there are certain circumstances when religious discrimination is allowed. This is when a person's religious belief is an important part of the work, known in law as a genuine occupational requirement. For example, a faith school could probably argue that it was a genuine occupational requirement for an RE teacher in the school to be a member of that faith. It would be more difficult, however, to make the same case for a teacher of maths or French.

Employers also have a duty to prevent employees from being harassed or intimidated because of their religious beliefs. If an employee makes an offensive comment about another employee's religion, the employer has a duty to take action to prevent this from happening again.

? Questions

1. Look at each of the case studies below, and decide whether you feel the person has a case for unfair religious discrimination.

   a) Sarah works for a charity that helps people with learning disabilities. The charity was set up a number of years ago, based on strong Christian principles. As the charity has grown, the proportion of practising Christians in the workforce has fallen. The directors of the charity feel that this is a mistake and write a letter to all employees saying that, although everyone's job is quite safe, anyone who is not a Christian cannot in future expect to be promoted. Sarah is an atheist; she has no religious belief, and feels that she is being unfairly discriminated against.

   b) Aisha, 19, has worked as a hairdresser since leaving school. She recently applied for a job at a modern stylish salon. During her interview, the owner asked Aisha if she would be prepared to work without the headscarf that she was wearing. 'No,' said Aisha, 'I wear it because of my religious beliefs. It's never been a problem elsewhere.' At this point the interview came to an end. The salon's owner said that she could not offer Aisha the job because people would need to see her hair. 'My hairdressers have to show off different styles,' she said, 'It's important for my business.' Aisha feels that this is unfair. 'My ability to cut and style hair does not depend on whether or not I cover my hair.'

2. In Britain today, the major Christian festivals of Christmas and Easter are both celebrated with public holidays. Followers of other religions, however, have to use part of their annual leave if they wish to celebrate their important religious festivals. Is it time for the Government to recognise the religious beliefs of those who are not Christians by allowing Hindus, Jews, Muslims, etc., to take a public holiday during their times of special religious significance?

Fairness at work

Sexuality

■ Taunts and jibes

Stephen Price, aged 25, was looking forward to starting his new job at an education centre in Wales. However, it wasn't long before his manager, Ms Jones, began to taunt him about his sexuality. She swore at him, said that he was vile, and called him, amongst other things, 'a stupid poof'. Hardly a day went by without Ms Jones making reference to sex or Mr Price's sexuality.

Although he complained about his treatment to his employer, Mr Price found it difficult to get anyone to take his claims seriously. Eventually he left his job, claiming unfair discrimination.

Ms Jones denied many of the allegations, but Stephen Price won his case and was awarded £37,000 in compensation.

■ Protection

Legal protection for gay and lesbian people is relatively new in Britain. Until 1967, male homosexuality was a criminal offence in England and Wales; it wasn't decriminalised in Scotland until 1980 and in Northern Ireland until 1982.

Regulations making it unlawful to discriminate against someone at work because of their sexuality came into force in Britain in 2003. By 2006 the law had been extended to protect people from discrimination on grounds of their sexuality in the provision of goods and services, for example in bars and hotels.

■ The law

Everyone has the right to be treated fairly at work, regardless of their sexual orientation. The law protects gay, lesbian, bisexual and heterosexual people from being treated less favourably at work or in training because of their sexual orientation. This includes turning down someone for employment, refusing to promote them and harassing or victimising them in any way.

Anyone who feels that they have suffered this kind of discrimination may take their case to an employment tribunal.

Age discrimination

■ Longer life

As a nation, we are living much longer than we did in the past. Since 1911, the numbers over the age of 100 has risen over 90 times – from 100 to more than 9,000 people.

Longer life expectancy has brought many advantages, but it has also meant that people who lose their job or retire in their fifties can spend at least 30 years without working or earning. This is often not good for them, or for the country's economy.

There has, and still is, a lot of prejudice against older workers. They are seen as slow to adapt to new technology, lacking new ideas and inflexible. Many employers, particularly in new industries, avoid recruiting older workers. Finding work is sometimes made even more difficult for older workers because they tend to have fewer qualifications than younger people, mainly because so few went to university in the 1960s and 1970s compared with today.

Age discrimination, however, is not only a problem for older people. In a survey undertaken in 2005–6, age was reported as the most common reason for unfair treatment at work, and it was younger, rather than older, employees who were more likely to make this complaint.

■ Any age will do

In order to combat what is known as 'ageism' in the workplace, a new law come into force in 2006, prohibiting employers from taking a person's age into account when deciding whether to offer them work – unless they could give a good reason for doing so.

The *Employment Equality (Age) Regulations 2006* state that it is unlawful to discriminate against an employee under the age of 65. This means employers must not advertise posts with minimum or maximum ages, nor can they dismiss workers or deny them training opportunities because of their age.

However, there are certain circumstances in which employers may discriminate, for example insisting that the part of a teenager in a film or play is played by a younger, rather than older, actor. It may also be acceptable to discriminate against a young person in work requiring a lengthy period of training but, in such a case, an employer would need to demonstrate that discrimination against a younger candidate was absolutely essential.

Like a number of other pieces of legislation designed to reduce discrimination, this law was introduced directly as a result of the UK's membership of the European Union, see page 156.

see page 156.

? Questions

1. Look at each of the job advertisements below and decide whether they break the age discrimination law in any way. Explain why.

2. At present, employees who reach the age of 65 may request to continue working, but the employer is under no obligation to allow them to continue. What are the arguments in favour and against removing all retirement ages, and allowing people to work for as long as they are capable?

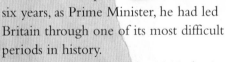

By the end of the Second World War in 1945, Sir Winston Churchill was 71 years of age. For most of the past six years, as Prime Minister, he had led Britain through one of its most difficult periods in history.

Although defeated in the 1945 election, he returned as Prime Minister in 1951, and finally retired in 1955 at the age of 81.

Nelson Mandela was 75 when he was elected President of South Africa, and Vivienne Westwood became British Fashion Designer of the Year at 65. Harland Sanders was also 65 when he started his Kentucky Fried Chicken business.

Fairness at work
Disability discrimination

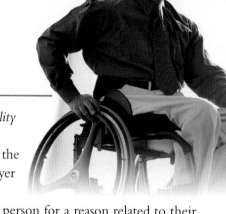

■ A problem made worse

Many people suffering from disabilities face an extra difficulty in their lives, which has nothing to do with their condition. It is other people's attitudes:

- Durrand, a wheelchair user, finds that some taxi drivers refuse to let him ride in their cab, saying that there is no room in the vehicle for his wheelchair.

- Caroline takes her brother, James, to a wine bar. James has learning difficulties and some physical disfigurement. Caroline is told that her brother will put off other customers from using the bar. They are asked not to come back.

■ The meaning of disability

Disability is defined in law as a physical or mental impairment that has a substantial and long-term effect on a person's ability to carry out normal everyday

activities. It covers a wide range of conditions, including cancer, diabetes, heart disease, learning difficulties, mental illness, difficulties with mobility, sight and hearing, and conditions that give rise to physical disfigurement.

■ The law

Under the *Disability Discrimination Act 1995* it is against the law for an employer to discriminate against a disabled person for a reason related to their disability, unless it can be justified. The law covers all aspects of work, including interviews, the terms and conditions of employment, training, promotion, benefits, dismissal and redundancy.

Employers also have a duty to make reasonable adjustments to the workplace so that a disabled candidate or employee does not face a substantial disadvantage.

There are certain circumstances when an employer *may* discriminate against a disabled person. This is most likely to occur if a person's disability prevents them from carrying out the essential requirements of a job, and if reasonable adjustments to help them cannot be made.

Disability Discrimination Act 1995

❓ Questions

1. Look at the following cases and decide whether you think the company concerned has broken the law. In each case, give reasons for your answer.

   Will is a wheelchair user and is unable to walk. He applies to work for a small firm of designers employing six people. He is well qualified for the job, but is turned down. It is felt that Will would find it very difficult to get to the firm's office, which is at the top of a spiral staircase with no access by lift.

Melissa is 22 and was born with a condition that prevents her growing to a normal height. She applies for work as a sales assistant in a women's fashion store. She attends an interview, but is not offered the job. Melissa phones the store manager to ask why she was not accepted. The manager tells Melissa that the company requires all employees to be smart and physically attractive. The manager apologises to Melissa and says that, unfortunately, her appearance does not fit the fashionable image of the shop and might discourage some customers from shopping there.

Paul is manager of a supermarket. He has worked for the company for several years and has done very well. A year ago, Paul discovered that he was HIV positive. This means that he has the virus that can go on to develop into AIDS. Although he is able to carry on with his work, he decides to tell his employer. The company worries that store sales will suffer if the public hears of his illness. Paul is dismissed.

David is 20 years old and applies for a job collecting trolleys in a supermarket car park. From David's application form, the store manager sees that David had attended a special school and correctly assumes that David has learning difficulties. David is not called for interview.

2. 'There is not a single job in the country that a person with a disability could not do.' Do you agree with this statement? Explain your point of view.

■ The Equality and Human Rights Commission

Until recently, help and guidance for people facing sex, race or disability discrimination tended to be dealt with by three separate public bodies.

In 2007, the three organisations were amalgamated, and today their work is handled by the Equality and Human Rights Commission (EHRC). The Commission is designed to be a single point of contact for individuals and businesses, providing advice and guidance on all aspects of unfair discrimination.

The Commission also has a duty to promote public understanding of the *Human Rights Act* (see page 30).

The EHRC is able to take on individual cases, particularly those that might result in an improvement or strengthening of the law. It also monitors and provides guidance to employers and organisations who are not giving their employers or other users the equal opportunities to which they are entitled.

Support During the 1990s, Raghib Ahsan was a Labour Party councillor in Birmingham. In 1997, stories appeared in two national papers claiming that local councillors of Pakistani origin were helping Birmingham residents jump the queue for housing grants, and Mr Ahsan's name was mentioned in this context. Although the allegations in both articles turned out to be untrue, and there was no evidence that Mr Ahsan had acted improperly, he was prevented from standing as a Labour Party candidate at the next election. Mr Ahsan lodged a complaint of unfair racial discrimination, but the Labour Party said that its action in this case did not come under race discrimination law. The EHRC felt the law needed clarifying here and supported Mr Ahsan's claim. The case reached the House of Lords, where it was decided that the Labour Party's actions did unfairly discriminate against Mr Ahsan.

Working for a living

This unit looks at the legal rights and responsibilities of employers and employees at work.

In work

Anit is 17 and still at school. He is looking for a part-time job. He lives in an area with high unemployment. Finding work is difficult. One evening, while he is in town, Anit sees an advert in the window of a restaurant.

He goes into the restaurant and asks to speak to someone about the job vacancy. Mr Bonner, the owner, explains that he can't speak to Anit right then, but asks him to come tomorrow evening at 6 p.m.

? Questions

1. Draw up a list of the things you think Anit needs to find out about the job during his interview.

■ Interview

Anit goes back to the restaurant. Mr Bonner asks why he has applied for the job and if he has ever done any similar work.

Anit says that he thinks the work would be interesting, but adds that he has never worked in a restaurant before.

■ Offer

Mr Bonner tells Anit that he would be required to work on Saturdays and Sundays, the busiest days of the week. He would be paid £3.50 an hour and each day would normally work a four-hour shift, either between 11 a.m. and 3 p.m. or 6 p.m and 10 p.m. Anit would also be required to wear a uniform of black trousers, orange shirt and black shoes, which he would have to provide himself.

Anit would be expected to wait on the tables, and help make sure that the restaurant itself was kept clean and tidy.

Anit is offered the job – and accepts.

? Questions

2. Look back at the list of questions that you thought Anit should ask. How many of these were answered? Is there anything else Anit needs to know before he starts work? If so, what is it?

■ Contract

In agreeing to take the job, Anit formed a contract with Mr Bonner, the owner of the restaurant. A contract of employment is a legal agreement covering the arrangements for work, such as pay, hours and the nature of the job.

Health and safety

Two days later, Anit begins his first evening at work. Carolyn, who has worked at the restaurant for more than a year, explains to Anit the various hygiene rules that the restaurant has for handling and storing food. Mr Bonner warns Anit that he is likely to lose his job if he breaks any of these rules.

Training

Carolyn shows Anit how to carry several plates of food to a table, how to serve food and also how to keep a record of customer orders. She also explains to Anit what is in some of the dishes – something that customers often ask.

Rights and duties

When a contract for employment is made, certain points are specifically agreed between the employer and employee. In law, these are known as express terms – specific things about the job that both sides have agreed.

However, employers and employees also have other rights and duties that both sides expect will be taken for granted. These are known as the implied terms of a contract.

Mr Bonner, for example, must provide Anit with a safe working environment. He must not unlawfully discriminate against him. Anit must obey all reasonable

instructions. He also has a duty not to damage Mr Bonner's business. Anit would be breaking the implied terms of his contract (and committing a criminal offence) if he let a friend eat at the restaurant for half price.

Written details

Within two months of starting work, employees should by law be given a written statement of the terms and conditions of their work. This should include details of:

- their starting date
- rate of pay
- hours of work
- holiday arrangements
- sick pay and pension
- the amount of notice that they and their employer must give if the contract is ended.

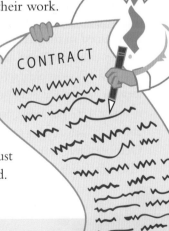

? Questions

3. Why would it be helpful for Anit to have the terms and conditions of his job in the restaurant set down on paper?

Working for a living

A working life

■ Pay

Almost everyone who is employed is entitled to a pay slip giving details of what they have been paid, and how it has been worked out. The only people to whom this does not apply are those working for the police and those with certain jobs in the fishing industry and merchant navy.

Generally speaking, employers are not allowed to take money from an employee's wage without the employee agreeing to this in writing beforehand. Again, there are a few exceptions. For example, employers can deduct money for tax or national insurance, or take back money from someone who has been overpaid.

Minimum wage The minimum wage was introduced in the UK in 1999. The rate payable depends on the employee's age. In 2008/9, the minimum rate for 16- and 17-year-olds, who are above compulsory school leaving age, was £3.53 per hour. For people aged 18-21 it was £4.77 per hour, and £5.73 for 22-year-olds and above. It is normally raised by a small amount in October each year.

Benefits such as free meals do not count towards the minimum wage, nor do tips if they are paid by the customer directly to the waiter.

However, they do become part of the minimum wage if they are paid through an employee's wages.

An employer who fails to pay the minimum wage can be fined, and employees may take their case to an employment tribunal.

Tax Everyone who earns over a certain amount each year (known as a Personal Allowance) pays income tax. This is normally deducted from their wages by their employer. It is illegal for an employer to pay 'cash in hand' without deducting tax and national insurance. Income tax payers are also required to pay tax on any tips or bonuses they receive.

? Questions

1. What is Anit's legal position in the following situations?

   Pay? At the end of his second week at work, Anit receives his first pay packet. He works out that his hourly rate is less than the national minimum wage.

   Mistake? At the end of the evening, the till is down by £15. The loss is traced to one of Anit's tables. It appears that a customer left without paying. Anit is told that the money will be deducted from his earnings over the next two shifts.

2. Why do young workers tend to get paid less than older workers? Is this fair? Is it fair if they are doing the same job?

3. Draw up a list of the consequences of a minimum wage of £6 per hour for all workers – regardless of age.

■ Health and safety

Under the *Health and Safety at Work Act 1974*, employers have a legal duty to take care of the safety of their staff.

This means that they must receive the proper training, the equipment that they use must be safe and the people they work with must behave safely and responsibly.

In an organisation with five or more employees, health and safety arrangements must be given to each employee in writing.

Anyone injured at work should immediately report the matter to their supervisor and get legal advice from their trade union or a solicitor.

? Questions

4. What is Anit's legal position in the following cases?

Fall? As Anit collected a customer's order from the kitchen he slipped on some cream that had just been spilt on the floor. His ankle was badly twisted and he missed two days' work.

Abuse? Anit receives some racial abuse from three customers, sitting together. Later he tells Mr Bonner, who says that he should just ignore it.

■ Contract

Contracts of employment are very important because they form the agreement upon which many of an employee's rights are based. A contract – whether written down or agreed verbally – sets out the kind of job the employee will do, their hours, pay, holiday arrangements and the kinds of things over which they can be disciplined by their employer.

Part-time workers It is against the law to discriminate against workers employed part-time. This means that part-timers should receive, for example, the same rate of pay as full-time workers. They should have the same training opportunities and have their holiday allowances calculated in the same way as full-time workers.

? Questions

5. If Mr Bonner did not provide Anit with either a written contract or a note of his terms and conditions at work, what is the basis of Anit's contract?

6. What is Anit's legal position in the following situations?

The wrong shoes? Anit leaves his black shoes at a friend's house, and comes to work in trainers. Mr Bonner sends him home. When he returns with the right shoes, Anit is told he must work an extra hour – the amount of time that he lost in collecting the shoes.

No work? If the restaurant is quiet Anit is sometimes sent home early. Although he appreciates the time off, it means that on some shifts he gets only two hours' pay.

Jobs? At the start of each shift, Anit is often told to mop out the men's toilets. He feels this is unfair. He is employed as a waiter, not a cleaner.

Hours? When Anit works in the evening he is expected to stay until the last customer leaves. Sometimes he is unable to get away until after midnight.

Holiday? Anit asks if he will be entitled to any holiday later in the year. Mr Bonner explains that he can take a week off but, unlike the other staff, he won't be paid, as he only works part-time.

Trade unions

This unit looks at the role of trade unions and employer associations today.

Trade unions

■ A changing role

Beginning   The first trade unions in Britain developed in the late eighteenth century. They were originally formed by workers to help them negotiate their wages with their employers but, as they grew, they began to represent their members over many other aspects of work and to try to influence government policy.

Union membership in Britain reached its peak in 1920, with 45 per cent of the workforce belonging to a union, but declined in the late 1920s and early 1930s when unemployment became a serious problem.

During the Second World War, industry and unions worked closely together in order to maximise production. Co-operation with the Government continued after the war and, with strong membership figures once again, unions were able to play a significant role in shaping national policies. Unions have always been strong financial supporters of the Labour Party.

Change   In the 1960s and 1970s, Britain was increasingly affected by industrial disputes for which, at the time, the unions were held to blame. The new Conservative Government in 1979 believed that the influence of the unions should be reduced and, over the next 15 years, introduced new laws designed to weaken their power. These included requiring unions to hold secret ballots before strikes, and making them legally liable for unauthorised strike action.

Today   After an increase in membership in the early part of the twenty-first century, it began to fall again in 2007–8. Today, the female workforce has a higher proportion of trade union members than the male workforce.

The role of trade unions has also changed. Nowadays, there is less emphasis on negotiating pay deals, and more on improving working conditions and helping workers claim their legal rights.

The Trades Union Congress (TUC) is the main association to which nearly all trade unions belong.

Employers' organisations

■ The Confederation of British Industry (CBI)

The interests of employers in Britain are promoted by the Confederation of British Industry, usually known as the CBI. Its membership is drawn from owners and leaders of businesses throughout Britain and, like the TUC, it works to promote the interests of its members.

Typically, the CBI campaigns on issues that are important for business, such as changes to the tax system, improving the transport system and public services, and changing laws and regulations in a way that will benefit businesses.

Working hours

A nation of workers

Figures released in 2008 showed that workers in Britain work longer hours than those in almost every other European country. Only workers in Romania and Bulgaria worked longer.

The average working week for full-time employees in Britain is 41.4 hours. This is one hour and 24 minutes longer than the European average. Often this extra work is unpaid. The TUC estimates that employees donate on average almost 60 days work per year through unpaid overtime.

? Questions

1. Draw up a list of what you feel might be some of the main consequences of employees working long hours. Divide your list into what you regard as good and bad consequences.

2. Suggest two ways of reducing the numbers of hours that many people spend at work. What are the strengths and weaknesses of each idea?

The Working Time Directive

The *European Working Time Directive* is a set of European Union regulations (see page 22) designed to protect the health and safety of workers in member states. It limits the working week in EU states to a maximum of 48 hours, averaged over a 17-week period. It also lays down regulations about the number of rest breaks that workers should have and the amount of holiday to which they are entitled.

The Directive came into force in Britain in 1998. Although it applies to most employees, workers in a small number of industries are exempt. These include certain groups of transport workers, along with the armed forces, the police and the emergency services.

The Government also negotiated a further concession that allows British workers over 18 to opt out of the Directive, if they wish, and to work longer than the permitted 48 hours. This has been very controversial, and something over which the CBI and TUC disagree.

The CBI:
- accepts the *Working Time* regulations and supports the idea of preventing the exploitation of workers
- believes that employees should have the choice of saying no to working more than 48 hours, but should also, if they wish, have the choice of working longer in order to earn more money.

The TUC:
- states that many employees are not given any real choice by their managers over whether or not they wish to work longer hours
- questions whether it is right to allow people to work longer hours, even when they wish to do so. Longer hours increase the likelihood of fatigue, accidents, and ill-health – all of which can have an effect on other people and be a cost to society.

? Questions

3. Do you support the view of the CBI or TUC over the right of workers to opt out of the Working Time regulations? Explain your reasoning.

Losing your job

This unit looks at the law surrounding dismissal from work.

Fired!

Graham worked as a van driver for a large firm of printers. He had done the job for three years, but on several occasions his boss had been unhappy with his work, complaining that he was too slow.

One morning, Graham got completely lost on a delivery and was, once again, running late. In trying to make up time he was caught speeding by a roadside camera.

When the company was served with a speeding penalty, details were checked and it became clear that Graham had driven the van in question. The following morning he was called into the manager's office and told that he needed to find another job. He was given three weeks' notice to leave.

■ Notice

Finishing work When someone wants to leave their job, they must normally inform their employer, in advance, of their intention to leave. This is called a period of notice. The amount of notice an employee must give is normally set out in their terms and conditions of work.

If there is no written statement, a person who has worked for an employer for four weeks or more is required to give seven days' notice, irrespective of length of service.

Sacked An employee's terms and conditions of work will usually give the length of notice to which they are entitled.

If there is no written statement, the law states that the minimum period of notice employers must give is as follows:

- after four weeks' continuous service, one week
- after two years' continuous service, one week for every year of service
- after twelve years' of continuous service, twelve weeks. This is the maximum entitlement.

An employer who does not give proper notice may be taken to a county court by the employee and sued for wrongful dismissal. If the employee is successful, they will be awarded damages for the amount of money they have lost by not being given the right notice.

? Questions

1. Dorothy was sacked from her office job after three months, because of the poor standard of her work. She was very slow and made many mistakes. She had no written statement of terms and conditions of work. How much notice was Dorothy entitled to?

2. Kassie worked for five years part-time, as a doctor's receptionist. After several warnings she was sacked for poor time-keeping. She had no written statement of terms and conditions of work. How much notice was she entitled to?

3. Bruno lost his job as a chef after he arrived at work drunk for the third time. Why do you think his boss gave him two weeks' wages and told him to leave immediately – instead of allowing him to work during his two weeks' notice?

■ Instant dismissal

If an employee does something seriously wrong at work, their employer may decide to bring their contract to an end immediately and to sack them on the spot.

Instant dismissal means that the employee loses their right to notice – but they should have first had an opportunity to defend themselves against the allegation before the dismissal takes place.

Serious misbehaviour is described in the law as gross misconduct and includes theft, violence, dishonesty and damage to the employer's property.

■ Go!

Claire worked as an office manager for an insurance company and was instantly dismissed after her boss discovered that she had been arranging her holiday while at work. Over a period of several days, Claire had been surfing the internet looking for cheap flights and hotels during her lunch breaks. She claimed to have spent less than two hours over the four days searching for a holiday, adding that there was no time to go to a travel agent after she had finished work.

Her boss reminded Claire that the company had written to all employees saying that office computers could not be used for personal use as they contained important and confidential data. Claire was told to leave immediately. Claire felt that her dismissal was unfair and took her claim to an employment tribunal.

? Questions

4. Did Claire's behaviour amount to gross misconduct? Give reasons for your answer.

Losing your job
Claiming unfair dismissal

■ Fair or unfair?

In this section, you will be asked to decide whether you think people have been dismissed from their job fairly or unfairly. But before you do that, you might like to consider (without looking at the section on the law on the next page) what makes a dismissal fair or unfair.

One way of doing this is to complete the following sentences:

A person is dismissed fairly when …
A person is dismissed unfairly when …

■ Greater rights

Until 1971, employers were able to dismiss staff as they pleased. They were required only to give the correct notice, and pay the employee the money due to them.

Nearly 40 years on, employees now have much more protection against unfair dismissal. A simplified summary of the law is given opposite.

? Questions

1. Using the information on this double page, decide whether you feel the person in each case was fairly or unfairly dismissed, giving reasons for each of your decisions.

 **Colette** had been employed as a secretary for two months when she was given the sack after taking a two-hour lunch break. Her employer felt that she worked too slowly and had previously warned her about poor time keeping.

Martine lost her job in a bank, where she had worked for two years, when her boss discovered that she had lied at her interview when asked if she had any criminal convictions. A year before joining the company she had been found guilty of theft.

John had worked for the ambulance service for ten years. He lost his job after he injured his back lifting a heavy patient. He was dismissed when it became clear that he could no longer do the same kind of work.

Evan was fired after failing to turn up for his job as a bus driver when his partner Nerys went into hospital to have a baby. In the ten months that he had been with the firm he had missed work twice due to the difficulties that Nerys was having with her pregnancy.

The law

Anyone who feels they have been unfairly dismissed, and has been working for their employer for a year, may try to obtain compensation for this by taking their case to an employment tribunal. The tribunal can order that the employee should be given their old job back – but this is rarely done.

An employer must show that they had a fair reason for sacking the employee and that – in the circumstances – they behaved in a reasonable way.

Fair   Under the *Employment Rights Act 1996*, fair reasons for dismissal are as follows:

- *employee misconduct* – such as theft, fighting or persistent lateness

Dean   had worked for three years in a sports shop. One morning he was told that he would be losing his job because profits were down. A week after he had left, Dean noticed that someone else had been employed in his place.

Natasha   made several mistakes during her first week as a cashier at a supermarket. Just before she went home on Saturday she was told that she was unsuitable, and was dismissed.

- *incapability* – the employee does not, or is not able to, do the job to the required standard
- *redundancy* – when the job done by the employee is no longer required
- *so as not to break the law* – when, for example, a van driver loses their licence for a drink-driving offence
- *any other good reason.*

Unfair   Some reasons for dismissal are seen in law as automatically unfair, and here an employer has no defence. In these cases, employees may claim unfair dismissal, even if they have been working for their employer for less than a year.

Some of the situations in which dismissal is automatically unfair are set out below.

- *Trade union* – it is automatically unfair to dismiss someone because they belong (or choose not to belong) to a trade union. It is also unfair to dismiss them because of their trade union activities outside working hours.
- *Pregnancy* – dismissing someone solely because they are pregnant, need to attend maternity classes or plan to take maternity leave is automatically unfair.
- *Health and safety* – anyone who is sacked because of reasonable concern about health and safety at work is automatically unfairly dismissed.
- *Family emergencies* – a person has the right to take a 'reasonable amount' of time off to deal with the illness of their child or other family member.

Warnings   A worker who under-performs or breaks a rule in a minor way and is sacked without a warning or a reasonable time to improve may have a case for unfair dismissal – although there is no law saying that warnings must be given before a person is dismissed.

An employer may dismiss someone immediately for gross misconduct. No warning is necessary.

Losing your job
The employment tribunal

■ Reason to leave?

One morning, Kirsty Brennan received a call at work from her son's school. Seven-year-old Robbie had a high temperature and an ear infection. The school felt he ought to see a doctor.

Kirsty immediately went to her boss, telling him that her son was unwell and that she needed to collect him from school.

Just as she was preparing to leave, a colleague came downstairs to tell Kirsty that she had been sacked. 'Mr Collier has given you one week's notice,' she said, 'because he can't rely on you.'

Kirsty felt that she had been sacked unfairly. She decided to take her case to an employment tribunal.

At the tribunal Mr Collier said that Kirsty was rude and aggressive. 'This really was the last straw,' he said. 'She would fling files onto my desk, and if I asked her to make any changes she would snatch the paper and storm out.'

'Ms Brennan did not ask if she could pick up her son,' Simon Collier went on, 'she just told me she was leaving. She had only been here six weeks, and this was the second occasion she needed time off for childcare arrangements.'

Kirsty said that she didn't have the chance to tell Mr Collier that she would return as soon as she had taken her son to the doctor and found someone to look after him.

? Questions

1. Using the information in this section on *Losing your job*, put yourself in the position of a member of an employment tribunal and decide whether Kirsty Brennan was unfairly dismissed. When you have reached your decision, write a short report outlining the reasons for your view.

■ A court of law

A person who feels that they have been unfairly dismissed may take their case to an employment tribunal. This is a special court dealing with employment disputes.

■ Procedure

Anyone claiming unfair dismissal must fill in a special form, available from a Jobcentre, on which they set out details of their case.

It is important to get help with this from someone with experience in dealing with these cases. This could be a solicitor, someone from the Citizens Advice Bureau or a trade union representative.

■ Paperwork

A lot of preparation is required in gathering evidence and arranging for witnesses to come to court. Often both sides are required to let each other inspect the documents that they will use as evidence.

Finding a solution

Before the case goes to tribunal one more attempt is made to help both sides reach agreement, and avoid going to court. Often this is successful.

At the tribunal

Tribunals are more informal than other courts of law. No one wears a gown or a wig, as they do in a county court.

The panel that will hear the case consists of three people: a legally qualified chairperson, and two lay people – one representing employers and the other trade unions. The three members of the panel should not all be of the same sex.

It was originally intended that people should put their case to the tribunal in person. This is still possible but today many applicants use the services of a lawyer or a trade union official. Employers also often engage specialists.

The decision

If members of the tribunal find in favour of the employee, they usually order that the person should be compensated for loss of income and the difficulties they have faced as a result of the unfair treatment.

Tribunals are allowed to order that the employee should be given their job back – but rarely do.

The cost

Tribunals were designed to be a cheap and effective way of settling disputes. There is no charge for taking a case to an employment tribunal, but a person's chances of success are statistically greater if they have advice and help from a solicitor or trade union representative.

All lawyers' fees must be paid privately or taken from any award that the person receives.

Unfortunately, if the employee wins, they are not always better off. The average award is around £4,000, and more than half the people who take their case to tribunal are in lower-paid jobs afterwards.

? Questions

2. It is estimated that about one and a half million people a year have a serious problem at work. Of the half who seek advice, only a quarter decide to take the matter further. Why do you think many people do not assert their legal rights and make claims for unfair dismissal or discrimination? Does it matter?

Managing the economy

This unit explains the Government's role in managing the economy and the place of the tax system within this.

All change

■ The business cycle

Boom, recession and recovery are words that are often used to describe a country's economic position. They refer to the fact that, over a period of time, most businesses and organisations go through a cycle of change.

During a boom, things are going well. Many businesses have full order books. They invest in new equipment, employ more workers, and generally make good profits. However, sooner or later, costs (such as wages or the price of raw materials) tend to rise. These push up prices and people start deciding not to buy some of the goods or services on offer.

The economy then tends to slow down and may move into a period of recession. A fall in demand means that businesses can't sell all the things that they make. They buy fewer supplies and, if things don't improve, begin to lay off workers. Some firms close down completely.

Eventually, business confidence begins to return. A recovery can take several years. Investment gradually increases and new jobs are created. Once again, the economy moves on an upward cycle.

Changing times   During the 1950s and 1960s, the cycle of boom, recession and recovery used to take place every four or five years. In the 1970s and 1980s the swings between boom and recession became much greater (in the mid-1980s, unemployment reached record levels). However, between 1992 and 2006 the cycles became much weaker and the UK economy enjoyed an unusually long period of sustained growth. But in 2007 this all began to change.

■ A global financial crisis

Most experts agree that the root cause of the economic downturn that began in 2007 was the very high level of borrowing that had developed in most western countries, particularly in Britain and the United States. With low **interest rates**, and sometimes less-than-thorough checks on a borrower's ability to repay their loan, credit could be very easy to obtain.

The sub-prime market   The widespread availability of credit led to record levels of borrowing. It also gave more and more people the opportunity to buy their own house, with greater demand leading to higher house prices. This gave rise to further lending, as banks became prepared to lend people more and more money against the value of their house.

Some of the loans, however, were not good. In the United States, in particular, many people had chosen, or been encouraged, to take out a mortgage that they would have difficulty repaying, especially if economic conditions worsened. When interest rates, fuel and food prices began to rise, many people found it difficult to keep up their repayments. These mortgages – sold to customers with a low income and a poor credit rating – became known as 'sub-prime'.

The banking crisis   When lenders realised that property had become over-valued and that borrowers were having difficulty in paying back their loans, they started to call in their debts. However, bad decisions about mortgages and loans had

not only been taken by banks in Britain and the USA, but by financial institutions throughout the world. As the extent of the problem became clear, lenders began to fear that almost any bank could go under.

British banks, however, were particularly vulnerable. In order to fund their loans, they had borrowed widely. With fears over their ability to pay back the money that they owed, their **creditors** demanded immediate repayment, placing banks under huge pressure to find money or risk going bust.

The British Government was vitally concerned to prevent the banking system from collapse, and large amounts of money (much of it raised from taxpayers) were pumped into the banking system in an attempt to protect people's savings and to prevent the failure of the banking system as a whole. Governments throughout the world took similar action, believing that a collapse of the banking system would damage so many aspects of people's lives.

The credit crunch The losses faced by the banking system made banks very reluctant to lend money – unless they could be absolutely sure of getting it back. Loans (i.e. credit) became very difficult to obtain, affecting individuals and businesses throughout the world. People cut their spending (particularly on non-essentials); businesses could not develop; and people began to lose their jobs.

Recession By the middle of 2008, there was general agreement that Britain was facing a period of recession.

During a recession, shops and businesses find it more difficult to sell goods and services, and some are forced to close. Certain groups of workers are likely to lose their jobs, and it's difficult to start a new business. People have less money to spend and are often cautious about the future.

? Questions

1. On several occasions in 2007 and 2008, the Government had to decide whether to intervene and protect the banking system. Try to put together a list of some of the advantages and disadvantages of a) intervening, and b) doing nothing at all.

2. What should the Government do in a recession? Look at the list below, and decide the five measures that you feel would be the most effective. Explain why.

Raise benefits helping those worst affected

Go green financing and encouraging the development of new green technology

Build more houses helping to overcome the housing shortage and keep people in work

Lower taxes giving people more money to spend

Improve public transport providing work and cutting pollution

Financial support helping businesses hit by the recession

Encouraging lower interest rates making it easier for people and businesses to borrow

More training and guidance helping people back into work

Key words

Creditor
A person or organisation to whom money is owed.

Interest rate
The price charged to borrow money.

Managing the economy

Taxation

Driven away

In 2007, news was announced of British Formula One driver Lewis Hamilton's plans to leave Britain and move to Switzerland.

At first, reports indicated that his reason for quitting was the lack of privacy he suffered in the UK as a result of his celebrity status. Later, however, it was confirmed that, by moving to Switzerland, Lewis Hamilton would avoid the need to pay UK tax rates on his income from racing and sponsorship.

Switzerland, in common with a number of other countries, has a different tax system for foreigners who live but don't work there. At the time of his move, reports indicated that on an income of £10 million, Lewis Hamilton would be required to pay something in the region of £35,000 tax in Switzerland, compared with a bill of up to £4 million had he remained resident in Britain. (However, this figure would almost certainly have been reduced, with advice from his accountant.) Lewis Hamilton is not alone in choosing to live overseas for tax reasons. Other successful sports stars, singers, actors and business people have followed a similar pattern.

? Questions

1. Some people criticised Lewis Hamilton for moving abroad to pay less tax. Others said that he was quite justified in doing so. What's your view? Try to explain your answer.

■ Tax demands

Taxes in Britain are commonly divided into two categories: direct taxes and indirect taxes.

Direct taxes   These are taxes paid on a person's income or capital. They include income tax, inheritance tax, national insurance contributions, capital gains tax and corporation tax.

Indirect taxes   These are taxes paid on goods or services that we buy. They include VAT, stamp duty, excise duty and council tax.

The taxes we pay

Capital gains tax Tax on the profits from selling shares, land or buildings.

Council tax   A local tax, which helps to pay for local services, based on the value of a person's property, whether owned or rented.

Corporation tax   Tax on the profits of companies.

Excise duty   An extra tax placed on items like fuel, alcohol and tobacco.

Income tax   Tax on earnings, pensions, certain benefits, savings and investments.

Inheritance tax Tax paid on the value of a person's money and property when they die.

National insurance Contributions entitling a person to certain benefits, including a state pension.

Stamp duty   Tax paid on the purchase of property.

VAT   Strictly known as value added tax, and paid on many goods and services.

Why do we pay tax?

Income tax, which was first introduced in Britain in 1799, was originally a means of getting money for the war that Britain was waging against France. Today taxes are raised for a number of reasons.

Paying for government expenditure The Government uses taxes to raise money for their expenditure programmes on health, defence, education, etc. In fact taxes make up nearly 90 per cent of all government revenue.

Managing the economy The tax system can be used by the Government to regulate the economy as a whole. For example, in 2008, the Chancellor of the Exchequer announced a one-year cut in the rate of VAT (from 17.5 to 15 per cent) as one of a number of ways of combating the deepening recession.

Redistributing income Income tax in Britain is charged at three different rates. People whose income is under £6,000–£7,000 do not normally pay income tax. Those earning up to £35,000–£40,000 are allowed £6,000–£7,000 tax-free, and the remainder of their income is taxed at 20p in the pound. Income above this figure is taxed at 40p in the pound. Taxing richer people at a higher rate can go some way towards making a society more equal.

An example of this is the case of Liverpool footballer, John Arne Riise, whose wage slip was mischievously posted on the internet in 2007, showing a monthly wage of just under £140,000 a month. It also revealed a monthly deduction of more than £55,000 in tax.

Changing behaviour Taxes may also used as a way of changing people's personal behaviour. For many years, governments have tried to discourage people from smoking by raising the excise duty on tobacco – making the price of a packet of cigarettes more and more expensive.

Taxation levels

Tax rates in the UK are broadly similar to those in most other developed countries. Rates in Belgium, France and Scandinavia currently tend to be higher, with the USA, Japan, Russia and Eastern Europe charging slightly lower rates.

However, the question of how much a government should take in tax remains controversial. Those taking too much risk unpopularity and being forced from power. A government that does not take enough risks being unable to provide the level of services that many people require.

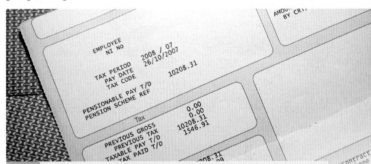

? Questions

2. Select two of the following statements and outline their strengths and weaknesses:

   a) 'Lower tax rates allow people to keep more of their own money, and encourage them to work harder.'

   b) 'The rich should pay more tax than the poor – it's only fair.'

   c) 'The government has no right to take part of our earnings.'

   d) 'A flat tax rate for everyone would be simple and fair.'

World trade

This unit examines some of the benefits and drawbacks of globalisation and the ways in which trading conditions for less economically developed countries might be improved.

Globalisation

Long haul

In 1994, one of the longest trials in British history began when McDonald's Corporation sued two protestors, Helen Steel and David Morris, over the contents of a leaflet that they and others had distributed on behalf of London Greenpeace.

The leaflet, entitled *What's wrong with McDonald's?*, strongly criticised the food that McDonald's sold and many of the ways in which the company operated. McDonald's hotly disputed these accusations, and asked those responsible to withdraw their comments. Some agreed, but Helen Steel and David Morris did not, and legal action followed.

It took almost *three years* for both sides to deliver their evidence. McDonald's used a large team of lawyers to present their case. Helen Steel and David Morris conducted their own defence. The judge decided that most of the serious allegations made against the company were untrue, and awarded McDonald's £110,000 damages, later reduced on appeal to £40,000.

Worldwide scale

One point raised in the leaflet was the scale of the McDonald's operations. The McDonald's Corporation has more than 31,000 restaurants in 120 countries. McDonald's is not alone in this. Many companies have a worldwide presence, and their products are household names.

Companies operating in a number of different countries are called *multinationals* and are a reflection and a part of the process of *globalisation*.

Globalisation refers to the process in which business, politics and culture operate on a world stage, no longer confined to single countries or continents.

The term was originally coined in the 1980s, but the idea itself goes back more than five hundred years.

The long view Between the fifteenth and nineteenth centuries, Britain and several other European nations colonised many parts of the world – in effect, trying to spread their rule and influence across the globe. In doing this, they exported their languages and their religions, and set up governments and administrations that often exactly mirrored the arrangements that they had at home.

Local people were used as cheap labour and were often forcibly moved from one area to another. These ideas added to the slave trade already existing in Africa to the point where millions of Africans were shipped to work in the Caribbean and America.

The colonisers also amassed huge amounts of wealth from their overseas colonies. Food, plants and other raw materials that had previously been restricted to certain parts of Africa, Asia or the Americas, arrived for the first time in Europe. Fruits, spices, coffee, tea and certain types of timber and fur became known for the first time on a *global* scale, no longer restricted to their region or country of origin.

The situation today

The process of globalisation is believed to have accelerated and developed over the last 25 to 30 years. It has also changed its nature. There are several reasons for this.

> WITH ACCESS TO A COMPUTER, THE *COST* OF SENDING AN EMAIL ANYWHERE IN THE WORLD IS VIRTUALLY *NIL*.

- *Communications* Technological developments in phones, faxes and computers have made communications throughout the world simpler, faster and cheaper.
- *Transport* Lower costs and improved technology have led to a massive increase in the movement of people and goods around the world.

> AIRLINE TICKETS ARE NOW SOMETIMES *CHEAPER* THAN RAIL FARES.

- *Politics and economics* The 1980s and 1990s were a period of great political and economic change. The Soviet Union was dismantled into separate independent states. There was also a big reduction in the role of the state in the USA and Europe (particularly in Britain, under the influence of Mrs Thatcher). Companies became much freer to move their operations to different parts of the world and to invest capital overseas.

> IN BRITAIN AND ELSEWHERE A NUMBER OF *STATE-OWNED* ENTERPRISES INCLUDING TELEPHONE, GAS, ELECTRICITY, WATER, RAILWAYS, AND THE NATIONAL AIRLINE WERE SOLD TO BECOME *PRIVATE BUSINESSES*.

Size matters There are ASDA supermarkets in many British towns and cities. The company was formed in 1965 by a group of farmers from Yorkshire. In 1999 it was taken over by Wal-Mart, an American corporation with stores throughout the United States – and in 2001, Wal-Mart recorded the largest sales of any company in the world.

The figures below give an indication of how large some businesses have become. The examples – a supermarket, a car maker, and two IT businesses – show companies with sales in excess of the value of all the goods and services (GDP) produced in some countries.

	2007 Sales				2007 GDP		
Wal-Mart Stores	Toyota	IBM	Microsoft	Belgium	Sweden	Ireland	Kenya
$403.9 billion	$264.1 billion	$105.5 billion	$61.7 billion	$376 billion	$335 billion	$186 billion	$59 billion

? Questions

1. A major multinational supermarket plans to introduce up to 50 new stores in southern Africa, promising lower prices, up-to-the-minute facilities, greater choice for consumers, and new employment opportunities for local people.

   What do you think are the strengths and weaknesses of this idea?

2. Put yourself in the position of a member of the local government in one of the areas where the supermarket is hoping to build several new large stores.

   What kinds of agreements or guarantees would you expect the supermarket to give to make sure that the new developments benefited the whole of the local community?

World trade
Anti-globalisation

■ Protest

In June 2007, thousands of demonstrators marched through Rostock in northern Germany, where world leaders were meeting. The protest was one of many that have taken place in various cities throughout the world – including Berlin, London, Moscow and Prague.

While the majority try to protest peacefully, many of the demonstrations have resulted in violence, with damage to buildings and shops and running battles with the police. In the Italian city of Genoa in 2001 a protestor was killed as he attacked the police.

Targets Large-scale anti-globalisation protests have tended to be held at meetings of the World Trade Organisation, the International Monetary Fund and the World Bank. These are international organisations that promote trade and provide loans to help countries in crisis.

The protestors believe that the rules governing world trade tend to meet the interests of large business corporations, rather than the needs of ordinary people.

Criticism 'Cheap sloganeering and mindless vandalism' was the description of the protests given by one person interviewed by the BBC after demonstrations in 2001 at Davos in Switzerland.

Others critics are more thoughtful. They agree that some protestors attend largely to stir up trouble and that many probably don't understand all the issues involved. 'But at least they are doing something,' they say. 'How else can you change things when many of the people with power are accountable to no one but their **shareholders**. If we don't like our politicians we can vote them out of office. How do we get these people to listen to us?

? Questions

1. How should people protest or make their opinions known over issues of this kind? What do you think are the limits to acceptable protest?

■ Too large?

As we have seen (page 90), a multinational company may be larger than the state in which it is operating. Some people have expressed concern over this, believing that large businesses can become a law unto themselves, riding roughshod over local regulations and law.

Whilst corporations may seek to have fewer controls and limits placed upon them (which states are sometimes willing to provide), all businesses have to face certain structures and limitations. In addition to the laws of the country in which they are operating, multinational companies also have to follow international regulations covering, for example, pollution, business practice, labour standards. These rules do guarantee good practice, but may have some effect in limiting the abuse of power.

■ The case for globalisation . . .

Japanese companies set up electronics factories and car manufacturing plants in Britain. A joint British-Dutch company produces and sells ice cream in China. Kenyan farmers send flowers and vegetables to Europe. These are some of the things taking place in the global market. Those in favour of these trends see them as the best chance of improving standards of living in the world as a whole.

Governments generally see multinationals as a force for good. They create work, spread wealth, introduce new technology and help people learn better ways of doing business. Many companies also work for the good of the local community, with projects to improve education, health and the environment.

Globalisation gives millions of people choices and access to goods and services. It increases wealth, enhances human liberty and helps us better understand our neighbours.

■ . . . and the case against

Opponents of globalisation are worried about the level of influence that large corporations and multinational companies have in the world today.

Although governments usually welcome foreign investment in their country, opponents state that the benefits of this can be short-lived. Promises of employment sometimes mean that measures to protect the environment are ignored. Critics also say that there is nothing to stop the foreign investor pulling out if better opportunities for profits appear elsewhere, leaving many workers without jobs.

Too many foreign imports damage a country's industry and culture. Giant companies, they say, squeeze out traditional local producers and limit choice.

Many multinationals set up plants or operations in less-developed countries in order to take advantage of cheaper labour or a plentiful supply of raw materials. Some companies are criticised for offering much poorer pay and working conditions to workers overseas than they do to those at home.

? Questions

2. Which of the following statements do you most agree with? Explain why.

   a) Globalisation is a force for good and should be encouraged.
   b) Generally the advantages of globalisation outweigh the drawbacks.
   c) Greater controls should be placed on large companies to make sure that they work for the benefit of the community and not just their investors.
   d) Globalisation should be opposed at all costs.

Key words

Shareholder
Someone who invests in a company.

World trade
A fair price to pay?

■ The end of the line

In 2007, after almost 20 years of clothes production at Treorchy in south Wales, Burberry, the garment manufacturer, decided to close the plant and transfer production to China. It was reported that about 300 jobs were lost in the move.

In explaining their decision, Burberry said that the cost of producing garments in China was much lower than in the UK. For example, it cost about £12 to make a polo shirt in the Treorchy factory, compared with only £4 in China. Moving some of the production, the company claimed, was essential if its products were to remain competitive in a world market.

Although Burberry continues to manufacture garments in the UK, there was considerable criticism of the closure of the Welsh factory, perhaps because the company and its style of clothes are regarded as quintessentially British. Burberry is also a holder of a Royal Warrant, awarded to companies who provide goods or services to the Queen, the Duke of Edinburgh or Prince Charles for a period of at least five years.

? Questions

1. Many firms in Britain have transferred all or part of their manufacturing or services to countries where costs are lower. What are some of the consequences of this? Who tends to benefit, and who tends to lose?

2. Can a firm still claim to be British if it moves its manufacturing base overseas?

■ Terms and conditions

One significant effect of moving production to another location is the new work it brings to that area. This can be of great benefit, but raises the question of how the factory should be run. What levels of pay and working conditions should companies like Burberry adopt for their factories overseas? Should they apply UK standards, or is it acceptable that the terms and conditions are not as good as those of their remaining or former employees in Britain?

Fair game? Since the late 1980s, there has been much criticism of the conditions of workers in less-developed countries who are employed to make clothing and equipment for sportswear manufacturers, supermarkets and other large retail chains.

In the mid-1990s, companies such as Nike and Adidas were singled out for criticism over the excessive working hours and low pay suffered by those who made their goods in countries such as Pakistan and Indonesia.

Today similar concern is expressed over the manufacture of fashion and everyday clothing in the less-developed world, which is sold at low prices through chain stores and supermarkets in Europe and the United States.

Fashion victims? The clothing factory, located just inside the Chinese border, a few miles from Hong Kong, employs about 800 people, making garments for a number of well-known British brands and stores.

A typical worker's basic pay is just over £50 a month, but this can go up to £100 through piecework and overtime. Quality is carefully controlled, but workers who make mistakes lose pay or have to redo the work in their own time.

Employees often work for up to twelve hours a day, with two weeks holiday per year. Most workers are migrants, sending part of their wages home to their families. Workers are housed in special dormitory buildings and have relatively few employment rights. There are no trade unions and staff say that they have little choice but to do as they are told by their supervisor. Anyone who protests faces instant dismissal.

Clothing workers face similar conditions in other parts of China, and in Vietnam, India and Bangladesh. In some countries, for example Bangladesh, wages are lower than in China, at around £30 per month, or 10 pence an hour.

Exposed In recent years, a number of clothing brands, stores and supermarkets have faced criticism for selling certain items of clothing at extraordinarily low prices, with tops and skirts available for £5 or £6 and jeans on sale at £10 or less.

The companies claim that these low prices are not a result of exploitation and poor working conditions, but due to reduced overheads and their ability to buy fabric in bulk at low cost.

These statements have been challenged, particularly by charities such as War on Want, who have identified a direct link between poor working conditions overseas and low prices in the shops in Britain and elsewhere.

In response to this criticism, many stores and clothing manufacturers have introduced strict codes covering pay and employment conditions, which all suppliers must

follow. Failure to do so may result in the supplier no longer being used.

However, a lot of manufacturing overseas is outsourced to many different suppliers, making it very difficult for companies to establish with certainty that their garments are being made in acceptable conditions. Despite spot checks, there is evidence to suggest that low pay and poor working conditions remain a reality for many workers.

? Questions

3. The manufacture and sale of a pair of jeans involves many different processes. Draw up a list of the stages that must be completed in the creation and sale of a pair of jeans – from the field where the cotton is grown, to the store where they are sold.

4. 'We have to be prepared to pay more for our clothes if workers are to be adequately rewarded for their labour. This means paying £30, rather than £10, for a pair of jeans.' To what extent do you agree with this view, and how would you answer it?

World trade
Ironing out the highs and lows

■ The problem of uncertainty

Most people in Britain with a job or pension have a fairly clear idea of their likely income over the next six months or year. It might not be as high as they would like, but – as long as they can keep their job – they can be fairly sure of the amount of money they will have for both the essentials and the luxuries of life.

In some parts of the world, however, the situation is very different. About a third of the world's population (around two billion people) work either growing or mining raw materials. These are crops such as rice, coffee beans and cotton, and minerals such as copper or tin.

They are known as primary commodities and are used throughout the world for food and industrial production.

Quite often the sale of a particular commodity forms a major part of country's economy. For example, almost three-quarters of the **export** earnings of the Republic of Mali, in West Africa, come from the sale of cotton.

However, unlike many of the goods that we routinely buy, the prices of commodities tend to fluctuate. For example, between 2008 and 2009, the price that farmers in Africa could obtain for their rice fell by a third; similarly, from 2000 to 2004, coffee prices ranged from $0.45 to $1.20 per pound. A sudden fall in prices can mean that a farmer's crop becomes almost worthless overnight.

? Questions

1. Draw up a list of some of the likely consequences of sudden shifts in commodity prices. You might like to look at this in terms of advantages and disadvantages and also perhaps on its impact on families, communities, and countries.

■ The terms of trade

In recent years, two further problems have arisen for developing countries that rely on selling their crops or materials on the world market:

- *Less purchasing power* Over the past 20 years, the prices of manufactured goods have risen faster than those of commodities. This has worked to the

benefit of industrialised nations, but has meant that developing countries have had to produce more for the same return.
- *Influence of multinationals* Today, many industries are dominated by large multinational companies, giving small individual producers little control over the price that they receive for their goods.

■ Problems of uncertainty

Fluctuations in the prices of commodities make it difficult for governments to plan for the future. A five-year road-building plan might easily run out of money if the price of the country's main export suddenly falls. High prices can bring problems too. Increases in the prices of soya or cereals can lead to farmers seeking more land on which to grow these crops. Sometimes this means the destruction of valuable forests – upsetting the ecological balance of the area.

Fairtrade

International organisations are trying several ways to overcome these problems. One of them is through a process known as Fairtrade.

In order to be able to display the Fairtrade logo, companies must guarantee to pay producers a minimum price for their goods, which covers the cost of production and ensures that the producer gets a reasonable return. If this figure is above the market price, then consumers who choose to buy these goods will probably pay a little more than they would for non-Fairtrade goods.

Fairtrade goods must meet certain minimum standards of production, and a very small part of the price paid goes to support social projects in the producer's community, a measure designed to help raise overall living standards in developing countries.

Britain sells more Fairtrade goods than almost any other country (only the USA sells more), and the names of some of the large Fairtrade organisations, such as Cafédirect, Traidcraft, and Divine Chocolate, are widely known. Major supermarkets stock Fairtrade goods and some stores will only sell items such as tea, coffee and bananas if they are from Fairtrade sources.

. . . but does it help? Organisations working to reduce world poverty, the UK government's Department for International Development and Fairtrade organisations themselves all believe that Fairtrade is an important and effective way of giving a better life to workers and producers in developing countries. But not everyone agrees. Here are some arguments that are made against Fairtrade:

- *It keeps countries poor* By guaranteeing minimum prices, Fairtrade props up inefficient producers who ought to be engaged in other forms of production that would bring them and their country more benefit.
- *Others suffer* Helping farmers and producers who are part of a Fairtrade scheme penalises all the others who are not.
- *Guilt* Fairtrade is mainly a marketing device that feeds on the guilt that people in developed countries feel about their high standard in relation to that of the rest of the world.

? Questions

2. Fairtrade goods are sometimes – but not always – slightly more expensive than others. Would you choose a Fairtrade option if it was available?

3. Is Fairtrade something you think should be encouraged? Explain your view.

Key words

Exports
Goods and services produced in one country and sold in another.

Poverty

This unit sets out the different kinds of aid that may be provided for countries in crisis and for those that are less economically developed.

Foreign aid

■ The Asian tsunami

Just after midnight on the 26 September 2004, the second biggest earthquake in recorded history took place off the north-west coast of Indonesia.

The jolt of the earth moving beneath the seabed sent out large waves from the centre of the earthquake. As these reached the land, they slowed down but gained height, reaching the coast as huge walls of water, up to 20 metres high. People living in the surrounding area had no warning of their approach and little time to escape or move to high ground.

The tidal wave – known as a tsunami – moved right across the Indian Ocean, reaching Thailand, Malaysia, India, Bangladesh, Sri Lanka, and even the African coast of Somalia. It is estimated that about 230,000 people were killed as a result of the earthquake and tsunami, and about 1.8 million were left homeless.

? Questions

1. What kinds of difficulties, would you imagine, were faced by those people most closely affected by the tsunami? (You may like to answer this for both the short term and the long term.)

2. What was the duty of the rest of the world when they heard news of the tsunami – and why?

■ Emergency aid

About $7.5 billion was raised by the general public in response to worldwide appeals for help for victims of the tsunami. A further $5.9 billion was pledged by national governments.

Helping people to overcome the effects of natural disasters is usually referred to as emergency or humanitarian aid. Like all aid, it tends to come from several sources – governments, international agencies (such as the International Red Cross and the Red Crescent societies), private foundations and individual personal donations.

■ Development aid

Crises, like floods and earthquakes, usually require immediate help to save lives. However, people's lives are in danger for other reasons, and one of the most significant is poverty – a problem faced by large numbers of people throughout the world.

The help given to people in these circumstances is usually longer term than humanitarian aid. Known as development aid, it is designed to eradicate poverty and to raise the general standard of living of a country or region.

The problem of poverty There will be few people who are not aware of the great differences in standards of living that exist throughout the world. Put simply, about 60 per cent of the world's population do not have a basic, decent, quality of life.

1 in 5
of the world's population lives on $1 a day or less

Almost half
the world's population lives on $2 a day or less

Almost half
of Africa's population lives on $1 a day or less

Source: Roger Riddell
'Does Foreign Aid Really Work?'

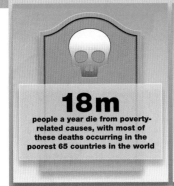

18m
people a year die from poverty-related causes, with most of these deaths occurring in the poorest 65 countries in the world

The annual number of deaths from poverty is equal to two and a half times the population of London

It is equivalent to 100 jumbo jets crashing each day

Every five days the same number of people die from poverty as died in the Asian tsunami

Help from aid Today the calls for aid to poorer countries are probably louder than ever before. In 2000, world leaders met at the UN to sign the Millennium Declaration - promising, by 2015, to try to get rid of extreme poverty and to halve the proportion of the world's population with an income of less than $1 a day.

The campaign involves many different kinds of action, including the provision of financial aid to help countries out of poverty.

Is aid the answer? In 2005, the 26 leading donor countries, including Britain, gave $106 billion in aid. Smaller, but still very significant, amounts were provided by non-governmental organisations (usually called NGOs) such as War on Want or Oxfam. However, despite the size and importance of aid, some people express doubt over the value of these programmes.

One criticism is that the money does not always reach those for whom it is intended. This may be due to bad management by the aid organisation, or because of corruption in the country that is receiving the aid. People also criticise the way in which aid is sometimes organised, claiming that donor countries do not always take note of the needs of those who are receiving aid, and sometimes attach 'strings' or requirements to aid, which don't always benefit the people in need.

Assessing the effectiveness of aid is very complex. Research shows that most aid programmes achieve their goals, although this could sometimes be done more efficiently. It also shows that, if there is to be a significant reduction in poverty, aid needs to be at least twice the level it is today.

? Questions

3. Sometimes aid is given only if certain conditions are met. For example, the country receiving the aid might be required to improve its human rights record or make changes to the way in which it is governed. What are the strengths and weaknesses of this approach?

4. Here are some arguments in support of giving development aid. Which do you feel are the strongest?

a) The rich have a duty to give to the poor.
b) Allowing the gap between rich and poor to grow is a threat to world peace.
c) Britain has a particular responsibility to help, because of its colonial past.
d) All lives are equally valuable; a reasonable standard of living should be available to all.
e) Helping others increases the level of happiness in the world.

Coming to Britain

This unit looks at reasons for and the impact of migration to and from the UK.

Migration

On the move

Almost everyone living in Britain today has their origins elsewhere. We are a nation of **migrants** – able to trace our roots to countries in all parts of Europe, the Middle East, Africa, Asia and the Caribbean. Romans, Saxons, Vikings and Normans came to Britain to invade and conquer. Some, particularly from Africa, were brought by force as slaves and servants. Refugees from France, Germany, Russia and other parts of Europe came to Britain to escape persecution and violence in their own country.

A better life

The other reason for many people coming to Britain has been the hope that they, or their children, would find a better standard of living here than in the country that they had left.

Economic migration, as this is called, goes back a long way. Records show that people from France, Germany, Italy and Holland were settling in London and elsewhere for this reason as early as AD 1130.

Skills

Many migrants bring useful skills. Merchants who came from France in the twelfth century brought an understanding of money and trade that was unfamiliar to the British – and were the founders of London's banking and financial services.

From the fourteenth century, other trades – connected with weaving, printing, brewing and engineering – were brought by French, Germans and Dutch immigrants.

Filling a gap

Migrants often move to countries where there is a shortage of labour or where it is difficult to get people to do certain jobs.

At the end of the Second World War in 1945, there was the huge task of rebuilding Britain, damaged by six years of war.

As there were not enough people available for work, the British Government started to encourage workers from other parts of Europe to help with this process of reconstruction. A year later, in 1948, the invitation was extended to people in Ireland and the West Indies.

Some industries launched large advertising campaigns to attract workers to Britain. London Transport set up centres in the West Indies to recruit bus crews, and textile and engineering firms in the north of England and Midlands sent agents to find workers in India and Pakistan.

For about 25 years, people from the West Indies, India, Pakistan, and later Bangladesh, travelled to work and settle in Britain.

Arriving from Jamaica, June 1948

Clinton Edwards 'I joined the RAF and came over to England in 1942, and was in the war for three years. When I went back to Jamaica there was no work. So I decided to return to England where the opportunity for jobs was better than back home.'

departed from Britain to settle in parts of Africa, the United States, Canada, Australia and New Zealand. In the 50 years between 1850 and 1900, five and a half million people emigrated from England, Scotland and Wales.

The importance of the Commonwealth

Britain's long-established links with Commonwealth countries have had a major effect on migration to (and from) Britain. A common language and certain similarities in culture have drawn many people to Britain from Commonwealth countries in search of work. Often, as we have already seen, this has been with the direct encouragement of the British Government and major British companies and organisations. During the 1960s, migrants from the Commonwealth faced tighter controls on entry by the British Government, and further restrictions were put in place in 1981.

The European Union

One of the fundamental principles of the European Union (see page 22) is the general right of people from member states to travel to, live and work in any EU country.

At the end of 2008, 1.1 million EU nationals were working in the UK. At the same time, about 290,000 UK citizens were working in other EU states.

Two-way traffic

Britain has also been a country that many people have left. From the seventeenth to the twentieth centuries, large numbers of people

> **EMIGRATION TO NEW ZEALAND PARADISE**
>
> Every industrious young man or woman in good health will, on approval, receive a **FREE GIFT** of *Forty Acres of Good Land* in the province of *Auckland, New Zealand*, together with *Forty Acres more for each person above 18 years* **AND** *Twenty Acres for each child above five.*

? Questions

1. It is quite possible that you and other students in your class will spend part of your working life in another country. If you had the opportunity to move, which country or countries would you choose? What would be the reasons for your choice?

2. What difficulties do you imagine that you might face? How could you try to overcome them?

3. Who would have responsibility for your safety and well-being in the country where you were working?

Key words

Migrant
Someone moving from one place or country to another. Emigrant describes a person who leaves their region or country. Immigrant refers to a person arriving from another region or country.

Coming to Britain

Migration

■ Coming to work

Agnieszka came to Wales from Poland with her fiancé in 2005 and settled in Wrexham. Like most economic migrants, they left their country in search of a better life, choosing to come to Britain where they hoped to make more money than they would at home.

In an interview for BBC Wales, Agnieszka explained that life was not always as easy as they hoped. 'In my country there is a myth that in the UK life is better and easier, so we migrate in search of a better future. All kinds of people go abroad. Some are young and well-educated; others are just ordinary people with families. They have one big aim – to earn more money than they could earn in Poland, and live like normal people do, without struggling and having to choose between food or bills.'

？ Questions

1. What do you think Agnieszka means when she says, 'In my country there is a myth that in the UK life is easier'?

2. Why do you think people might have such views of Britain?

■ A wider view

For thousands of years, people have moved from one part of the world to another, in search of a better life. In the nineteenth and early twentieth centuries, for example, there was mass emigration from Europe to the United States.

Between 1868 and 1914, more than a million people moved from Sweden to America.

Migration remains of huge importance today. At the moment there are about 200 million people in the world who have migrated from one country to another. Many will make an important contribution to the economy of the country where they settle, often doing work that local people cannot or will not take on. They may also contribute to the country they have left by sending money back home. Some economically less-developed countries receive more money in this way than they earn through production or foreign aid. Migrant workers can play an important part in reducing poverty.

■ A controversial issue

As we have already seen on page 100, migration to Britain has been taking place for centuries. However, it has not been without controversy. In the 1960s, for example, although workers from overseas had been encouraged to come to Britain to meet labour shortages, some people opposed their arrival, fearing a threat to jobs and a change in the character of the population. Migrants often faced open discrimination.

Concern and debate over the Government's migration policy has also developed in recent years, particularly since 2004. Probably the main reason for this is that the level of inward migration to Britain has been higher during this period than at any time over the past 100 years. Until 1982, more people were leaving Britain each year than were arriving.

In 2008, a report compiled by two British MPs stated that, 'in the last ten years, nearly 2.5 million immigrants have arrived, and almost three-quarters of a million British people have left, thus adding 1.6 million directly to our population'. Their report suggests that the Government should try to balance the number of people coming in with the numbers that leave. This idea has, however, been criticised as impractical.

The European Union

The origins of the European Union go back to the period shortly after the Second World War. One of its fundamental principles is the free movement of people from one member state to another, allowing EU citizens to seek work in any member state, with the same employment rights as local workers. (However, citizens from Eastern European member states must register for work and, until 2011, those from Bulgaria and Romania must not work without official permission.) In 2006, just under a third of migrants to Britain were from EU member states.

Government policy

In 2008, the Government overhauled and revised the very complicated system that had developed over the years, determining whether a person would be allowed to work in Britain.

Today, workers from outside the EU require a certain number of 'points' to be allowed to come to Britain either to seek or to take up work. Highly skilled workers are awarded the highest number of points; those with few employment skills, or with skills that are not in demand, receive fewest points. Points are also awarded according to an applicant's chances of success in Britain. These are affected, for example, by a person's age and whether they have a criminal record.

Although the points system, described above, has been broadly welcomed in Britain, some have criticised it for failing to place a limit on the numbers allowed into the country.

Ella 'Economic migrants make a valuable contribution to our economy and our way of life. Often they take on the jobs that the British either don't want or can't do.'

Anil 'There are too many people in Britain, and limiting migration is one way of dealing with this. Over-population puts pressure on services and means that towns and cities continue to expand, further damaging the environment.'

Dan 'I don't think the government should interfere. Let people come to this country when we need the labour; and when we don't, they'll leave and go elsewhere.'

Frances 'Surveys show most people think that too many people come to Britain. Are these people wrong? Should they be ignored in a democracy?'

? Questions

3. What kind of immigration policy do you feel the Government should follow? Here are three alternatives that have been discussed. Select one and outline its strengths and weaknesses:

   a) Place fewer restrictions on people who want to come and live and work in Britain.

   b) Make sure that only those with the right skills or able to make the right kind of contribution will be able to come to work in Britain.

   c) Make sure that the numbers of people who are given permission to come into the country broadly equals the number who leave.

Coming to Britain
Seeking asylum

▪ Moving images

Statistics published by the United Nations in 2008 indicated that there were about 31 million people worldwide who were either **refugees** or **asylum seekers** or had been **internally displaced** in their own country. The word 'refugee' is often used in a general way to describe someone who is fleeing their home or country because everyday life is almost impossible. It also has a very specific legal meaning, referring to someone who has been given permission to remain in a country where they have sought refuge because of a well-founded fear of persecution. For more information on this, see page 106.

Reasons to move There tend to be three main reasons why people become refugees and seek safety elsewhere.

In 2008, several thousand people fled their homes in the region of Ossetia to escape the fighting between Georgia and Russia. War places people in great danger. It is not surprising that individuals and families seek safety elsewhere.

When war takes place in a country where many people are already poor, the problems become worse. Fighting stops the distribution of food. People leave to escape famine and serious outbreaks of disease. A recent example of this is the war that has been taking place in Somalia in north-east Africa, where figures show that about half a million refugees left the country in 2007.

Many people who become refugees have been targeted because they belong to a particular ethnic or religious group. This difficulty has faced many Jewish people in the past and also now affects others – such as the Kurdish people in Iraq and Turkey.

❓ Questions

1. What feelings do you have as you look at these pictures?

2. What do these pictures reveal about the kind of problems that refugees are likely to face? What other difficulties might refugees encounter?

Leaving home

Jingmei In 1989, many protests were held in China against the Chinese Government, which people felt was too harsh and brutal. Students, workers and many others took part in demonstrations telling the Government that it should give people more freedom.

Jingmei was a police officer at the time and was arrested for helping students who were taking part in the demonstrations. He came from a family that had frequently opposed the government and he feared that he would be sentenced to hard labour, as his father had been several years earlier. Jingmei left Beijing and fled, without any possessions, to Hong Kong, and then to London, where he sought **political asylum**.

Benjamin In 1973, the government of Chile was overthrown by a military dictatorship. Benjamin was a member of the former government and, like anyone who opposed the coup, was in constant danger of death.

He went into hiding and joined a resistance movement, plotting to restore a democratically elected government. He was eventually arrested and tortured for information, with a doctor on hand to resuscitate him.

Benjamin was in prison for three years, but was released as part of an international deal in which the Chilean military government released political prisoners in return for money from the international community. He received help from students at Oxford University, and eventually sought asylum in Britain.

Majid Originally from Afghanistan, Majid was born in 1981, and grew up during the war between Afghanistan

and Russia. Eventually, the dangers from the bombing and fighting became too great, and Majid fled with his parents to Pakistan.

Within two years, despite working long hours, all their money had run out. Majid's father went back to Afghanistan, but lost contact with his family and no one has seen or heard of him since. Majid and his mother were terrified to return and, encouraged by his mother, Majid decided to try to reach Europe, where he hoped to find a better life.

With ten others, he crossed illegally into Iran and then Turkey. He paid someone to smuggle him into Germany, but was abandoned when they reached Hungary, where Majid decided to claim political asylum.

? Questions

3. Why did each of the people in these stories leave their country? Are any of these reasons more important than others? In your opinion, are they all refugees?

4. Does anyone have responsibility to help the people in each of these cases? If so, who has responsibility and how far does it extend?

Key words

Asylum seeker
A person seeking political asylum.

Internally displaced
People who are forced to leave their homes, but remain within their own country.

Political asylum
Protection given to someone who is fleeing persecution in their own country.

Refugee
A person who has been granted political asylum.

Coming to Britain
Seeking asylum

■ Permission to stay

When someone seeks asylum in Britain, they are asking to be officially recognised as a refugee. If their application is successful they can generally stay in Britain for a period of up to five years. Unsuccessful applicants are generally instructed to leave the country or face deportation.

If refugees wish to remain in Britain after this five-year period is over, they must show that they have knowledge of life and language in Britain, that they have been law-abiding citizens and that the conditions in their home country have not improved significantly.

■ Refugee status

Deciding whether a person can stay in a country permanently is a complicated process. In simple terms, immigration officials have to decide whether the person making the application fits the definition of 'refugee' as set out in the *Convention Relating to the Status of Refugees*. This is an international agreement passed by the United Nations in 1951, which most countries in the world have signed. Under the Convention, a refugee may be defined as follows:

refugee \Ref `u*gee"\ n.

A refugee is a person who has left their country and cannot return because of a well-founded fear of persecution for reasons of race, religion, nationality, membership of a particular social group or political opinion.

CONVENTION
AND
PROTOCOL
RELATING TO THE
STATUS OF
REFUGEES

UNHCR

Application   A person may claim asylum in Britain in two ways – as they enter the country (at an air or sea port or railway station) or after they have arrived, at a Border and Immigration Agency office.

People who are waiting for a decision on their asylum claim are known as asylum seekers. Some have their case dealt with quickly but others may have to wait several months for a decision.

Not eligible   A person who claims asylum because they hope to earn a better living in the new country does not fit the definition of a refugee, and is unlikely to be successful.

Rights and freedoms   Asylum seekers generally have the same legal rights as UK citizens, but their access to social benefits is restricted. Most asylum seekers are not allowed to work and therefore have to rely on the state. Benefits are set at 70 per cent of Income Support.

Asylum seekers also have little choice where they live. Accommodation is allocated to them and is often in a property that is hard to let and not popular with other people.

Many of these restrictions are removed if the person is allowed to remain in Britain.

Reaching a decision

Muna's brother, along with 25 other army officers, was executed for plotting to overthrow the government in Sudan. Muna helped to form an organisation to support the families of those who had been killed by government forces and was herself repeatedly arrested and threatened with rape. She came to England with her young daughter to stay with friends, and then asked for asylum, feeling that she could not return and face the danger any more.

Milan is a Roma from Slovakia. He asked for asylum for himself and his family in Britain after being attacked many times in Slovakia by skinheads. He said that there was a lot of prejudice against Roma people in Slovakia. 'We have slogans like "Gypsies to the gas chamber" daubed on our wall. We want to be free, but get no protection from the police.'
The British Government recognises that Roma people do have difficulties in Slovakia, but believes that the police there do provide some protection.

Seeking refuge

Oliver, aged 32, was a teacher in Zimbabwe. He came to the UK in 2003 after receiving threats to his life following his outspoken opposition to the president, Robert Mugabe. Since coming to the UK he has been living without his wife, son and daughter – and without work, for as an asylum seeker he is unable to work.

When his asylum application was refused, Oliver immediately lost all benefits and was forced to live on handouts from friends. After appealing against this decision he was awarded a weekly voucher of £35, which could not be used as cash and only exchanged in certain shops.

A short while later he was suddenly taken, without warning, to a detention centre, ready for deportation. With the help of a solicitor he appealed against this decision. After being held for three months, Oliver was allowed to remain in Britain temporarily, because of the continued risk to his life in Zimbabwe. He has again applied for asylum and is awaiting a decision.

? Questions

1. Look at the details of the two cases above and decide whether each one passes the refugee test. If they do, the person should be granted refugee status and be allowed to stay in Britain for up to five years.

2. Some people try to come to Britain to escape from very poor living conditions in their own country. In many ways their lives are also in danger, but they don't fit the official definition of a refugee. Should they be allowed to stay in Britain? Give reasons for your answer.

? Questions

3. Oliver is fit and able-bodied and would like to contribute to society, but is not allowed to work. Can you suggest why this rule was made? What is your view?

4. Oliver is very critical of his treatment in Britain, saying that it is inhuman to treat people fleeing from persecution in such a way. How do you react to this? Are asylum seekers and refugees treated fairly?

Coming to Britain
Seeking asylum

■ A long history

Britain has a long history of providing safety for those escaping persecution and violence.

France Britain's reputation as a country offering safety from persecution began with the arrival of the Huguenots from France. These were Protestants who had been persecuted for their beliefs by the Roman Catholic Church for more than a hundred years, between 1560 and 1685. Thousands died, but about 150,000 people escaped to safety, mainly in England, Ireland, Germany and America.

Russia Jewish communities have lived in Russia for 2,000 years. During this time they have faced periods of great persecution (there and elsewhere). In 1835, the Tsar (the ruler of Russia), ordered all Jewish people

to move to the western edge of the Russian empire. Much of this is now in Poland, Ukraine and Belarus. Restrictions were placed on where Jewish people could live, where they could travel and how they could earn a living.

In 1881, Tsar Alexander II was assassinated, and one of those responsible was a Jewish woman. The result was an outbreak of violent attacks (called pogroms) on Jewish people throughout Russia.

Groups were organised by the Russian Government to break up and destroy the homes and businesses of Jewish people, and to murder members of Jewish communities. Thousands of Jews were slaughtered, often with the support and encouragement of the authorities, and the leaders of these groups were publicly honoured.

For their own safety, many Jewish families left. Between 1880 and 1910 about two million people fled from Russia, seeking safety in the United States, Germany, France, Britain and Australia.

■ Not always welcome

In the news In 1888, the *Manchester City News* wrote of the refugees coming from Russia to Britain:

In the 1930s, Jews again faced persecution. A large number of Jewish families tried to leave Germany, but were not always welcome in many countries, including Britain, as shown in this extract from the *Daily Mail* in 1935:

> *Their unclean habits, their wretched clothing and miserable food enable them to perpetuate existence upon a pittance. They have flooded the market with cheap labour.*
> *Manchester City News 1888*

> Once it was known that Britain offered sanctuary to all who dared to come, the floodgates would be opened, and we would be inundated by thousands seeking a home.
> **Daily Mail 1935**

This article (right) is a more recent report of asylum seekers from Kosovo coming to Britain in the late 1990s.

KOSOVANS, ALBANIANS AND YUGOSLAVIANS COME TO TOWN
FLOODGATES OPEN AGAIN TO REFUGEES

SOCIAL SERVICES were forced to use an emergency centre as 70 asylum seekers flooded into Dover. Poulton's Family Centre, in Folkestone Road, was opened on Friday evening after 35 Kosovan, Albanian and Yugoslavian refugees were discovered by immigration officers. The accommodation problem became even worse the following day with another 35 arrivals. They are the latest in a growing tide of asylum seekers flooding the area.

❓ Questions

1. Certain kinds of emotive words are used in each of these extracts. What are they, and what pictures or images do they create? What do these reports omit to say about refugees?

The picture today

During the late 1990s, the number of people seeking asylum annually in Britain rose sharply, reaching a peak of 84,000 in 2002. Since then, however, the number of applicants has fallen steadily to 23,000 in 2007.

Most current asylum applications to Britain are made by Afghan, Iranian, Chinese, Iraqi and Eritrean citizens. In recent years, about 40 per cent of applicants have been granted asylum or other forms of protection.

On a worldwide scale, in 2007, the United States and Sweden received the largest of asylum applications, followed by France, Canada and the United Kingdom. A number of other countries, however, particularly Pakistan and Syria, have large numbers of refugees who have moved within their borders over a more extended period of time. In Pakistan, this figure is estimated to be about two million people.

ASYLUM CAMP

Should Britain keep taking immigrants? No, Britain does not have the space and economic capacity to absorb the same number it allowed in during the past 40 years. Walk in London and watch refugees thrusting babies at passers-by demanding money. I will not welcome other people here. We need a guarantee that if admitted, refugees will be returned when appropriate and no political asylum will be accepted.

J M Potton, Middlesex

❓ Questions

2. Make a list of the key points contained in J M Potton's letter.

3. In the light of what you have ready in this and previous sections, assess the accuracy of each key point.

4. Write a letter in reply to J M Potton.

There are many examples of refugees who have come to Britain and led successful lives, making a great contribution to their local community or to wider society (see panel right).

Success . . .

Yasmin Alibhai-Brown
Journalist and author, Ugandan refugee

Omid Djalili
Comedian and actor, Iranian refugee

Ben Elton
Author and comedian, grandson of Czechoslovakian refugee

Jacob Epstein
Sculptor, son of Polish-Jewish refugees

Lucien Freud
Artist, German-Jewish refugee

Lew Grade
Founder of television company, responsible for many successful series, Russian refugee

Paul Hamlyn
Founder of major publishing company, German-Jewish refugee

Alec Issigonis
Designer of the Morris Minor, the Mini, and the Austin 1100, refugee from fighting between Turkey and Greece

Michael Marks
Co-founder of Marks & Spencer, Russian refugee

Lakshmibhai Pathak
Founder of successful food manufacturing company, Kenyan refugee

Identity

This unit asks whether greater efforts should be made in Britain to develop a sense of community and identity, and, if so, what forms these might take.

Parallel lives

After the riots in 2001: Oldham and Burnley (below left).

■ Trouble

How well do people get along together
* *different issues people consider:*
* *community cohesion means how people live together*

Between April and June 2001 disturbances in England for the north of England between groups of young men, in areas with high unemployment and poor housing.

One of these towns was Oldham, in Lancashire, where at the time around 11 per cent of the population was British Asian. During the 1960s and 1970s, many people from Pakistan and Bangladesh came to Oldham to work in the textile industries – by the turn of the century, however, many of these factories had closed down, leaving large numbers without work.

Most people of Asian background in Oldham lived close together in the poorest areas, and were more likely to be unemployed than their white counterparts. Over the years, districts of the town became divided along ethnic lines, with a number of schools becoming largely white or largely Asian. A report into the causes of the riots criticised Oldham Council for not doing enough to prevent this 'segregation', or separate development.

? Questions

1. What are the effects of this kind of segregation? List as many as you can.

2. What might be the causes?

■ Making changes

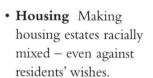

The official report into the riots suggested that many things needed to be done to prevent further trouble. Suggestions included:

- **Housing** Making housing estates racially mixed – even against residents' wishes.
- **Jobs** Improving job opportunities in the area to create wealth and give people a better chance in life.
- **Schools** Ensuring schools are racially mixed, and discouraging them from having pupils from just one religious faith.
- **Councils** Increasing the number of people of ethnic minority origin who work for the local council. In Oldham at the time of the riots, only 2.5 per cent of the workforce was from an ethnic minority.
- **Democracy** Listening more to what local people say, and encouraging people from all communities to become more involved in local politics.

A sense of belonging During the discussions that took place after the riots, David Blunkett, then Home Secretary, added his own suggestions for the future. He said that anyone living in Britain should be able to speak English. Without this, Mr Blunkett said, it was difficult for people from different backgrounds to mix and to play a full part in the community life.

? Questions

3. Are there any of the above report's proposals that you would not support? Explain why.

4. Some people believe that communities should be left to develop naturally, without being engineered or interfered with. To what extent do you agree?

5. How far do you agree with David Blunkett that everyone living in Britain should be able to speak English?

6. What are the implications of this view?

■ The 2005 London bombings

On 7 July 2005, starting at 8:50a.m., four bombs exploded in London, within an hour of each other. Three were detonated on Underground trains and the fourth on a double-decker bus; 52 people were killed and more than 750 injured. The motivation for these attacks is not entirely clear, but it is generally taken to be anger against perceived injustices committed against Muslims throughout the world and certain un-Islamic practices of Western countries.

When the identities of the four men who carried out the attacks were discovered, three of them were found to have been born in Leeds while the fourth was originally from Jamaica. In the debate and discussion that followed two questions were commonly asked.

How could a group of British-born people deliberately plot to kill so many of their fellow countrymen and women? And what needs to be done to prevent the same outrages from occurring again?

■ Living together

The events of 7 July (and a similar, but unsuccessful, plot two weeks later) led, once again, to a number of further official reports and recommendations – all of which stressed the importance of all people feeling attached and part of mainstream society. This idea is commonly referred to today as **community cohesion**.

Although a lot of the discussion about community cohesion has taken place as a result of religious or ethnic tensions, they are not the only reasons for separation and division in society. Factors like class, income, age and a perceived lack of opportunities can also cause groups to feel isolated from the rest of society.

? Questions

7. Not everyone agrees that mixed communities are a good idea. How do you react to the following statement? 'I prefer to live in a community with people who share my culture, my religion and my general outlook on life. I don't want to be surrounded by people who do not.'

8. Write a short description of the kind of community you would like your children's generation to live in. What qualities would it have? What would be its strengths?

Key words

Community cohesion
People sharing a sense of belonging and community identity.

Identity
Being British

■ Going back

Migration has traditionally played an important part in British life (see page 100). The impact of people travelling to (and from) this country has had a widespread influence.

The English language, for example, is largely derived from those who invaded Britain between one and two thousand years ago, from Denmark, France, Germany, Italy and Norway.

Our diet also has strong overseas influences. Recipes originating in Italy, France, the United States, India and China are well-established in Britain today, but even some of the food and drink thought to be most traditionally British have origins elsewhere. The fashion for drinking tea reached England via Portugal, after King Charles II married the King of Portugal's daughter in 1662. The idea of frying fish in batter also came from Portugal and Spain, and chips are almost certainly an invention of the French or Belgians.

Even our monarchy is not entirely British, with the present Royal Family being partly descended from German nobility.

The British are, historically, a mixed people, with roots and traditions derived from many parts of the world.

■ The pace of change

Until the 18th century, most people in Britain lived in small village communities. Their family commonly lived close by, and they shared the same language, ethnic group, religion and culture as did all, or most, of their neighbours.

Although this situation still exists in a few parts of Britain, life in the 21st century for most people is very different, particularly for those living in large cities. Globalisation and population movements have meant that an increasing number of people living in Britain, whether for a long or short time, were born overseas. Figures released in 2009 indicated that these made up one in nine of the population.

The development of a society so much more diverse than was the case in the past has caused the Government to look for ways in which all people in Britain might develop a greater sense of shared national identity.

■ Personal and national identity

Most people asked about their personal identity will describe themselves in a number of different ways. This might be in relation to their family and friends, where they live, or their interests, age, occupation, gender or ethnic group. Our personal identities tend to be multiple, often changing over time, according to our circumstances.

Our national identity is rather different – and, for people in Britain, the choice may be more complicated than elsewhere. Are we English, Irish, Scottish or Welsh – or are we British, or a combination of more than one? What is our national identity if we, or our parents, were born overseas?

❓ Questions

1. How would you describe your own personal identity?

2. How would you describe your national identity? On what basis do you say this?

■ A stronger national identity

After the London bombings in 2005 (see page 111), the Government stressed the need for a greater sense of national identity in order to combat intolerance and religious extremism. In 2007, the Government announced that it believed it was important to find a British statement of **values** that could bind the whole population together.

This idea is commonly reported in the press through questions such as 'What makes us British?', or 'What is Britishness?', or 'What are British values?'.

❓ Questions

3. Do you agree with the Government's wish to create a stronger sense of national identity? What are the strengths of this idea? What are the weaknesses?

4. What values do you feel are important to many people in Britain?

A problem with values? In a speech in 2005, Gordon Brown listed some of the values that he thought characterised the British way of life. These included: *tolerance*, *liberty* and *fairness*.

Many people – although not everyone – would probably agree that these are good values, but are they something that can be used to bind people together and strengthen their feelings of Britishness? Liberty, fairness and tolerance are not unique to British society; they are values that many people throughout the world support. Also, perhaps more significantly, they are not entirely straightforward. What exactly do we mean by 'fairness', for example? There is every chance that my view of fairness in some circumstances will be different from yours.

Binding the nation A number of other suggestions have been made of ways to increase people's sense of national identity:

- Celebrate Britain with a new national holiday, as they do in Australia, France and the United States.
- Introduce citizenship ceremonies for young people when they leave school.
- Alter some of the content of history and geography so that children learn more about *British* history and the *British* way of life.

❓ Questions

5. How do you react to each of these proposals? Are there any that you support? Explain why.

6. What do you value from this society that you would like to pass on to future generations?

Key words

Values
Beliefs or principles that we hold to be important.

Unequal Britain

This unit looks at some of the inequalities that exist in [B] efforts that are being made to bring them to an end.

Racism

■ Death in custody

At the beginning of 2000, Zahid Mubarek, aged 19, from London, was sentenced to 90 days in a **Young Offenders Institution**. He had been found guilty of a series of small-scale theft offences, committed to fund his drug habit.

Towards the end of his sentence he was placed in a cell with Robert Stewart, aged 20, who was known by the prison authorities to be dangerous and disturbed. Robert Stewart was being held, charged with sending racist hate mail. The prison authorities knew about his racist feelings. He had a Ku Klux Klan sign on display in his cell and his letters home had referred to the number of 'niggers on the wing'.

On the day before he was due to be released, Zahid Mubarek was battered to death in his cell by Robert Stewart, using the leg of a table.

After his son's death, Mr Mubarek said, 'There was always a lot of racist abuse going on, a lot of trouble. The wardens just used to keep their heads down and let prisoners get on with what they were doing.'

Racial equality is an important issue, for both staff and prisoners

? Questions

1. Who do you think was responsible for the death of Zahid Mubarek? Who was at fault? Give reasons for your answer.

2. How could Zahid Mubarek's death have been avoided?

■ Racism in prison

Robert Stewart was convicted of murder and jailed for life.

After a long campaign by Zahid's family, a public enquiry was held to examine the circumstances of the young man's death. The enquiry found that prison officers had completely failed to recognise the dangers of requiring a young man from an Asian background to share a cell with a known racist – despite Zahid himself asking for a transfer to another cell.

The enquiry's chairperson also criticised the prison service as a whole for failing to place enough importance on maintaining good race relations in prison – amongst and between both inmates and staff. There was a failure to take racist language seriously and to deal adequately with victimisation suffered by officers from ethnic minorities. The prison service, he stated, was institutionally racist.

■ Institutionalised racism

Institutionalised racism takes place when an organisation collectively fails to provide a proper service to people because of their colour, culture or ethnic origin. It can be shown through prejudice, ignorance and racist stereotyping.

The prison service is far from being the only organisation criticised for this.

Equality and Human Rights Commission

Second class citizen When Farouk Stemmet climbed on board the 16.22 train from Liverpool to Sunderland he headed for the first-class accommodation. As he approached the carriage he was stopped by the train conductor and told that he should sit elsewhere. Mr Stemmet explained that he had a first-class ticket.

When the conductor came round to check his ticket, Mr Stemmet protested about his treatment. The conductor replied that he was only doing his job, and suggested that Mr Stemmet had a chip on his shoulder because he was black.

Mr Stemmet decided to make a complaint. He wrote to the rail company and reported the matter to the Commission for Racial Equality (CRE), now part of the Equality and Human Rights Commission (see page 62). The CRE helped Mr Stemmet bring a case against the train company. Mr Stemmet successfully showed that he had been unfairly discriminated against.

? Questions

3. How might you account for the behaviour of the conductor?

4. Was his behaviour unusual, in your opinion?

5. How do you think Mr Stemmet should be compensated for his unfair treatment?

6. What action could be taken to try to make sure that the conductor or other employees do not behave in the same way again?

7. What actions should schools take to promote good race relations?

■ The law

Under the *Race Relations Act 1976* it is unlawful to discriminate against anyone on grounds of race, colour, nationality, or ethnic or national origin. It is also against the law for public bodies – such as the police, schools, hospitals, prisons – to discriminate while carrying out any of their functions.

The *Race Relations (Amendment) Act 2001* outlaws all race discrimination by public bodies such as the police, prisons, schools, hospitals, social services, etc.

It also places a duty on public bodies to promote good race relations. In practice, this means making sure that working practices are fair and that organisations meet the needs of all ethnic groups.

Key words

Young Offenders Institution
Secure accommodation where young offenders between the ages 15 and 21 are held in custody.

Unequal Britain
Sexual equality

■ Aiming high

Rosie is 15 and has everything to live for. She is clever, with lots of friends and a cheerful personality that

everyone seems to like. Her hobbies are gymnastics and football and she is very good at both. One day she hopes to represent her country at one of these sports. Her mum is a nurse and her dad works for a pipeline company. Rosie would like to be a lawyer – and perhaps eventually a judge. She'd also like to do something that helps people – which is why she thinks that she could, one day, become an MP.

? Questions

1. How likely is Rosie to realise all her ambitions?

2. Which do you think she will find most difficult to achieve? The information on the right might help you with this.

■ Life chances

Education Qualifications play a large part in determining the kind of job a person will do. People with low qualifications are more likely to be unemployed or in low-paid work.

Men, as a whole, have better job qualifications than women. However, the picture changes among young women and men under 25 years of age.

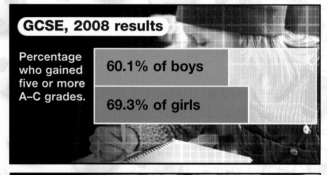

GCSE, 2008 results

Percentage who gained five or more A–C grades.

60.1% of boys

69.3% of girls

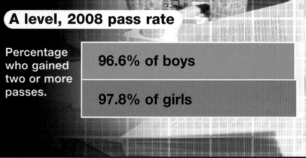

A level, 2008 pass rate

Percentage who gained two or more passes.

96.6% of boys

97.8% of girls

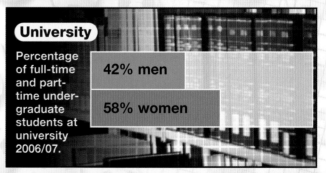

University

Percentage of full-time and part-time under-graduate students at university 2006/07.

42% men

58% women

University
It was not until 1895 that women were eligible to obtain a degree at most British universities. Women wanting to graduate from Oxford had to wait until 1920, and those at Cambridge until 1948.

Work

Employment by occupation 2003

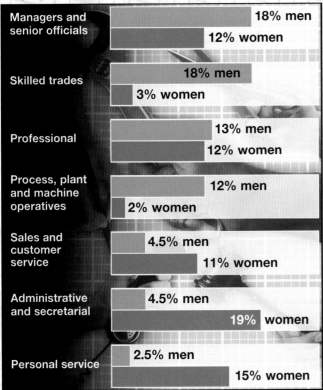

Occupation		
Managers and senior officials	18% men	
	12% women	
Skilled trades	18% men	
	3% women	
Professional	13% men	
	12% women	
Process, plant and machine operatives	12% men	
	2% women	
Sales and customer service	4.5% men	
	11% women	
Administrative and secretarial	4.5% men	
	19% women	
Personal service	2.5% men	
	15% women	

Source: http://www.statistics.gov.uk/cci/nugget.asp?id=1654

The weekly earnings of women are, on average, 21 per cent less than men (*Office for National Statistics, 2007*).

Men's work?

The idea of married women not working and staying at home to look after the children developed in the nineteenth century. Until then, women were responsible for much of the farm work – and shared many of the trades that we normally associate with men. Records show women working as butchers, printers, carpenters, brewers and blacksmiths.

Politics

Source: Year 2005

MPs	80% men	
	20% women	
Welsh Assembly members	53% men	
	47% women	

Women in Parliament

The first woman elected to Parliament in 1918 did not take her seat, as her party, Sinn Fein, did not recognise the British government. The first woman actually to take her seat in Parliament was Nancy Astor, MP for Plymouth Sutton in Devon, after an election victory in 1919.

? Questions

3. Who or what is standing in the way of Rosie's success?

4. What would you say to someone who believes that full equality between men and women cannot be achieved because men and women are different?

5. Now that girls appear to be doing better at school than boys, should special efforts be made to help boys? If so, what should they be?

■ The law

Under the *Sex Discrimination Act 1975* it is against the law to treat a person less favourably because of their sex. This applies in particular to work, training, education and the provision of goods and services.

The *Equal Pay Act 1970* gives women and men rights to equal pay and benefits for the same or similar work.

Women should not lose their job because of pregnancy, childbirth or the care of their children. The law also states that parents of children born after 14 December 1999 have the right to take up to 13 weeks' unpaid leave during the first five years of their child's life.

Unequal Britain
Sexual equality

The long struggle

Before the *Married Women's Property Act 1882*, married women were not allowed to own property. Once a woman got married, everything she possessed belonged to her husband.

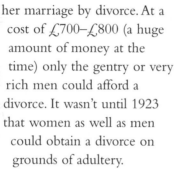

In the nineteenth century it was almost impossible for a woman to end her marriage by divorce. At a cost of £700–£800 (a huge amount of money at the time) only the gentry or very rich men could afford a divorce. It wasn't until 1923 that women as well as men could obtain a divorce on grounds of adultery.

With very little support for single parent families, many women who were trapped in an unhappy marriage had no choice but to endure it. They remained, in effect, their husband's property.

Campaigners

Some women were not content with this situation. They realised that progress would be slow if all the laws continued to be made by men. By 1885, almost all men (and not just the rich landowners) had been given the right to vote – but women had not. No woman had the right to choose her MP, and certainly no woman could stand for election as a Member of Parliament.

For this reason, in the early 1900s, women began to campaign seriously for the vote. They were called 'suffragettes', from the word 'suffrage' meaning 'the right to vote'.

By 1906, their leader, Emmeline Pankhurst, decided that more pressure was required, which marked the beginning of the suffragettes' militant campaign. They broke windows, damaged government buildings, burnt railway stations and even attacked MPs.

War intervenes

When the First World War broke out in 1914, the suffragettes halted their campaign and persuaded women instead to work for the war effort, by going into industry or joining the armed services.

With so many men fighting overseas, women did much of the work previously carried out by men, in factories and elsewhere. This changed many people's views about the capability of women.

In 1918, immediately after the war, women over 30 were given the vote, and in 1928 this was extended to women over 21. At last women were on equal terms with men.

In 2002, however, the law was changed. *The Sex Discrimination (Election Candidates) Act 2002* allows political parties to discriminate in favour of women when choosing candidates – but does not require them to do so, if they don't wish to.

In favour and against

Here are two statements about positive discrimination – both made by women MPs, and both from the Conservative Party.

'We whinge and whine and demand special treatment. If that isn't an insult to women, I don't know what is.'
Ann Widdecombe MP

'There are many women not being selected who would make first-class MPs and Parliament is missing out on a pool of talent that would strengthen this house.'
Theresa May MP

Women in Parliament

Women were first allowed to stand for Parliament in 1918. There were 17 female candidates, but only one was successful. Until 1987, the maximum number of women elected at any general election was 30.

After the 1997 election, women comprised 121 out of the 659 MPs. At the 2005 election, 128 women were elected MPs, the highest number ever. Women now make up 20 per cent of MPs.

Britain now ranks thirty-third in the world in terms of women MPs.

? Questions

1. Do you think it matters that women make up more than half the population of the UK, but make up only 20 per cent of the MPs? Explain why.

2. Do you think Parliament would be very different if it had equal numbers of men and women? If so, how?

Positive discrimination

Before the 1997 election, the Labour party decided to increase the number of women in Parliament by allowing only female candidates to stand for election in a number of their 'safe' constituencies. Some male candidates thought that this was unfair and challenged the idea in court. The court agreed with the men, ruling that women-only shortlists broke existing sex discrimination law.

? Questions

3. Are women-only shortlists for election to Parliament a much-needed measure or an insult to women? List the arguments on either side and outline what advice you would give to a party leader who was contemplating positive discrimination of this kind.

Unequal Britain
Challenging disability

◼ David and Goliath

David is 17 years old and lives in Sheffield. He has muscular dystrophy, an inherited condition from which sufferers face a progressive weakening of their muscles, requiring them to spend much of their life in a wheelchair.

David decides to open a bank account. The website of the bank he chooses indicates that his local branch has wheelchair access. However, when he goes to the bank he is unable to gain entry. Bank staff suggest he uses the staff entrance – but again this is inaccessible. His interview about opening an account is held on the street outside.

When David complains about the treatment he has received, the bank points out that he was free to use their telephone or online banking service, or to visit one of their three other branches in Sheffield – all of which have disabled access. These measures, the bank claims, indicate that it is doing everything it reasonably can to enable David to use its banking services. It also points out that the cost of installing disabled access can be extremely high.

❓ Questions

1. Read the information in 'the law', on the opposite page, and decide whether you feel the bank has unfairly discriminated against David. Explain your answer.

See you in court? David's mother decides to take action against the bank, on her son's behalf, believing that he should be able to access the bank like all his friends.

She applies for the case to be heard in the small claims court, which is designed to be a simple and informal way of settling disputes without having to pay for a solicitor. The court deals with claims up to £5,000. However, David's claim involves much more money than this, particularly if the bank loses and is required to carry out expensive alterations. The case is transferred to the county court (on what is known as the multi-track system). This works in a much more formal way, with barristers or solicitors presenting the case on either side, and possibly with expert witnesses being called to give their opinion. It can be a very expensive way of settling a case, and the person or organisation that loses may have to pay the costs of the winning side in addition to their own.

❓ Questions

2. What decision does David's mother now face?

3. The bank offers David's family £1,500 to drop the case. What would you advise David's mother to do? Should she accept their offer or proceed with the case? What risks does she face? Can you suggest any ways in which these may be overcome?

Pressing on David's mother feared that, by continuing with the case, she was leaving herself open to expensive legal costs, which she and her family could not afford.

She was on the verge of giving up the case when she received help from Sheffield **Law Centre** and the backing of the Equality and Human Rights Commission (see page 62). These two organisations enabled David's case to be prepared and presented in court by a solicitor and a barrister, and ensured that, if they lost the case, David's parents would not have to sell their house in order to pay the legal fees.

A decision   The court decided in David's favour. The judge said that the bank had made significant errors and ordered it to pay £6,500 in compensation. It also ordered the bank to pay for the costs of the case and, within nine months, to install a platform lift at the bank. The cost of these together is estimated to be in the region of £250,000.

? Questions

4. Do you agree with the court's decision in this case? Was the bank treated fairly? Explain your answer.

5. A judge in the 19th century once said 'In England justice is open to all – like the Ritz Hotel.' What do you think he meant by this? Does David's case support this idea?

What is a disability?

When we hear the word 'disabled' we often think first of wheelchair users. But disability also includes blindness, deafness and having learning difficulties. Many other people are affected by mental illness or have brain damage from accidents or strokes that make it difficult for them to function properly. In fact, there are 8.5 million people with some form of disability in Britain. That is about one person in seven.

■ The law

Under the *Disability Discrimination Act 1995*, it is against the law to treat a person less favourably because of their disability. The law applies in particular to employment, education and buying or renting property, and also access to services and facilities.

Employers, schools and organisations providing a service all have a duty to make reasonable adjustments to enable a disabled person to be employed or to use the facilities. There may be some circumstances, however, when discrimination is justified. If reasonable adjustments are not possible, then discrimination on grounds of disability will not be against the law. For example, it would be unreasonable to expect a nightclub to change all its lighting to enable people with epilepsy to attend – by doing so, it would no longer provide the atmosphere that its customers expect.

Key words

Law centre
Law centres provide free legal advice, on matters such as discrimination, housing or employment; they try especially to help people who would not otherwise be able to afford legal help.

Older people

This unit examines the lives of older people in the UK and, in particular, how they are seen and treated by others.

The future is grey

■ Getting older

? Questions

1. Which of the people in the picture on the right would you describe as old? All of them, or just one or two? What makes people describe someone as being old?

2. What kinds of things do you associate with becoming old? What kinds of things *don't* you associate with older people?

3. What sort of stereotypes do we have about older people? How accurate are they?

4. What do you imagine are the best and worst things about getting old?

■ Too old?

By the end of the Second World War, in 1945, Sir Winston Churchill was 71 years old. For most of the previous six years, as Prime Minister, he had led Britain through one of its most difficult periods in history.

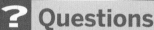

Although defeated in the 1945 election, he returned as Prime Minister in 1951, and finally retired in 1955 at the age of 81.

Nelson Mandela was also 81 when he stepped down as President of South Africa in 1999. In 1965 he had been imprisoned for his political activities against apartheid – the then official South African government policy of racial segregation. In 1990 he was released, and in 1994, at the age of 76, was elected President.

? Questions

5. Few achieve as much as Nelson Mandela or Winston Churchill, but most older people have worked, had a family, and faced some difficult times during their lives. What do you think older people have to offer to society?

■ One hundred and rising

In 1950, there were 300 people in Britain aged 100 or over. Today there are more than 9,000 centenarians. It has been predicted that by 2031 this figure will have risen to nearly 40,000 and by 2066 to 95,000.

Life expectancy Not everyone lives to such a great age. At the moment average life expectancy for men in Britain is 77, and for women it is just over 81.

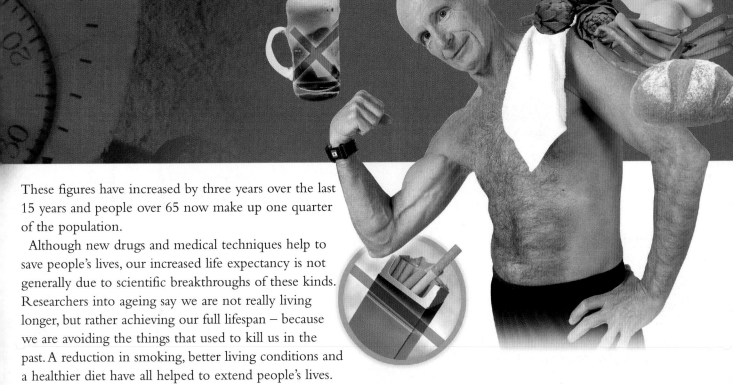

These figures have increased by three years over the last 15 years and people over 65 now make up one quarter of the population.

Although new drugs and medical techniques help to save people's lives, our increased life expectancy is not generally due to scientific breakthroughs of these kinds. Researchers into ageing say we are not really living longer, but rather achieving our full lifespan – because we are avoiding the things that used to kill us in the past. A reduction in smoking, better living conditions and a healthier diet have all helped to extend people's lives.

Health Although people are living longer, statistics show that the proportion of our life during which we may be in poor health has increased. Two-thirds of people over 75 have a long-standing illness.

Change

Many countries around the world now face decisions about how to adapt to having larger numbers of older people.

Here are some of the things that people say need to be done in Britain.

- *Accommodation* Older people usually need help with their living arrangements, either to stay in their own home or with special purpose-built accommodation.

- *Education and leisure* Many people now live for 20 or 30 years after they retire. If this time is to be enjoyable, more education and leisure facilities are required.

- *Help and support* It is now much less common for older people to live either with or close by their family. More need support and care with everyday living.

- *Healthcare* More medical facilities are required as the proportion of older people in society increases.

- *Pensions* People now draw a pension from the state for much longer than they have in the past. More money needs to be set aside for this – which means that taxes will have to be raised and people will have to save more themselves.

- *Retirement* Many people now retire before they are 65. If they stayed at work longer less money would be needed for pensions, and more would be paid in tax - which could be used for public services like education, hospitals and transport.

- *Transport* Better public transport services will be needed, as most elderly people don't have the use of a car. Without frequent and low-cost public transport, many elderly people will be almost housebound.

HIS **DAD'S** POPPING ROUND TO VISIT LATER ON...

102 TODAY

? Questions

6. How much responsibility does the state have to help older people, and how much should they be responsible for themselves?

7. If the Government had the resources to adopt only three of the above measures, which would you recommend? Why?

Older people
An age-old problem

Wards A-C
X-ray Dept

■ Standards of care

It was a cold day in February. Two elderly patients, Edith Vance and Dorothy Gately, needed to have an X-ray. The hospital was on a large site and the distance from the ward to the X-ray department was so great that an ambulance was used to carry patients between buildings.

As they were helped into their wheelchairs, neither patient was wearing a dressing gown or slippers. The blanket that they were each given did not properly cover their legs and feet.

A porter took the two patients together from the ward. He pushed Edith ahead of him. Dorothy was towed behind, travelling backwards.

When they reached the waiting ambulance, Edith was left in the roadway while Dorothy was put onto the ambulance lift. This process was reversed as they were taken from the ambulance outside the X-ray department.

While she waited, Edith asked what was happening. Neither the porter nor the ambulance driver replied.

The porter wheeled both patients into the X-ray building, and used the footrest of the first wheelchair to push open the door. As they moved through the entrance the heavy plastic doors swung back hitting Edith, who was coming through in reverse, on the back of her head.

While they waited for their X-ray, neither Dorothy nor Edith was told how long they would have to wait.

? Questions

1. Read the account of the two elderly patients. Make a note of anything about their treatment that you feel was wrong. Explain why.

2. A friend of one of the patients reported the matter to the hospital. An investigation took place. All the facts in the account were found to be correct. What action do you think the hospital should take?

Rationing

Medical treatment can be very expensive. There is no health service in the world that can give every patient everything that they need. There are always a lot of people who are ill and only a limited number of medical staff, drugs and medical equipment available to treat them.

Hospital staff therefore have to make decisions about who will receive the limited treatment that is available. Sometimes they decide that this will be based on age.

Unfair? Charlie Hughes is 85 years old. He has a heart problem, which his GP said could be helped by having by-pass surgery. This is an operation to repair an artery to the heart. Mr Hughes's GP sent him to see a specialist.

At the hospital, the surgeon said that he couldn't understand why Mr Hughes was there. 'There are men in their fifties still capable of earning a living who need this operation,' he said, adding that, at his age, Mr Hughes had little chance of ever having the operation.

Mr Hughes said he realised that only a limited number of people could be treated at any one time. But he felt that it would be much fairer if everyone, no matter what their age, put their name on a waiting list and received their treatment in turn.

❓ Questions

3. Do you agree with Charlie Hughes? Should older people have the same right to medical treatment as younger people?

4. Does a 17-year-old who needs treatment for cancer deserve to be treated ahead of someone who is 70? Try to explain the thinking behind your answer.

Age discrimination

In 2006 it became illegal to discriminate against someone at work because of their age, but the law applies only to people under 65. People over 65 have the right to ask for their employment to be extended, but employers do not have to agree.

However, age discrimination is allowed when an employer can show a sound reason for it. Discrimination against an older actor for a part written for a much younger person would almost certainly be acceptable.

A new law In 2008, the Government announced plans to replace all the different pieces of legislation, covering age, race, sex discrimination, etc., with one new equality law.

The Government also proposes to extend the coverage of age discrimination law to ban discrimination against older people in the provision of goods and services. This means that it would no longer be legal to turn down someone's application for a credit card or insurance policy simply because of their age.

❓ Questions

5. If local authorities or other public bodies want to develop a new scheme – such as a new hospital or school, or change a bus route – they have to assess its impact on ethnic minorities, disabled people, men and women. Some think that older people should be added to this list. Do you agree? Should older people automatically be consulted over developments of this kind?

Age discrimination at work? Not in my court!

Housing

This unit outlines the main rights and responsibilities of tenants and landlords and indicates further sources of legal help and advice.

A place of your own

■ Moving in

Tom has decided to live on his own for the first time, and finds a flat in a small block. Before moving in, he signs a written tenancy agreement with the landlord, who owns all of the flats in the block. This sets out the rights and responsibilities of the tenant and the landlord, which include:

- the length of the tenancy
- the amount of rent to be paid each month
- whether the rent can be increased, and by how much
- the notice that must be given to end the tenancy
- the landlord's responsibilities for repairs.

A tenancy agreement can be written or spoken. Written agreements are better, particularly when problems arise.

THE TENANCY AGREEMENT

Each tenant in the block has the same agreement.

- The tenant will pay rent of £625 per calendar month, payable a month in advance by cheque or standing order. The landlord reserves the right to increase the rent by up to £50 each year.
- The tenant will pay a deposit of £500, returnable at the end of the agreement, subject to any reasonable deductions for repairs or unpaid bills.
- The tenant will not make any alterations to the property without the landlord's written consent.
- The tenant is responsible for keeping the interior of the premises clean and in good working order.
- The tenant must report any disrepair in the property to the landlord.
- The tenant must not spend money on repairs without the landlord's written permission, except when acting reasonably to carry out emergency repairs for which the landlord is liable.

■ Moving out

Abyese and Michael, who live opposite Tom, are giving up their flat. On the day they move out, the landlord comes to check the condition of the flat and finds one of the wardrobes has been damaged. Abyese says that the hinge broke by accident earlier that week, and agrees to pay for the repair. The landlord says that she will take the cost from their deposit.

Deposits   Anyone moving into rented accommodation is normally required to pay the landlord a deposit, which is returned at the end of the tenancy. The landlord may keep some or all of the deposit to cover the costs of repairing anything that has been broken in the property that is covered by the tenancy agreement. However, the landlord cannot keep back a tenant's deposit to pay for the replacement of items that have deteriorated due to general wear and tear.

Since 2007, landlords have been required to use a

? Questions

1. Look at the terms in Tom's tenancy agreement. Are any unclear or unfair? Explain your answer.

tenancy deposit protection scheme, designed to protect the tenant from having their deposit withheld unreasonably.

Abyese and Michael have £400 of their deposit returned, and realise that the landlord has taken £100 to fix the wardrobe door. The landlord's receipt shows that she did the work herself, charging £40 an hour for labour, and £20 for materials.

? Questions

2. Abyese and Michael feel that the landlord's charges are excessive. Do you agree? What would you advise them to do? Explain your answer.

■ Repairs

One day, Tom notices a large damp patch in his bedroom ceiling. He calls upstairs to Arjit, who lives in the flat above. Arjit explains that that one of the bathroom pipes has been leaking for several weeks and that the landlord has promised to deal with the problem. Two days later, the problem worsens and water begins to drip into Tom's bedroom.

? Questions

3. What would you advise Tom and Arjit do? Should they contact the landlord or go ahead and arrange a repair? How should the work be paid for?

The landlord's responsibilities Landlords are responsible for looking after the structure of the building (windows, gutters, etc.) along with essential services, such as heating appliances (but not cookers), sinks, baths,

toilets, water, gas and electricity supplies. The local authority has a duty to intervene if the condition of the property is affecting the occupier's health or might cause problems for a neighbour.

■ Rent

The person who takes on the tenancy is legally responsible for paying the rent up to the end of the agreed period. If they want to leave sooner, they will have to pay the remaining rent due, unless a 'break clause' has been agreed beforehand. This allows the tenant to leave early after serving an agreed period of notice.

A landlord's right to increase the rent depends on the type and conditions of the tenancy agreement. If it is for a fixed term, the rent can only be increased if this is written into the agreement or if the tenant agrees to the increase. If there is no fixed term in the tenancy agreement the landlord can increase the rent if it is written into the agreement or by giving the tenant a written notice. A person who cannot afford to pay their rent may be able to claim housing benefit.

? Questions

4. All the tenants in the building receive notice of a £50 per month increase in rent. Gemma feels that she cannot afford to pay this. What would you recommend she should do?

Housing
Dealing with problems

■ While she was gone

During her final year as an art student, Mari – who is from Norway – shared a house with four friends. Each person had their own tenancy agreement and was responsible for the payment of their own portion of the rent.

Towards the end of her final year, Mari failed to keep a check on her personal finances. When she discovered that she was heavily overdrawn at the bank, she decided that not paying her rent was the best way of getting through to the end of her course, which was now only two months away. A fortnight after her rent was due Mari got a letter from her landlord's agent, saying that legal action would be taken if her rent was not paid within ten days.

Mari ignored the letter and the following month's rent. She felt completely overwhelmed by work and so decided to sort out the problem of the rent once her course was over.

Two days before her final assessment, while Mari was at college, the landlord's agent let himself into the house, went into Mari's room and took her passport, which was on a table by the bed. The agent then locked Mari's door and left a note saying that the door would be opened, and her passport returned, when she had paid all the rent that was due.

When Mari got home, she could not get into her room. She still had her coursework to complete – and nowhere to stay.

■ Help and advice

Although Mari's case is quite extreme, many people who rent (or lease) property have a problem at some stage with the landlord or tenant and need legal advice.

Negotiation with the landlord or tenant

Discussing the problem with the landlord or tenant is usually the first thing that should be done. This can take place face-to-face, on the phone or in writing. A written record of the discussion or any decisions taken is useful, particularly if further action becomes necessary.

Some landlords, especially local authorities and housing associations, have set enquiry and complaints procedures that tenants are expected to follow.

Advice agencies

A number of organisations provide help and advice for people with housing problems:

- *The Citizens Advice Bureau (CAB)* offers a free, independent and confidential service advising and helping people with a range of problems, including housing. The CAB has offices in most towns and cities, but their hours of opening are sometimes limited.
- *Shelter England and Wales* are housing and homelessness charities able to give advice on a wide range of housing issues. They have a number of offices in large towns and cities and a free advice line, open seven days a week.
- *Local council housing departments* can also provide advice for private and council tenants, and usually offer an out-of-hours emergency contact number.

Solicitors and law centres

Solicitors give advice, take action and represent their client in court. As a rule, solicitors charge for their services, but free legal help on housing matters is available to people on a low income. Public funding may also be available for a solicitor to represent a client in court, although this will depend on the type of case and the client's personal circumstances.

Law centres provide free legal advice and can represent clients in court. They tend to specialise in welfare matters, such as housing, employment, benefits and immigration, and were originally set up in the 1970s to help the legal needs of the poor and disadvantaged. There are 54 law centres in Britain, about half located in London.

The Ombudsman Service

The Ombudsman Service investigates complaints brought by the general public against a particular organisation. There are separate ombudsmen for financial services, estate agents, health and prisons. Council housing matters are dealt with by the Local Government Ombudsman; other housing issues are handled by the Independent Housing Ombudsman (IHO) – although the IHO has authority only over private landlords who are members of the scheme.

The word 'ombudsman' derives from a Swedish word describing someone who looks after the legal affairs of a group, such as a trade union. Before an ombudsman can hear your complaint, you must first have done everything you can to sort things out yourself with the person or organisation concerned. If you are successful, you may receive an apology or compensation, or your landlord may be required to change their procedures to prevent a similar problem from happening again.

? Questions

3. Read the following cases, and decide what actions should be taken by the person concerned.

Simone lives alone in a privately rented flat. Her landlord has a set of keys and regularly turns up, without notice, saying that he wants to check the condition of the flat. This makes Simone feel very uncomfortable, particularly when he looks around her bedroom, sometimes opening drawers and doors. Simone is reluctant to ask him not to come around unannounced in case he tries to evict her.

Harit moved into his flat in October and reported that one of the windows could not be closed. He called the landlord again two months later to ask why the job hadn't been done. The landlord said that this, and all the other repairs, would be done together in the summer – the most cost-effective way of getting the job done. Harit finds this unacceptable.

4. Look through the list of services available to people with problems over rented accommodation. What are their strengths and weaknesses? What suggestions can you make about how they might be improved?

Voting and elections

This unit looks at the different ways in which people can vote and asks if parts of our voting system should be changed.

A problem for the council

Labour councillors in Bristol had a problem. The cost of providing **public services** in the city was going up and up. The biggest expense was education. Like most other councils, Bristol spends more on education than on anything else.

To continue to provide people in Bristol with the level of education services that they were used to would mean the Council having to find more money. There was only one way to do this – by increasing the amount of **council tax** people had to pay.

What made it even more difficult for the Labour councillors was that they had only a small majority on the Council over their rivals, the Liberal Democrats – a majority of two.

Local elections were coming up in May. If there was just a small swing towards the Liberal Democrats, then Labour would lose control of the Council.

A decision had to be taken about spending more on public services – and it had to be taken quickly.

? Questions

1. Bristol City Council needed to decide two things. Firstly, whether to spend more money on education, and secondly, if they did decide to do this, how the extra cash would be raised.

   What are the different ways in which they can make these decisions?

■ What the Council did

Instead of deciding the issue themselves, the Labour councillors chose to let the people of Bristol decide. They held a referendum in which people simply voted on whether to increase council tax or keep it at the old rate. Voters were warned that if they voted against a tax rise there would almost certainly have to be cuts in the education service.

Out of the 278,000 electors in Bristol, 40 per cent voted in the referendum. Of these, 54 per cent voted against an increase in council tax.

Teachers were furious at the result and threatened to go on strike if any teacher lost their job. They pointed out that about 20 per cent of secondary students in Bristol go to private schools and don't therefore use the Council education service. They also said that some people in Bristol send their children to school in neighbouring authorities.

? Questions

2. Do you think the Council's decision to hold a referendum was a wise one? Give reasons for your answer.

I DISAGREE! IT'S MY RIGHT!

Democracy

■ What does it mean?

The decision on whether to increase council tax in Bristol was taken through a process of democracy.

This is a system of government where decisions are taken either by people directly or through representatives they have elected.

There are two types of democracy. Direct democracy is when people make their decisions together as a single group. Representative democracy is when people elect representatives to take decisions on their behalf, for example. a local councillor, an MP or a school councillor.

Representative democracy, as we practise it today, contains a number of further characteristics. It is a form of government that:

- reflects and responds to public opinion
- has regular and free elections
- allows people to criticise what it does
- protects the rights of individuals and minority groups.

? Questions

3. Which of the following issues do you think would be best decided by representative democracy and which by direct democracy? Why?

   a) whether to adopt the euro as our currency
   b) whether the country should go to war
   c) whether we should have more religious or faith schools
   d) whether to introduce identity cards.

4. What do you think are the advantages and disadvantages of each of these different types of democracy?

■ Referenda

A referendum is the process of putting a specific political issue to the people as a whole, rather than their elected representatives.

In 1975 there was a referendum of the British people asking if they agreed with Britain's continued membership of the European Community. In 1998, the people of Wales were asked if they wanted a separate assembly.

Some would like to have more referenda because they feel that they give people more of a say in decisions that affect them. Others disagree, believing that some issues are too complex to be reduced to one or two simple questions and that referenda can work to the disadvantage of minority groups.

? Questions

5. Are there any issues in Britain on which you think we ought to have a referendum? Explain your reasoning.

Key words

Council tax
A tax paid to the council by most householders based on the value of their property.

Local elections
Elections to choose councillors for the local council.

Public services
Services needed by the community as a whole, e.g. street lighting, education, waste disposal.

Voting and elections
The right to vote

Before 1918, only men in Britain were allowed to vote in elections for Parliament – and even then it depended on their age, wealth and class.

In 1918, the vote was extended to all men aged 21 and over, and to women of 30 and over. In 1928, the voting age for women was lowered to 21 giving them, for the first time, the same political rights as men. The present voting age of 18 was set in 1969.

Low turnout

The number of people turning out to vote in UK **general elections** has generally fallen in recent years. From 1964 to 1997 turnout ranged from 71 to 79 per cent. In the 2001 election it dropped to 59 per cent, rising to 61 per cent in 2005.

Natalie's story 'I did not vote in the last election. Do you want to know why?

'Imagine this. There are two blokes who fancy me. I'm not that impressed by either, but I am beginning to think I shall never ever meet anyone nice. If I was forced, I suppose I would say that one of them is not quite as bad as the other. My best friend said she thought he was "really quite nice". But my heart's not in it – even the thought of going out with him makes me feel slightly sick. So I decide to ignore them both and hold out for someone better.

'That's why I didn't vote in the last election. It wasn't because I had better things to do, or it was raining, or I think politicians are all alike or just because I couldn't be bothered. It was because there wasn't any party that really reflected my views.'

? Questions

1. What was Natalie's reason for not voting? Was it a good reason?

2. Is it important if people don't vote in elections? What are your views?

3. Some people would say that Natalie was wrong for not voting. Here are some arguments they might use. Which do you think are the strongest, and why?

No respect It is disrespectful to those who fought and died in two world wars not to protect the rights we have today.

No control By opting out she is letting politicians do what they like.

No say She is throwing away her chance to have a say in the way the country is run.

Responsibility She has a responsibility to vote as a citizen.

Sets a bad example Where would this country be if nobody voted at all?

Struggle She should remember the struggle that women had to get the right to vote.

Reasons

After the low turnout in the 2001 general election, researchers tried to find out why fewer people were voting.

It was discovered that the largest drop in voting was among those in the 18–24 age range, with 20 per cent fewer voting than in 1997.

Several explanations for the low turnout have been put forward:

Contentment People didn't vote because they were happy with the way things were.

All the same Many saw little difference between one political party and another.

Foregone conclusion Many thought that the Labour Party would almost certainly win the election (which it did) therefore there was little point in voting.

Irrelevant Some didn't vote because they felt that politics didn't affect them.

What can be done?

Here are some suggestions to increase the numbers who turn out to vote at elections.

Easy vote Let people vote from home by phone or the internet – or in their local supermarket.

Education Teach more about politics at school.

Incentives Allow people who vote to pay less in tax, say £10, or make voting compulsory, as they do in Australia.

Presentation The political parties should do more to interest voters and make clearer exactly what they stand for.

Real people Make a big effort to make politicians more like ordinary people. Try to increase the number of female, black and Asian candidates.

VOTER CARD

Please return this card to the Election Official after voting.

Lower the voting age to 16

Some people argue that it is time to lower the voting age to 16 as has already been done in three parts of the British Isles – the Isle of Man, Jersey and Guernsey.

? Questions

4. What is your opinion of the proposals to increase turnout at elections? Are there any that you particularly favour? Why? Have you any suggestions of your own?

5. There was a small increase in turnout in the 2005 general election. Can you suggest any reasons why this might have happened?

Key words

General election
An election to choose the MPs who will form a new Parliament, held every five years or less.

Voting and elections

Election to Parliament

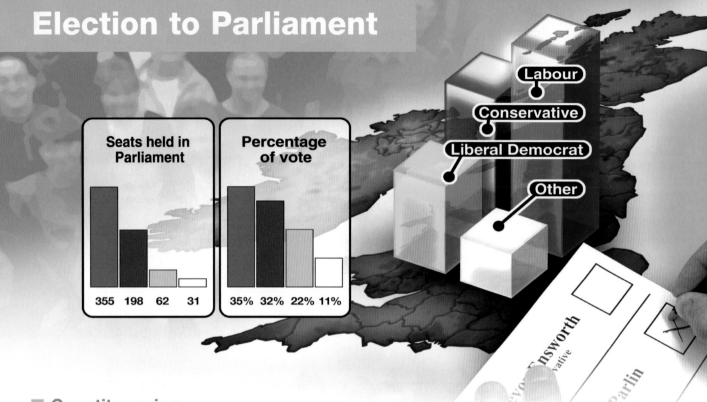

Seats held in Parliament

355 198 62 31

Percentage of vote

35% 32% 22% 11%

Labour
Conservative
Liberal Democrat
Other

Constituencies

There are 646 MPs in Parliament, representing the whole of the United Kingdom – that is England, Northern Ireland, Scotland and Wales.

Almost all MPs represent a registered political party and each represents a defined area, called a constituency.

Elections

If an MP dies or resigns, a by-election is called to allow people to elect a new MP for their constituency.

At least once every five years, a nationwide election must take place. This is known as a general election and voters in every constituency have the chance to re-elect or change their MP.

At the end of the general election, the party with the greatest number of MPs forms the new government, with the party leader becoming Prime Minister.

Voting

First-past-the-post Votes for general and by-elections in the United Kingdom are counted on a 'first-past-the-post' system. People each cast one vote and the winning candidate is the one with the most votes.

Above are the results of the United Kingdom general election, 2005.

? Questions

1. Which party won the election in 2005?

2. If the 646 seats in Parliament had been allocated according to the percentage of the vote that each party had gained, how many seats would the Conservative, Labour and Liberal Democrat parties have each obtained? Can you see any criticisms that might be made against the first-past-the-post system?

Other voting systems

In recent years people in Britain have had the opportunity to vote for their representatives in the European Parliament, the National Assembly for Wales, the Scottish Parliament, the London Assembly and the Northern Ireland Assembly.

The process of counting the votes is complicated because it uses (or transfers) people's second, third and fourth choices, etc., to decide who are the most popular candidates overall.

In a constituency where four seats are available, the four candidates who come top of the poll become the local representatives. People who favour this system argue that it allows voters the most choice and gives a fair reflection of the popularity of each party.

CANDIDATE	PARTY	YOUR ORDER OF CHOICE
EVANS, Annabel	Labour	
FERGUSON, Robert	Conservative	
KINGSLEY, Mica	Liberal Democrat	
JONES, Martin	Plaid Cymru	
RAMIREZ, Joseph	Green Party	
SAMPSON, Emma	Independent Socialists	

None of these has used the first-past-the-post system described above.

Instead, other systems have been used, designed to produce a more representative result. Three of these systems are described below.

List system In the election of Members of the European Parliament, voters cast one vote – not for individuals, but for a party. When the votes were added up, each party got the number of seats equal to the share of their vote. In this way a party that won 20 per cent of the vote was awarded 20 per cent of the seats.

Additional member system Everyone voting under this system has two votes. The first is cast for the *person* they want to be their constituency representative. The winner in each constituency is simply the person who gets the most votes.

The second is used to vote for their favourite *party*. After all these votes have been counted, further seats are awarded to additional representatives in such a way that the overall party representation in each area reflects that party's share of the vote. This system has been used in the elections for the Assemblies for Wales and for London, and also for the Scottish Parliament.

Single transferable vote This system is complicated for election officials to count, but very simple for the voter to use.

Each ballot paper indicates the number of seats available in the constituency and the names of all those standing for election. All the voter has to do is to number the candidates in order of preference.

? Questions

3. You can test the different ways of voting for yourself through a mini-election in your classroom.

- **Step 1** Select a number of candidates from the class. Choose at least one for each of the three main parties, but ideally include one or two minority parties, such as the Green Party.

- **Step 2** Make sure everyone has: a list of the candidates; an outline of their policies; a ballot paper.

- **Step 3** Everyone puts a 1 against the candidate of their first choice, and a 2 against the candidate of their second choice.

- **Step 4** Collect in the ballot papers and count the first choice votes. This produces the winning candidate (and party) by first-past-the-post.

- **Step 5** Now add the second choice votes to the first choice ones, and work out the total number of votes for each candidate. This uses the system of the single transferable vote.

4. Compare your results using the two systems. What do you notice?

Party politics

This unit looks at political parties and asks what influence the mass media has on our political views.

Join the party

Imagine

When Channel 4 conducted a poll of the British public to find the all-time top 100 British Number 1 singles, first place went to John Lennon's *Imagine*.

The words of the song carry a political message – a vision of the way in which society could be run. Many people probably wouldn't want to live like this - imagine no possessions – but for some, the words of the song do say at least something about the kind of society that they would like to see.

? Questions

1. Imagine you had the opportunity to change three things that you believe would benefit society as a whole. What would they be? You might like to think about this at three levels – locally, nationally and internationally.

2. Select one of your suggestions and describe how it might be achieved.

Political views

Many of the answers you gave to Question 1 were probably similar to those of the others in your group. Most of us would like to see an end to war or poverty, or an improvement in the environment.

Where we tend to differ, however, is in deciding *how* these things might be achieved. Do we end fighting by heavy bombing? Do we help the poor by taxing the rich? Do we reduce pollution by building nuclear power stations?

Ideas into action

Protest Sometimes we become so concerned about a problem we take action ourselves. When a local school or hospital is threatened with closure, parents, children and teachers may protest either as individuals or as a group.

Pressure groups If the issue is of wider significance we might join or support a national or international group. The RSPCA and Oxfam are examples of these. Campaigning organisations of this kind are known as pressure groups.

Political parties Political parties are organisations interested in a much wider range of issues than pressure groups. They also tend to have certain principles or ideas that run through many of their policies and have the overall aim of governing the country.

The Conservative Party has its roots in the landowning and business classes of the eighteenth and nineteenth centuries. It has traditionally stood for free enterprise – the right of people to make the most of their talents – and opposes excessive interference by government. It traditionally supports the monarchy and sees Britain playing an important and independent role on the world's stage.

The Labour Party was jointly formed in 1906 by the trades unions and a left-wing political group called the Fabian Society. It has almost always been associated with ways of improving the situation of working people, for example through council housing and the National Health Service, which it introduced in 1945. Until recently, the party has also believed that key industries – such as coal and rail – were so important that they should be run by the state.

The Liberal Democrat Party emphasises the need to protect individual rights and freedoms, particularly from abuse by the State, and supports close links with the remainder of Europe. Other policies include greater action to protect the environment, a reduction in tax for people on low and average incomes, and opposition to the introduction of identity cards.

Other parties include *Plaid Cymru*, which aims to secure self-government for Wales; the *Green Party*, which seeks to change the way we live to produce a fairer society, and one that ceases to damage the ecology of the planet; the *United Kingdom Independence Party (UKIP)*, which campaigns for Britain's withdrawal from the European Union; and the *British National Party (BNP)*, which seeks largely to repesent the interests of the UK's population that has Celtic, Anglo-Saxon and Viking roots.

In Scotland, the *Scottish National Party (SNP)* campaigns for Scotland to become an independent state.

? Questions

3. Try to find out these parties' policies on a number of issues. You could choose from a list that includes crime, education, environment, taxation, transport, etc.

4. It is sometimes said that there is little difference between the main political parties. What does your research (above) show about this?

■ Smaller parties

Candidates from 110 different political parties stood in the British 2005 general election. Nearly all of them were very small, often with just one candidate, and many focused on a single issue, frequently a problem in the immediate locality.

LEAVE THE KIDDERMINSTER HOSPITAL AS IT IS

KEEP OUR HOSPITAL SAFE

SAY NO TO HOSPITAL REDUCTION

Save our hospital! In 1998, the Government announced proposals to reduce the size of the hospital at Kidderminster in Worcestershire. Many local people opposed this, with 10,000 joining a protest rally outside the town hall. In 2001, the campaign received a major boost when retired local doctor, Richard Taylor, stood as an independent candidate for Kidderminster in the general election, campaigning against the Government's health reforms, and won – with a majority of more than 17,000 votes. In 2005 election, he was the only independent MP to be re-elected and hold his seat.

The party that Dr Taylor and his supporters formed is called *Health Concern* and campaigns mainly for the provision of proper medical care.

? Questions

5. What are the strengths and weaknesses of single issue parties?

Party politics
Where do you stand?

Left and right

Among the most common ways of describing people's political views are the terms left wing and right wing.

They originate from the days immediately before the French Revolution, in the late 1780s, when political power in France was largely in the hands of the aristocracy and the Church – those whose power and wealth had generally been inherited. There were huge differences in the standard of living between rich and poor. Ordinary citizens had no influence in government at all. Pressure began to build inside the country for change.

As this was debated in the French national parliament, those who supported keeping things as they were, sat on the right of the Assembly. Their opponents, who wanted greater equality and to break away from tradition, sat on the left.

The words 'left' and 'right' are still used today to describe types of political belief, although it is difficult to define each term accurately. Probably the most that can be said is that left-wing views tend to emphasise the need to make society more equal and to give greater support to the poor and weak. Right-wing views stress the importance of allowing individuals and businesses as much freedom as is practicable.

The political spectrum

Despite their shortcomings, the words 'left' and 'right' can provide a useful shorthand way of describing political views and policies by setting them along an imaginary line or spectrum, with 'far left' at one end, and 'far right' at the other. Quite often a person will have right-wing views on some subjects, and left-wing views on others.

Left wing Traditionally, this position has been occupied in Western countries by socialist parties, who believe in a society in which property is largely owned by the state, with little private ownership or wealth. The benefit of this, socialists argue, is that production is geared to the benefit of society, rather than the creation of the greatest profit for individuals. Socialism also, it is claimed, produces a fairer society, with less poverty and greater equality.

Right wing People with right-wing views tend to emphasise values of self-reliance, authority and obedience, and often argue for a smaller role for government in people's lives. They also usually support the existing patterns of order and authority although, in some circumstances, they may be in favour of moving society back to an earlier and different kind of social order.

? Questions

1. Look at the list of political views below and decide whether each one is broadly 'right wing' or 'left wing'.

   a) People earning a high income should be heavily taxed.
   b) We should abolish the minimum wage and allow employers to pay workers what they feel they can afford.
   c) Anyone who commits a serious crime should be given a long sentence in prison.
   d) Important industries, such as rail, power and water, should be in the hands of the government.

■ Political change

In recent years, the main political parties in Britain have moved away from some of their traditional values and beliefs in an attempt to appeal to the majority and become more electable.

During much of the 1980s, the Conservative Party, under the leadership of Margaret Thatcher, dominated British politics. Between 1979 and 1992, it won four general elections in a row. Many believed that the reason for the lack of success of the Labour Party, the main opposition, was Labour's determination to hold on to many of its left-wing policies and to continue to oppose changes brought in by the Conservatives.

By the mid-1990s, the Labour Party was changing. As it tried to persuade the public that it should become the new party of government it no longer rejected key Conservative policies, such as the sale of council houses and the privatisation of nationalised industries, nor did it promote nuclear disarmament or higher tax rates for the rich, as it had done in the past.

In 1997, Labour, led by Tony Blair, regained power and, for the following ten years, it was the Conservatives who faced a series of election defeats. Just like Labour before it, the Conservative Party responded by rejecting some of their previously held policies (like opposition to the minimum wage). Instead, the party aimed to offer a 'modern conservatism', more in tune with the events and values of the day.

e) Generally speaking, it's a good idea for the government to spend money on housing and benefits for the less well-off.

f) Eye tests, dental treatment and prescriptions should all be free for everyone.

g) The Royal Family is an important and valuable part of the British way of life.

2. Where would you rank your own views on the political spectrum? What number would you give yourself on a scale of one to ten, if one represented the extreme left wing and ten the extreme right? Explain how you came to decide on this figure.

3. Traditionally, Labour has been regarded as a left-wing party, with the Conservatives towards the 'right', and the Liberal Democrats somewhere between the two. How useful and accurate is this description today?

In order to answer this, you will probably find it helpful to look at the policies of each political party, which are available online on the Conservative, Labour and Liberal Democrat websites.

4. It is sometimes said that the main political parties have become too much alike. Do you agree with this? Would it be helpful for voters if there were greater differences between each party? Would it be better for the country as a whole?

Party politics
Newspapers

■ Read all about it

In 1995, not long after becoming leader of the Labour Party, Tony Blair travelled to Australia to meet Rupert Murdoch, owner of the *Sun* newspaper. His aim was to get the paper's support for Labour at the next election, whenever that would be.

Three years earlier, during the previous election, Labour had seemed to be cruising to victory until the *Sun* launched a series of personal attacks on their leader, Neil Kinnock – and Labour lost.

The support of the *Sun* was seen to be vital; and when the general election finally did take place, in 1997, the *Sun* gave Labour its support – and Labour won. Both Tony Blair and the newspaper itself believed that the *Sun*'s support had contributed to Labour's success.

Not everyone agrees that newspapers are as important as this, believing that people cannot be instructed how to vote, but there is little doubt that papers can exert a lot of negative power by criticising politicians and damaging their reputation.

■ Party preference

Most national newspapers tend to favour one political party in particular – although this is not as rigid as it used to be.

Until the mid-1990s the *Mirror*, the *Guardian*, and the *Independent* were the only national daily papers not to support the Conservatives. But, by the 2001 general election, most newspapers were recommending that their readers should vote Labour. In 2005, the *Mirror*, *Sun* and *The Times* supported Labour; the *Mail*, *Telegraph* and *Express* supported the Tories, with the *Guardian* and coming out in favour of the Liberal Democrats.

Bias Newspapers also exert political influence through how and what they report.

Michael Foot, Labour Party leader in the early 1980s, is remembered by many people for what he wore, rather than for what he did. At a Remembrance Day service in London he was photographed wearing an old jacket, which some thought was not suitable for such an occasion. Those newspapers that were critical of the Labour Party at the time gave this picture great prominence, suggesting that a party whose leader dressed in this way was not fit for government.

We have already seen (page 108) how some newspapers have used words such as wave, flood and tide to describe the arrival of asylum seekers, deliberately raising readers' concerns.

Profit All newspapers, and much of television and radio, are businesses trying to make a profit for their shareholders. Four companies publish 84 per cent of our daily and Sunday newspapers. This means that a relatively small number of people have a major influence over what we read.

■ Balance

Radio and television stations are under much tighter control than newspapers over the way they broadcast news and political information. By law, both state-run (the BBC) and independent radio and television stations must present and report news in a fair and balanced way. But this does not prevent radio and television from being criticised at times for the way in which they do report the news.

Unlike newspapers, radio and television stations must not tell their listeners and viewers whom to vote for in an election. In fact, on the day of the poll, the only political news that may be broadcast is simply that an election is taking place. There is no discussion of policies, winners and losers, or even the numbers turning out to vote, until the election is over and polling stations have closed.

JOHN MURRAY reporting from Tel Aviv

■ Public opinion

SO, GENTLEMEN, ARE YOU FOR OR AGAINST THE *EURO?*

Newspapers, radio and television, and the political parties themselves regularly carry out surveys into which party people favour and how they intend to vote. Opinion polls can be an important way of measuring what voters think.

However, some people feel we should follow the example of France and ban opinion polls completely during the period of an election. They say that knowing that the Conservatives are well ahead of Labour (or vice versa) distorts the whole election process.

? Questions

1. What factors do you think determine how people vote? Draw up a list and decide what you think are the most significant.

2. What is your impression of the way in which political events are reported? When people vote, do you think they really understand the political issues? Can you suggest any ways in which people can be better informed?

? Questions

3. The BBC undertook a survey in Wales asking people how they would vote in a referendum on the euro. These were the results.

- 41 per cent said they would vote *Yes* to joining the common currency
- 40 per cent said they would vote *No*
- 15 per cent replied *Don't know*
- 4 per cent said they would not vote at all

a) How might a newspaper in favour of Britain joining the euro present these figures?

b) How might they be presented by a newspaper that is against our membership of the euro?

c) How would you interpret the figures in an accurate and balanced way?

Campaigning

This unit shows how community action can be used to bring about change and asks what people need to do to improve their chances of success.

Home alone

Florence Okolo arrived in Britain from Nigeria to join her husband, who was a student in Manchester. Florence brought with her their two daughters, Awele and Anwuli. A year later, she gave birth to their third child, a baby boy.

The family had been together in Britain for two years when Florence and her husband separated. Florence's husband went back to Nigeria, taking his small son with him.

Florence stayed in Manchester with her daughters. She had a home, a job and she belonged to the local church. The girls attended primary school, and the whole family felt that they had become part of the community.

However, when her husband returned to Nigeria, Florence and her family ceased to have any legal right to remain in Britain as they did not have British citizenship. It took some time for this to come to the notice of the authorities – but four years after arriving here, Florence received a letter from the **Home Office** ordering her, Awele and Anwuli to leave.

Florence did not want to return to Nigeria. She decided to do as much as she could to ensure that she and her daughters stayed in Britain.

? Questions

1. Florence had to persuade the Home Office that she and Awele and Anwuli should not be deported. This would be difficult to do alone, as she had no family in Britain and relatively little money.

   What do you think Florence could do? Who could she find to help her with her case?

■ Help

Florence went to a solicitor who specialised in immigration cases of this kind. He agreed to take up her case, but also suggested that she should ask for help from Awele and Anwuli's school.

As soon as he heard about the problem, the head teacher, Mr Dalby, said he would do as much as he possibly could. He told the teachers and school governors and explained the situation to the whole school.

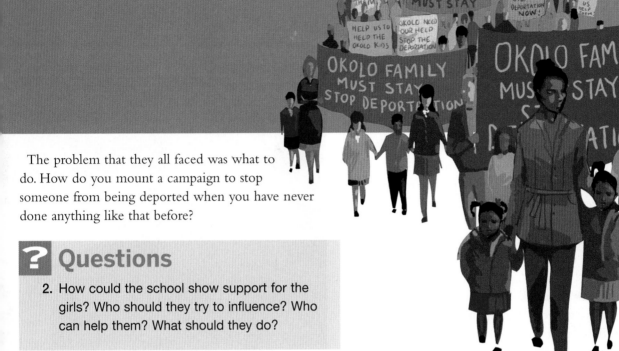

The problem that they all faced was what to do. How do you mount a campaign to stop someone from being deported when you have never done anything like that before?

? Questions

2. How could the school show support for the girls? Who should they try to influence? Who can help them? What should they do?

■ Tactics

Over the next four years Florence, her lawyer, the school and the church did as much as they could to make sure that Florence and her family stayed in Britain. This is what they did.

- *Putting the case* The lawyer prepared the documents that set out why Florence should be given special permission to remain in Britain. He made sure they were filled in correctly, presented on time, and clearly set out to show why it would be unfair to require Florence and her family to leave Britain.

  When Florence's application to stay in Britain was turned down, her lawyer prepared the papers for an appeal to the Home Secretary. Again he had to make out the best possible case on Florence's behalf.

- *Support* Letters, asking for help, were written to Florence's local MP and the city council in Manchester. The MP, the mayor and the city council all gave Florence their support.

- *Publicity* Florence and her supporters needed to get members of the general public to support her case.

  They wrote letters, made posters and talked to the media. They organised marches and demonstrations and always tried to make sure that the newspapers, radio or television covered them.

  They held rallies in Manchester outside the city hall and in one of the parks, and also took their case to London – with demonstrations outside the Houses of Parliament and the Royal Courts of Justice.

  They didn't just involve adults, but children too, particularly those from Awele and Anwuli's school.

■ Success

The Home Office at first turned down Florence's application to stay in Britain, but did allow her to submit an appeal. This too was rejected. With few chances remaining, her supporters were able to arrange for her to meet the Home Secretary, with her solicitor, to put her case in person. A month after this meeting, Florence received a letter giving her permission to stay in Britain.

? Questions

3. What do you think were the three most important reasons why Florence's campaign succeeded?

4. Who benefited from the campaign? Explain why.

Key words

Home Office

A government department with responsibilities that include law and order and immigration. The Home Secretary is the head of the Home Office.

Campaigning
We want our bus back!

■ Bus stop

The notice in the paper read 'As from 1 March the 7.55 a.m. service to Bedford will be withdrawn.'

'It is so annoying,' said Lena to her mum. 'We rely on that service to get us to school. If they take it off, we'll have to leave home at five past seven.'

'You could find out why they are doing it,' said her mum, 'and a letter of complaint wouldn't do any harm either.'

The following day Lena asked the bus driver why they were taking the service off. 'Not enough passengers,' said the driver. 'If they put it on half-an-hour later at 8.25, they can almost fill this bus with people going into town for shopping and work.'

? Questions

1. The next morning Lena asked some of her friends on the bus if they could do anything together to save the service. Here are some of the answers she received.

   - 'It's not our responsibility.'

   - 'No one will listen to us, we're just kids.'

   - 'We won't go to school.'

   - 'It's up to the bus company what it wants to do.'

   - 'We should get teachers or parents to do something about it.'

   - 'It's too complicated.'

   Do you agree with these comments? Write down what you would say in reply.

■ Starting off

Lena and two of her friends decided that they would write to complain. The next day they sent a letter to the bus company asking why the 7.55 bus was being discontinued and explaining how much they relied on the service.

A week later they received a reply saying that not enough people used the service and that it was therefore uneconomic. Although the company regretted the inconvenience, the service would still be changed in just under two months, as planned.

? Questions

2. If they are to continue with their campaign, what can Lena and her friends do next? Draw up a list of ideas, and then select those that you think would be the most effective.

■ Action

The three friends decided to organise a petition, collecting signatures from everyone who used the bus. They took some photographs of this and sent the pictures to the local newspaper and the petition to the bus company. They also made posters for display in local shops.

CHILDREN'S PETITION to save bus

'We also thought it would be a good idea to ask the school for help,' said Lena. 'After all, that's why we need the bus.'

The head suggested that Lena wrote to the county council, which has the power to keep important loss-making services going. She added that she and the school governors would also write a letter supporting Lena's case.

'We arranged a meeting with our local county councillor, and wrote to our MP. We also kept the paper informed about our campaign,' said Lena. 'We met the reporter several times and always tried to find a way of getting a photograph in as well. Twice we made it onto the front page.

'Eventually we managed to persuade the county council to talk to the bus operator about ways of getting the service put back on. The council has some money that they can use to subsidise a service if they feel it is worthwhile. Finally they reached an agreement, and, six weeks after our campaign began, the bus company decided not to cut the 7.55.'

? Questions

3. Make a list of the tactics used by students in their campaign.

4. What do you think were the most significant things that brought them success?

■ Pressure groups

Groups of people campaigning for change or trying to influence government policy are known as pressure groups. They can be local, very small and short-lived, like Lena's group, or they can be much larger, working all over the world, with a long history of involvement. Greenpeace and Amnesty International are examples of these.

Sometimes pressure groups work to represent or promote the needs of particular groups of people who all share something in common. This could be a trade union, a motoring organisation or even a group of people who suffer from a particular medical condition. These are sometimes known as *sectional* groups.

Other pressure groups are based around a particular *cause*, such as world poverty or cruelty to animals. Members of these groups come from all walks of life, often with no direct connection with the pressure group's purpose or subject.

Some pressure groups work closely with the Government – as *insiders* – and may often be consulted over proposed changes to policy or law. Others remain on the *outside* – perhaps because they choose not to become involved with the Government, or because the Government does not wish to become associated with them.

? Questions

5. Try to identify a different pressure group for each of the above categories – *sectional*, *cause*, *insider* and *outsider*.

Campaigning

How far should you go?

Police were involved in violent clashes with protesters today at a farm in Oxfordshire where cats are bred for medical research.

About 800 people gathered at Hillgrove Farm, near Witney, to try to force the closure of the business run by Christopher and Katherine Brown, who breed kittens for use in medical and other scientific experiments both in Britain and other parts of the world.

Ten arrests were made as protestors tried to break through a cordon of police surrounding the farm. At one stage a group of activists managed to climb over security fencing surrounding the farmhouse and pelt the building with stones, dislodging and damaging roof tiles.

The farm has become a constant target for animal rights groups, as they try to force its closure. Protest organisers said that breeding cats for medical research was completely unacceptable. 'We've waited too long for politicians to act,' they claimed. 'If we want these hell holes to close, we have to do it ourselves.'

Complaints about the demonstrations have been voiced by local traders who say that campaigners are costing them thousands of pounds in lost business. 'I've had so many customers ringing me up telling me that they are not coming to Witney,' said the owner of a furniture store.

Mr Brown claims that the kittens he bred were healthy and well looked after. 'These demonstrations will not drive me out of business,' he said.

POLICE IN VIOLENT CLASHES WITH PROTESTER

■ The use of animals in medical research

Animals are used for the benefit of human beings in many different ways; for food, clothing, sport, pleasure – and research. Some of these uses are more accepted than others, but the question of the use of live animals for medical research (known as vivisection) remains controversial.

The case in favour . . . A key argument of those who support using animals for medical research is that the outcomes and benefits of the experiments outweigh the pain and suffering caused to animals.

The Medical Research Council, a government-funded organisation supporting medical research throughout the UK, states that:

- Studying disease patterns in animals and their reaction to treatment, helps scientists understand much more about the ways in which the human body works.
- Many important drugs and treatments in use today have been developed with the assistance of animal experimentation. These include treatments for diabetes, heart surgery, organ transplantation and breast cancer.
- Complex parts of the human body, such as the brain, cannot be studied by using simple organisms alone.

About 30 per cent of the work that is funded by the Medical Research Council involves animals. However, the Council states that researchers must give sound scientific reasons for using animals, and explain why there are no realistic alternatives.

. . . and against Groups who oppose the use of animals in medical research believe that animals have rights, and should not be made to suffer for the benefit

? Questions

1. What is your position on the use of animals for medical research? Try to put forward at least three arguments in support of your view.

BREAKING NEWS

...RDSHIRE FARM THAT BREEDS ANIMALS FOR EXPERIMENTS

of humans. They also argue that:

- The data obtained from using animals in research is not always applicable to humans. Animal organs can function differently from those of humans.
- The laboratory conditions in which tests are undertaken do not reflect the same sets of conditions and circumstances that apply in real life.
- More use should be made of other forms of research, such as growing cells and tissues outside the body, using advanced computer modelling, and working with human volunteers, from which they state a great deal has been learnt about the functioning of the brain.

These groups are also concerned that the number of experiments in the UK using animals for research has risen slightly in recent years.

■ Closure

After facing demonstrations and protests by animal rights groups for more than three years, Mr Brown decided to end the cat-breeding side of his business. The activists were pleased that their campaigning and protests had succeeded 'We have forced this obscene business, that offends everyone, to close,' said a spokesman.

Mr Brown denied that he had given in to the protestors, but agreed that they had made his life almost unbearable. He said that his house had been damaged, his car fire-bombed, and that he, his wife and his staff had all been attacked. 'I am surprised how vicious some of these people are,' he said. 'I have simply bred cats and no medical research has taken place here.'

Thames Valley Police estimated their costs for the entire campaign to be £4.8m. This included the cost of bringing officers into the area to police demonstrations, providing protection for those targeted by protestors and the effects of having fewer officers available to carry out other police work.

? Questions

2. What comments would you make on the actions of the protestors? Do you agree with, or oppose, what they did?

3. At what stage does a protest or pressure group activity become unacceptable? Here are some views. Select one that you broadly agree with and one that you do not, and explain why.

   a) 'all protests should be peaceful and remain within the law'
   b) 'if you want to win, you just have to do what it takes'
   c) 'protests should stop when they start making life difficult for other people'
   d) 'you can't claim to be a force for good when you attack and terrify other people.'

4. Are some unlawful protests more acceptable than others? Explain your view.

National government

This unit looks at some of the roles and responsibilities of MPs and at the ways in which the conduct of a government may be examined and challenged.

Governing Britain

Members of Parliament

MPs have a mixed and varied job, generally dividing their time between working in Parliament, working in their constituency, and working for the political party they represent. Many MPs are also given extra responsibility for special subjects, such as transport or defence.

In Parliament, MPs attend debates, work on committees and vote on new laws, amongst other things. In their constituencies, they listen to constituents' concerns, and – if it's a matter for central government – may be able to help them deal with the particular problem.

A working week

Supporting the party

MPs are generally expected to support their party in debates and votes in the House of Commons, particularly over important pieces of legislation. An MP who fails to do this may damage the party's reputation and chances of success. MPs who are disloyal to their party usually find it difficult to gain high office.

Sometimes, however, MPs take a stand and forcefully speak out against their party. In 2003, a senior MP, Robin Cook, felt so strongly about the Government's decision to invade Iraq that he resigned his position as a **Cabinet** minister and returned to the **backbenches**.

You can find out how your MP voted in the House of Commons on various issues by accessing www.theywork foryou.com.

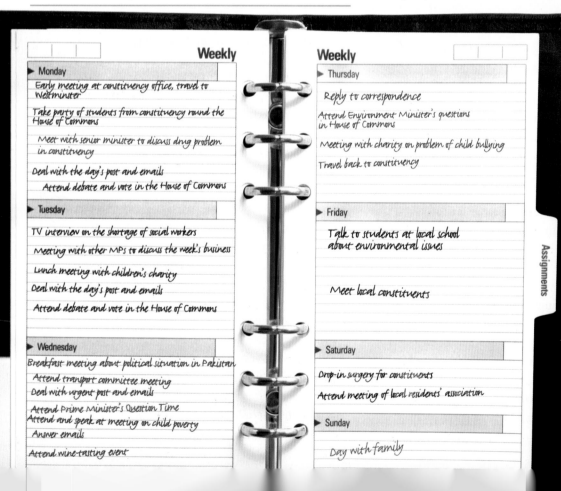

Weekly

▶ **Monday**
Early meeting at constituency office, travel to Westminster
Take party of students from constituency round the House of Commons
Meet with senior minister to discuss drug problem in constituency
Deal with the day's post and emails
Attend debate and vote in the House of Commons

▶ **Tuesday**
TV interview on the shortage of social workers
Meeting with other MPs to discuss the week's business
Lunch meeting with children's charity
Deal with the day's post and emails
Attend debate and vote in the House of Commons

▶ **Wednesday**
Breakfast meeting about political situation in Pakistan
Attend transport committee meeting
Deal with urgent post and emails
Attend Prime Minister's Question Time
Attend and speak at meeting on child poverty
Answer emails
Attend wine-tasting event

Weekly

▶ **Thursday**
Reply to correspondence
Attend Environment Minister's questions in House of Commons
Meeting with charity on problem of child bullying
Travel back to constituency

▶ **Friday**
Talk to students at local school about environmental issues

Meet local constituents

▶ **Saturday**
Drop-in surgery for constituents
Attend meeting of local residents' association

▶ **Sunday**
Day with family

Assignments

? Questions

1. Read the information in the diary opposite.

   a) What are the main types of work done by the MP?
   b) Most MPs have special areas of interest, such as education or defence. What do you think is the special area of interest for this MP?

▮ Constituency interests

In July 2003, it was announced that 13 disused American military and cargo ships would sail across the Atlantic to be broken up in the Teesside port of Hartlepool. The company proposing to carry out the work insisted that the ships contained only small amounts of asbestos and dangerous chemicals, and that all necessary safety precautions would be followed.

Although the work was expected to bring several hundred new jobs to the area, a number of groups immediately expressed their opposition. Environmentalists were concerned about pollution and damage to local wildlife, and some local people believed that it would give outsiders a bad impression of the area. One objector asked, 'If breaking up these old ships is so safe, why aren't the Americans doing it for themselves?' Members of Hartlepool Borough Council were also unhappy about the work.

The subject was discussed in the local media; all kinds of people were asked for their opinion, including Hartlepool's then local MP – Peter (now Lord) Mandelson.

▮ Conscience

Lord Mandelson chose to speak up for the project. He said he was satisfied that it would not pose a danger to health to people living in the area, and would bring much-needed work to the town.

Sometimes difficulties arise for MPs because of their personal beliefs. An MP with moral or religious objections to divorce, for example, may find it difficult

? Questions

2. Privately, Mr Mandelson felt that the work on breaking up the ships should be allowed to go ahead. However, as MP he had the job of representing the interests of everyone who lived in his constituency. What do you think he should do? Should he express his own views, or support the wishes of many of his constituents?

to support proposals for laws extending the grounds under which it might take place.

▮ Standards

MPs are expected to follow high standards in public life. They are required to be honest and open, and should not use their position for financial benefit. MPs who are found to have failed in this way may be required to make a public apology or be suspended from the House with loss of pay.

? Questions

3. As your local MP is about to buy a ticket for her car in a public car park, another motorist offers her a free ticket with an hour of unexpired time. What should the MP do? Explain your answer.

Key words

Backbenches
Seats, towards the back of the House of Commons, occupied by MPs who do not hold office in government or opposition.

Cabinet
The group of about 20 senior ministers responsible for final decisions about all the important areas of government policy.

Prime Minister's Question Time
A weekly opportunity for MPs to question the Prime Minister.

Controlling the government

Government power

In February 2003, at least a million people marched through the streets of London protesting against the Government's decision to go to war in Iraq. Smaller demonstrations were held in many other British towns and cities, but, despite this show of public protest, the Government continued with its plans for war.

Governments in Britain are, in theory, free to do whatever they wish, as long as their actions remain within the law. However, although Governments have wide powers, there are a number of ways in which they can be challenged.

Parliament

Parliament has an important role in examining the work of the Government. Members of both the House of Commons and House of Lords debate ideas for new law, and carefully check the proposed wording (see page 19).

The House of Commons   All MPs have the chance to comment on and debate government actions. A fixed number of days are also set aside for the **Opposition** parties to choose the subject for debate. This is an opportunity for them to criticise the Government's record.

In addition to this, each Wednesday between 12:00 midday and 12:30p.m., when Parliament is in session, the Prime Minister must go to the House of Commons to attend Prime Minister's Question Time, to answer questions from the Leader of the Opposition and other MPs. Other senior ministers must, at least once a month, also answer questions in Parliament about the work of their department.

Select committees   In 2009, a group of MPs criticised the Government for failing to do more to reduce the number of deaths on Britain's roads. (Road accidents are the largest cause of death of people between the ages of five and 35.)

The MPs were on one of a number of select committees with the job of examining and checking the work of the Government, with powers to call and question ministers and civil servants. Their findings are made public and the Government is normally required to respond to any criticisms. Select committees can investigate any area of government.

The House of Lords

The House of Lords is the Second Chamber of Parliament, and sometimes known as the Upper House. It has over 740 members, about 90 of whom have a hereditary title. Almost all the remainder are Life Peers, whose title is not passed on when they die.

Members of the House of Lords have two main functions in government: to make laws (see page 19) and to keep a check on the Government. In 2007, the Government decided not to go ahead with a plan to develop 17 large gambling casinos in various parts of the country after its proposals had been defeated in the House of Lords.

Judicial review

In 2006, the Mayor of London (then Ken Livingstone) announced plans to raise the congestion charge on 4x4 vehicles coming into London from £8 to £25 per day. The same charge would also apply to 4x4 drivers who lived inside the congestion zone, who were then paying only 80p a day. For them, the proposed charges represented an increase of 3025 per cent.

German car maker Porsche believed this was unfair, claiming that the increases were 'disproportionate' and would do nothing to reduce emission levels in London. They took their case to a court in London, for judicial review. This process allows individuals or groups to challenge decisions made by government departments, councils or other public bodies.

After hearing the evidence, the judges agreed with Porsche and ordered the increased charges to be dropped.

Elections

An important restriction on a government's power is the requirement for a general election to be held at least every five years (see page 132). In this way, a government that has become unpopular may be removed by the voting public.

Freedom of information

Under the *Freedom of Information Act 2000*, anyone can ask for information from a public body, including government departments. There are certain set procedures to follow and information may be refused if it is felt that handing it over is not in the public interest. Since the Act came into force, a great deal of information has been released.

? Questions

1. Draw up a list of those areas of life where you feel the Government 'could do better'. Identify the two or three areas that you feel are most significant and draw up a question about each one that could be put to the Government, and identify the person to whom this should be addressed.

   The names of ministers and the chair of each select committee can be found on the A–Z index on the UK Parliament website. Your local MP can be reached via www.theyworkforyou.com.

2. A request is made for the release of details of the Cabinet meetings in which the decision to go to war in Iraq was discussed. Normally these are not published for 30 years.

   Should the information be released? Is it in the public interest for details of Cabinet discussion to remain confidential – or is the public better served by understanding more about how the decision to go to war was actually made?

Key words

The Opposition
Political groups in Parliament who oppose the Government and its policies.

Devolution

This unit gives details of the Scottish Parliament and Northern Ireland and Welsh Assemblies and asks whether greater independence should be given to the people of Scotland and Wales.

Governing ourselves

A United Kingdom?

The United Kingdom is made up of England, Northern Ireland, Scotland and Wales. It hasn't always been so; at one stage the countries were quite separate. It wasn't until 1536 that Wales was formally united with England. Union with Scotland took place in 1707, and with Ireland in 1800.

'Union', however, is possibly not the word that people in Ireland, Scotland or Wales would have used at the time to describe their link with England. The 'union' was dominated by England, with power and influence largely resting in London.

The United Kingdom achieved its present form in 1922 when southern Ireland separated from the north with the creation of the independent Republic of Ireland. Today, about 84 per cent of UK residents live in England.

Differences and similarities Today the United Kingdom has three separate court and legal systems. England and Wales have one; Scotland and Northern Ireland each have another.

The main law-making body, however, remains the United Kingdom Parliament, based in London.

Devolution

The word 'devolution' means passing authority from central to regional government. In the United Kingdom there is now devolved government in Northern Ireland, Scotland and Wales.

The new Northern Ireland Assembly
A devolved parliament was created in Northern Ireland in 1922, but was abolished in the early 1970s because of the conflict between Protestant and Catholic groups. In 1998, following the Good Friday Agreement, the new Northern Ireland Assembly was established. It has 108 elected members and has the power to decide on matters of health, social services, environment, education and agriculture that affect the people of Northern Ireland. Arrangements are in place designed to make sure that both Catholics and Protestants share in the decision-making process.

The Assembly has been suspended several times because of a breakdown in trust between the political parties. The most recent suspension ended in 2007.

The National Assembly for Wales In 1997, a referendum was held in Wales proposing devolution. The 'yes' vote was just large enough to enable a National Assembly for Wales to be created in 1999. Its 60 elected members make decisions about some of the local issues affecting people in Wales; since 2006, the Assembly has had greater powers to pass legislation in areas such as education, transport and housing. However, central government at Westminster still has the power of veto.

The Scottish Parliament In the 1960s and 1970s an increasing number of people began to support the idea of greater independence for Scotland. A devolution referendum, held in 1979, did not get enough support, but in 1997, when another was held, people in Scotland gave a clear 'yes' to the creation of their own new parliament.

The Scottish Parliament opened in Edinburgh in 1999. The 129 Members (MSPs) have the power to pass laws affecting domestic policy in Scotland, including health, education, the environment, and the police. Scotland also has its own justice system (Scots law is different from

the law in England and Wales) and the Scottish Parliament has the power to make small changes in the rate of income tax, although it has not yet been used. The Scottish Parliament has far greater control over internal affairs than the Welsh and Northern Ireland assemblies.

Controversy A side effect of devolution was first raised by Tam Dalyell, a Labour MP for West Lothian in Scotland. During a debate in the House of Commons in 1977, he pointed out that the introduction of a Scottish Parliament would prevent MPs from England, Wales and Northern Ireland having a direct influence on domestic affairs in Scotland, whilst Scottish MPs would continue to be able to vote on matters affecting people in England (or elsewhere in the UK). This dilemma has become known as 'the West Lothian question'.

Heading for independence?

Devolution is sometimes seen as a first move towards independence, and this has particularly applied to both Scotland and Wales. Supporters of independence argue that Scotland and Wales can never be properly represented in a UK Parliament that is dominated by MPs from England. They also campaign for a Scottish and a Welsh voice on the global stage, with independent membership of the European Union and United Nations.

Supporters of independence for both Wales and Scotland deny that the countries would be too small to exist outside the UK, and that independence is the only way in which both countries can have full control over their own affairs.

Opponents argue that Scotland and Wales benefit greatly from being part of the UK, and would struggle to survive outside the union. They also add that a break-up of the UK would reduce the well-being of everyone in Britain.

? Questions

1. Draw up a list of arguments both in favour of and against independence for Wales and Scotland. Points in support of independence are given on the Plaid Cymru and Scottish National Party websites.

2. Which of the arguments on either side do you find most convincing? Explain why.

3. How would you answer 'the West Lothian question'? What changes, if any, would you recommend to the way in which matters are organised today?

Local councils

A day in the life

As Leah leaves the house in the morning, her mum asks her to put out the rubbish and recycling bins for collection. A few minutes later, Leah meets her friends at the bus stop at the end of the road, and they wait for the bus to school. Today it takes longer than usual, as the road is being resurfaced and a new pedestrian crossing installed. Leah gets to school a couple of minutes before registration.

At the end of the day, Leah goes to the public library to change a book, and then to the leisure centre where she trains with the local swimming club. Back home, that evening, Leah's mum tells her that her granddad had put his name down for one of the new special flats for the elderly, and that work would begin tomorrow morning on their neighbours' new extension.

? Questions

1. Read the passage above and try to identify all the local government services to which it refers.

Local services

Although the work done by local councils is not covered by the media in the same way as national government, local services play an important part in many people's lives. Local councils are responsible for about 25 per cent of **public spending** and employ more than two million staff, making them one of the biggest employers in the UK.

Education and social services tend to be the largest services provided by local councils. Other services include libraries, waste disposal, roads, planning, housing, fire and rescue, trading standards, parks, recreation and environmental health. Local councils are also responsible for civil defence and emergency planning.

Structure Local services in Wales and in large towns and cities in England are provided by just one body – known variously as a unitary, metropolitan or London borough. The remainder of England has a two-tier system of local government in which responsibilities are divided between district and county councils.

Funding Local government is funded by a combination of grants from central government, council tax, business **rates** and fees for local services. The amount of council tax per household is based on the historic value of the property in which they live. People living in households where they are the only adult pay a reduced rate of council tax, and those on a low income, with little savings, may be eligible for council tax benefit. Every year, local councils fix their own council tax rates, usually trying to maintain or improve their services *and* keep tax increases as low as possible. Sometimes this balance cannot be achieved and services are withdrawn or people face sharp increases in the amount they are required to pay. Older people, in particular, can find this difficult as the increase is almost always higher than any increase they receive in pension.

? Questions

2. Council tax rates are broadly based on the value of the property in which a person lives. People living in high-value properties generally pay more council tax than those in low-value properties.

   Do you think there is a better or fairer way of raising money to pay for local services? Consider the three alternatives below:

   Local income tax: 'Base the tax on a person's income. This would mean that rich people would pay more tax than the poor – which is fair.'

   Charging for local services: 'Keep council tax low by charging people only for the services they use. This would mean, for example, that people who put out large amounts of rubbish or recycling for collection would be charged more than people who leave very little. Small charges could be made for libraries and other services, and people who have cars would be required to pay more for using local roads than those who have not.'

   A population tax: 'Raise money on the basis of the number of people living in a house or flat. This means that a family of three or four would pay more tax than someone living alone – which is fair, because they are likely to use more services.'

■ Becoming a councillor

There are over 21,000 elected councillors in England and Wales. Candidates must be 18 or over, have their name on the **electoral register** of the authority in which they wish to stand, or have worked in the area for the past year. People who work for the local council are not allowed to stand for election in their local council area, and people in senior posts cannot stand for election in any local authority. People with a criminal conviction *may* also be barred from standing.

Generally speaking, fewer people vote in local than in national elections. In some areas the figure may be as low as 15–20 per cent. The national average turnout in local elections is around 30 per cent.

? Questions

3. What reasons can you suggest for a lower turnout in local council elections than in national elections?

4. What kind of qualities would you look for in someone standing for election to the council?

Key words

Electoral register
A list of names and addresses of everyone in the area who is registered to vote in local, national or European elections.

Public spending
Spending by government, at either local or national level.

Rates
A tax on property, imposed by the local council.

European government

This unit provides a simple outline of the basic nature of government in the European Union and asks students to consider how it could be made more democratic.

Governing Europe

A different way

The government of the 27 states that make up the European Union is very different from our own local and national government. Government of the EU is built around five separate bodies:

- European Council
- Council of the European Union (also known as the Council of Ministers)
- European Commission
- European Parliament
- European Court of Justice

European Council

The European Council is the name given to regular meetings, usually held in Brussels, between the heads of EU member states, including the British Prime Minister. One of the purposes of these meetings is to decide on important issues that the EU needs to examine. For example, in 2008 and 2009, the Council discussed ways of combating climate change and of dealing with the world's economic crisis.

Council of the European Union

The Council of the European Union (often known as the Council of Ministers) is the main decision-making body of the EU. It consists of government ministers from each member state with powers to decide policy, take decisions about how the EU is run, and negotiate with non-member states on behalf of the EU. It's at the centre of EU government, rather like the Cabinet in Britain.

Ministers from member states attend Council meetings according to the issues being discussed. If the subject is about farming or the environment, for example, the UK will be represented by the Secretary of State for Environment, Food and Rural Affairs.

Decisions Until the 1980s, decisions by the Council had to be unanimous; if a nation disagreed with a proposal, the measure could not be passed. However, as EU membership grew, this way of working proved to be more and more difficult. Today, votes are generally taken by a system of majority voting, with each member state having a certain number of votes, broadly based on the size of its population.

Currently, France, Germany, Italy and the United Kingdom each have 29 votes; smaller countries, such as Cyprus and Latvia, have 4 votes.

European Commission

Based in Brussels, the European Commission is the civil service of the European Union, taking care of the day-to-day running of the organisation. About 25,000 people work for the Commission, making it one of Europe's largest institutions. The Commission does several different jobs, including:

- drafting proposals for new EU laws or policies
- checking that EU laws and treaties are properly applied
- beginning legal action against member states or businesses that it believes are not following EU law
- representing the EU on the international stage.

European Parliament

The European Parliament is the only body within the EU that is directly elected. The Parliament meets in Brussels and Strasbourg, with offices also in Luxembourg.

Elections are held every five years, and it currently consists of 785 members (known as MEPs) – although there are plans for this figure to be slightly reduced. In the UK, as in all other EU member states, voting in European Parliamentary elections is open to any EU citizen, provided they are on the local register of electors. Voters in UK constituencies are directly represented by 78 MEPs.

Until recently, MEPs received the same salaries as the MPs of their national government – but this resulted in some huge differences in earnings. Today, all MEPs receive about 7,000 euros per month, together with certain expenses.

Powers Members of the European Parliament have the power to decide on many (but not all) aspects of EU law, together with the Council of the European Union. In recent years, MEPs have also been given some control over the money spent by the EU, and there are plans in future years for these powers to be extended.

European Court of Justice

The European Court of Justice (ECJ) is responsible for making sure that members states correctly follow and apply EU law. Located in Luxembourg, it is the highest court in the European Union and overrules all national courts. Member states must follow its decisions. The Court is made up of judges from each member state. They are amongst the most experienced in their field and are appointed for a period of six years. Cases brought before the Court cover a wide range of subjects. Recent cases include air quality standards in Britain; failure to protect fish stocks by allowing undersized fish to be sold in France; and the rights of workers in Britain over the age of 65 to carry on working.

? Questions

1. A criticism that is sometimes made of the European Union is that it is not democratic enough. Read through the information on each of the five main EU bodies, described above, and give each one a 'democratic score'. *Zero* would represent a body or structure without any democratic qualities, and a score of *five* would indicate a highly democratic organisation.

   Before undertaking this task, you may wish to do further research into how each body works.

2. On the same basis, what 'democratic score' would you give your local council and the British Government? How do your EU results compare?

Forms of government

This unit uses a case study of a dictator to ask
'How should a country be governed?'

The power to govern

■ The other 9/11

On the morning of 11 September 1973, two Chilean Air Force jets attacked the Presidential Palace in Santiago, the capital of Chile. At least 17 bombs are reported to have been dropped. One scored a direct hit. Tanks and armed forces were brought into position around the Palace and the President was called on to resign.

The **coup** was a complete surprise to the Chilean President, Dr Salvador Allende, who had been elected three years earlier. The attack was led by the Commander-in-Chief of the army, General Augusto Pinochet, whom Dr Allende himself had appointed only a few weeks before.

As President, Dr Allende had introduced a major programme of reforms designed to improve the Chilean economy and to give more power and wealth to poorer people. His policies, however, did not work well; soon the country faced chronic shortages, strikes and demonstrations.

General Pinochet explained later that he felt his forces had to take over government in order to save the country from further chaos.

? Questions

1. Do you think General Pinochet was right to act in the way that he did? Explain your answer.

2. What alternatives did he have? Were any of these more acceptable than taking power by force? If so, explain why.

3. Are there any circumstances in which it may be acceptable to force a government from power? If so, try to explain what these might be.

Taking control President Allende refused to resign, but committed suicide shortly before the General's forces stormed the Palace. There was little resistance in the remainder of the country, but over the following three months tens of thousands of President Allende's supporters were rounded-up and detained. At least 30,000 of Pinochet's opponents were tortured during this period and more than 3,000 killed. It was not uncommon for a group of prisoners from a slum or poor community to be executed as a way of forcing their neighbours to accept the military rule.

President Pinochet Soon after taking power, General Pinochet declared himself President of Chile. He banned all political parties and scrapped the country's **constitution**. He dissolved the Chilean Parliament (known as the Congress), and appointed military officers as city and regional leaders.

The press became heavily censored, and workers were banned from forming trade unions or going on strike. Political opponents (at home and overseas) were persecuted, and sometimes executed.

In 1980, President Pinochet's government drafted a new national constitution. This document said that Augusto Pinochet would remain as President at least until 1989, after which Chile would gradually return to **democratic government**.

A return to democracy In 1988, the people of Chile were allowed a referendum to decide whether Augusto Pinochet could remain as President for eight more years. They opposed the idea, and elections for President were held a year later. General Pinochet was defeated, and in 1990 he stood down as President (but remained in command of the army).

General Pinochet died in 2006, at the age of 91. Most people were pleased to see him go – but not everyone. Some believed that he had been a good leader, taking Chile from the chaos of the early 1970s to a country with one of the strongest economies in South America.

Dictatorship During his 17-year rule, General Pinochet had sole and complete political power in Chile. This form of rule is known as dictatorship. Dictators in the past include Hitler (Germany), Mussolini (Italy) and Stalin (USSR).

Democracy rules OK?

Britain, and most other developed nations, have what is known as a liberal democracy. Under this system, a small number of representatives are elected to government (the democratic part), but are required to govern in such a way as to protect basic civil rights. Without a requirement for justice and fairness (the liberal part), a dominant ethnic or religious group could deny all rights to other smaller groups. Although democratic, it would be unfair.

Western political leaders often urge less-developed countries to follow the liberal democratic route. In 2006, Prime Minister Tony Blair said that the world's security lay in spreading 'freedom and democracy'.

? Questions

7. It is sometimes argued that democracy should be introduced more slowly in less-developed countries. It is a mistake, the argument goes, to expect uneducated or inexperienced people to understand what is good for the country as a whole. These same people may vote for benefits that the country can't afford and could easily be led astray by parties that are not working in the national interest. How do you react to this view? Explain your answer.

? Questions

4. Look carefully at the information above outlining some of the ways in which President Pinochet ruled Chile. Write down those you find unacceptable.

5. Now try to explain why you feel these were not a good way to govern.

6. How should a country be governed? (You may like to answer this by drawing up five to ten principles of government.)

Key words

Constitution
The powers, rights, rules and procedures of government. May be written or unwritten.

Coup
Sometimes called a coup d'état: a sudden and violent overthrow of a government, usually by the military.

Democratic government
A system of government in which decisions are taken, either by the population directly or through representatives they have elected.

The power of the media

This unit looks at the influence of the media on our lives and asks whether there should be any changes in the way that it operates.

The front page

Almost every newspaper puts its main story on the front page. It is the section of the paper, apart perhaps from the sport, where most readers look first. It can also determine whether people choose to buy the newspaper.

The decision about which of the big stories a newspaper will use, and where they will go, is taken each day by a small group of the newspaper's senior journalists, including the editor.

A sample of the news in November 2008

Politics: The last few hours of the US presidential election campaign

Economy: Banks charging borrowers too much

EDUCATION: Schools breaking guidelines for pupil admissions

HEALTH: Terminally ill patients more likely to get drugs to give them an extra month or two of life

Sport: Racists claim that Lewis Hamilton's winning race was 'fixed'

Entertainment: Call to reduce the amount of swearing on television

Science: Scientists create clones of a mouse that has been dead and frozen for 16 years

HEALTH: Don't stretch before taking exercise

POLITICS: Presidential candidate's grandmother dies on eve of presidential election

? Questions

1. Put yourself in the position of the people deciding which stories their newspaper should use. Are there any on the list on the left that you feel should not be included?

2. Many papers today put three stories on the front page. Which three from the list would you select? Which story would you place first? What criteria did you use in reaching this decision?

3. The articles that you selected in question 2 show something about the kind of job that you think a newspaper should be doing. What is the purpose of a newspaper? Explain your views.

■ In the know

There are very few people whose job places them at the centre of events. Most of us learn what is happening through the media – newspapers, radio, television and more recently the internet.

This places people who either own or work for the media in a powerful position – giving them a huge influence on how people interpret world events.

MAIN SOURCE OF WORLD NEWS

72% Television
10% Newspapers
8% Radio

Source: Ofcom research, 2006

Newspaper sales and distribution 2008

Newspaper	Percentage
The Sun	26%
Daily Mail	17%
Daily Mirror	12%
METRO.co.uk	11%
The Daily Telegraph	7%
DAILY EXPRESS	6%
Daily STAR	6%
THE TIMES	5%
FINANCIAL TIMES	4%
Guardian	4%
Independent	2%

Source: Audit Bureau of Circulations, 2008

Television The main source of world and national news for most people in Britain is the television, although newspapers are more important for local news.

Newspapers More than half the adult population reads a newspaper every day. The *Sun* is the most popular.

? Questions

4. Since 1999, the percentage of UK homes with multi-channel television has risen from 26 to 87 per cent. This means that most of the population has access to 50–100 channels. Some programmes, on BBC World and CNN, will be seen by people throughout the world – others, on minority issues, will have a tiny audience.

   What do you imagine will be the advantages and disadvantages of such changes?

■ Ownership and control

Television The BBC began broadcasting radio programmes in 1922. Television transmission started in 1936, but was suspended with the outbreak of war in 1939. BBC programmes are financed through the annual licence fee that must be paid, with some exceptions, by every household with a television set.

Independent Television (ITV) came into existence in 1955. The terrestrial channels 3, 4 and 5 are funded through advertising, and cable and satellite services through subscription. Some additional channels are available through Freeview.

Newspapers Newspapers are commercial ventures. They depend for their survival on making money for their owners and shareholders. Most of the national newspapers in Britain (84 per cent of sales) are produced by four companies. The largest, News International, owns the *Sun*, *The Times*, the *Sunday Times* and the *News of the World* and has a 31 per cent market share.

? Questions

5. Over the past 30 years a relatively small group of companies has taken control of large sections of the media in Britain. It is now also common for newspaper groups to own a significant share of independent radio and television stations.

   What are the advantages and disadvantages of this situation?

The power of the media

Managing the news

■ Somewhere in Britain

During the Second World War many towns and cities in Britain were heavily bombed. Whilst those who were directly affected knew exactly what was going on, certain information was always kept from the public at large. Pictures and details of bomb damage were deliberately kept out of the papers for fear of giving information to the enemy and lowering public morale.

Most people are prepared to accept a certain degree of censorship in times of war, but is there a point at which it becomes unacceptable?

■ No publicity

After the September 11 attacks on New York and Washington, the British and American governments asked the media in both countries to limit broadcasts of Osama Bin Laden and his associates, who praised the attacks and warned that more would follow.

A spokesperson for the American President said that broadcasting propaganda statements from the man held responsible for the deaths of around 3,000 people could not be in the interests of the United States.

The material, he said, might encourage some people to volunteer to fight with the Taliban and could also contain hidden codes ordering further attacks on the West.

Some people thought that this approach was a mistake. They believed that if Osama Bin Laden and his group wanted to communicate with followers there were many other ways in which they could do it – such as via the internet or by mobile phone.

They also said that the real reason for this censorship was both governments' fear that publicity for Osama Bin Laden and the Taliban could reduce support for the war against them.

Bomb damage after an air raid on London, 1940. Photographs like this were not published until the war had ended.

? Questions

1. The difficulties of deciding whether or not to censor Bin Laden's videos was discussed at great length on the internet. Here are three extracts from messages published on the BBC site.

> **>Phil H, UK**
> 'By showing these tapes, the media are acting as pawns in Osama Bin Laden's campaign.'

> **>C.Meyer, US**
> 'Not to censor these tapes would be extremely short-sighted and ultimately irresponsible.'

> **>Safarali Senego, India**
> 'Let the truth be told. Do not give to the people only the western or eastern version of the truth.'

How do you respond to each of these points? On balance, what action would you recommend?

■ The role of the media

In 1988 Independent Television made a programme called *Death on the Rock*, investigating the circumstances surrounding the death of three members of the IRA (the Irish Republican Army), shot by the SAS (Special Air Service) in Gibraltar.

Since the 1970s, members of the IRA had carried out terrorist attacks in Northern Ireland and on the UK mainland.

Despite strong pressure from the Government, the programme was broadcast. Margaret Thatcher, Prime Minister at the time, complained that the media provided terrorists with 'the oxygen of publicity'.

More recently, certain sections of the press have been criticised for failing to support wholeheartedly the wars in Iraq and Afghanistan.

? Questions

2. What do you feel should be the role of the media in time of war?

■ A hidden message

News reports rarely give just the basic facts. The emphasis, the choice of subject, and the language used are all subtle influences on the reader.

A report in the *Daily Express* of a local council's decision to award its chief executive a pay rise of £9,000 contained words and phrases like 'fat cats', 'obscene' and 'credit-crunch busting'. Although, towards the end of the article, the newspaper did explain why the awards were being given, it was clear from the story as a whole that the *Express* regarded the case as a typical example of excess and waste by local councils.

Sometimes the process of managing the news is taken a stage further by those who are creating it. When Mrs Thatcher wanted to draw attention to the need to clear our towns and cities of litter, her staff arranged for papers and cans to be *deliberately* dropped on the grass in a London park so that the Prime Minister could be photographed doing something about the problem by picking them up!

Another example of an attempt at news management was the message sent to colleagues by a British Government adviser shortly after the second plane hit the World Trade Center in New York on September 11. 'It's now a very good day to get out anything we want to bury. Councillors' expenses? – Jo.'

? Questions

3. How was the Government adviser attempting to manage the news after the tragedy in New York?

4. 'There's nothing wrong with governments wanting to put themselves in the best light. It's quite natural. Everyone does it.' How would you reply to this view?

5. Finally, you might like to look at the evidence of bias in this unit on the media. What kinds of message do you think the authors are trying to give?

The power of the media
Freedom to publish

Violence There is concern that violence in the media desensitises us to the horrors of injury and suffering and encourages some people to copy the things that they hear, read or see on the screen. Violence is often represented as a way of resolving problems. Why not, critics argue, place greater emphasis on discussion, cooperation and compromise?

Some research has shown a connection between viewing habits and violent behaviour, but other work questions this. One of the difficulties in making a link is that anti-social behaviour is the result of many factors, and not only exposure to media violence.

Sex Until the 1960s the American film industry followed what was known as the Hays Production Code. This was an agreement that film makers were required to follow setting out what could and could not be shown. 'Excessive and lustful kissing' was forbidden and when a man and woman were pictured on a couch, each was required to have at least one foot on the floor.

Film and television today would be very different if the Code was still in force. Today there is criticism that there is too much sex on television. An official report recently warned that too many programmes with a sexual or violent content were broadcast before 9 p.m. One of the parents interviewed said, 'If there's not blatant sex, it's the sexual innuendos. I know it goes over a lot of children's heads, but it shouldn't be there.'

■ Number one

In 2001, Eminem received four nominations for the prestigious music industry's Grammy awards. Outside the Staples Center in Los Angeles, where the ceremony was held, hundreds of protestors gathered to demonstrate about his songs.

The violent and obscene content of the lyrics and anti-women and anti-gay sentiments have led people to call for his music to be banned. One album describes a rape fantasy and murder.

However, not everyone is offended. 'I don't think people will go out and start beating and killing people because of this album,' said one singer. Others defended Eminem's right to freedom of expression.

? Questions

1. How do you react to this problem? Would you place any limits on a singer's freedom of expression? If so, why, and what would they be?

? Questions

2. It is often said that if a person doesn't like what they see on television, they can always turn it off. How far do you agree with this argument? To what extent does it deal with the criticisms that are made about sex and violence on television?

Private lives

When author J K Rowling was out one day in Edinburgh with her family, she did not expect their picture to be taken and published in a Sunday newspaper. The picture concerned showed Ms Rowling pushing her 19-month-old son in a buggy.

Ms Rowling believed that there was no good reason for her son's picture to appear in the paper, and decided to take legal action to ban further publication of this and any other picture of the little boy without her permission.

Eventually, she succeeded in her claim. The case hinged on whether her little boy's right to privacy, as the son of a famous writer, was greater than the newspaper's right to publish the photograph.

The court decided that, in these circumstances, it was. The judge said that the little boy should have a reasonable expectation of privacy, and that it made no difference that he was the son of a famous parent.

Privacy Anyone who believes that their privacy has been invaded by the press may take their complaint to the Press Complaints Commission – a body run by the newspaper industry. If the Commission finds that the complaint is reasonable, it will order the newspaper to publish an apology.

The standard test in cases of this kind is whether the information revealed by the newspaper is '*in the public interest*'.

Additionally, the person concerned may take their case to court – either to obtain an order banning publication or to seek damages. However, this can be expensive and beyond many people's means.

Balance A difficulty here is the balance between press freedom and respect for privacy. Too many restrictions prevent newspapers and television reporting important information. Too few allow unreasonable intrusion into people's lives.

? Questions

3. Look at the following cases and decide whether you think that publication is acceptable. Explain your thinking in each case.

- The ex-boyfriend of a Coronation Street star sells his account of their life together to a newspaper. This includes intimate details of their sex life, which the paper publishes.

- A Premiership footballer, married with two children, has affairs with two women who both sell their stories to a newspaper. The footballer asks a court to order that his name should not be published.

- A radio presenter is photographed naked with her husband by the pool at their holiday villa. A photographer had rented the house next door in order to take pictures of the couple.

- A television personality visits a female prostitute, who sells the story to a newspaper. The man tries to stop the story being published.

Climate change

This unit asks what action should be taken in view of what we know about changes in world climate.

The problem

■ Breakaway

The Antarctic ice sheet is the largest body of ice on the planet. At its thickest, it is more than 4.5 km deep and holds 90 per cent of the earth's fresh water.

The amount of ice contained in the sheet fluctuates, with more in winter than in summer. It is quite normal for small parts of the ice sheet to break off – these form icebergs, which gradually melt as they drift north.

Scientists have known for many years that ice caps over both the North and South Poles are melting. However, in 2008 the British Antarctic Survey reported that a large plate of ice 'the size of Northern Ireland' was breaking off from the main Antarctic ice sheet.

For scientists who study the climate of the world, this is further evidence of climate change.

■ Evidence

Temperatures throughout the world are gradually rising, with a significant increase recorded over the past 25 years. Temperatures in the 1990s were the warmest on record. Scientists identified a further rise in world temperatures early in 2002.

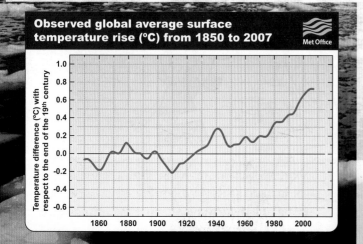

Observed global average surface temperature rise (°C) from 1850 to 2007
Met Office

? Questions

1. Look at the graph below showing changes in global temperature between 1850 and 2007. Make at least two observations about the information shown.

■ Explanation

Climate change over long periods of time is quite normal. There is evidence that a mini ice age began in Europe about 500 years ago and pictures painted of the River Thames in the early 1700s suggest that winters then were probably much colder than they are now.

However, scientists now almost universally agree that the changes that we have experienced since the 1980s are not part of this 'natural' variation in climate, but are caused by the burning of fossil fuels.

The greenhouse effect The atmosphere of the earth is warmed by energy from the sun. Much of this heat is reflected back into space, but some is trapped inside a layer of gases that surround the earth. This is called the greenhouse effect and stops the earth from cooling down too quickly. Without it, temperatures on earth would be 30° Celsius lower.

The layer of gas surrounding the earth is made up of water vapour, methane, nitrous oxide and carbon dioxide, all of which occur quite naturally as part of the cycle of life on earth.

However, the burning of fossil fuels over the last 200 years for power, manufacturing and transport is believed by most scientists to have changed the composition of this insulating blanket. Raising the level of greenhouse gases in the atmosphere has trapped energy from the sun that would otherwise escape – creating what we know as global warming.

Consequences

Scientists cannot predict exactly how the climate in specific parts of the world will change. But there is a general belief that the number of hot summer days in Europe, North America and parts of South America will increase and the number of exceptionally cold days will decline.

It is also predicted that higher overall temperatures will produce an increase in extreme weather conditions, such as high winds, floods and droughts.

The floods that have affected many parts of Britain in recent years have frequently been linked to global warming. But not all scientists agree that this is the prime cause of climate change. One of America's most experienced meteorologists argues that some of the predictions about climate change have been made from computer models that are based on an inaccurate view of the way in which climates work, and that most of the observable global warming is of natural origin.

Predictions

- *Sea levels* The melting of glaciers and ice caps could, by the end of the twenty-first century, cause sea levels to rise by between 15 and 90 cm. This would put a number of places at risk. Low-lying parts of Bangladesh would be flooded, as would parts of major coastal cities such as London, New York and Bangkok.

- *Farming* Patterns of agriculture will change as some crops become impossible to grow. This is likely to be expensive, to give rise to shortages and to affect some parts of the world more severely than others.

- *Flora and fauna* Some species of animals and plants will disappear, unable to adapt to changing climatic conditions.

- *Natural disasters* Forecasters predict an increase in natural disasters such as flooding, drought, disease and forest fires. All areas would be vulnerable, but experience suggests that disasters would occur more often in developing countries, where there are fewer ways of combating them.

? Questions

2. A very basic question facing governments today is whether they should take any steps to reduce global warming. What are the arguments in favour of taking action now? What are the arguments against? What would you recommend?

Climate change
The solution

■ Warning

The first person to use the phrase 'greenhouse effect' was the French mathematician Jean Baptiste Fourier in 1824. In 1938, a British meteorologist, G S Callender, gathered information from 200 weather stations around the world and found a rise in world temperatures over the previous 50 years.

However, it was not until the early 1970s, at a United Nations conference in Stockholm, in Sweden, that the nations of the world began to discuss global warming in any detail.

Despite this early effort, environmental problems, such as pollution and the destruction of natural resources, continued to increase. In the race for greater wealth, industrialised nations were causing environmental damage in their own countries and elsewhere, and risked leaving future generations with a whole range of environmental problems – and fewer natural resources.

In the 1980s, discussion also began to include ideas of 'sustainable development' – that is, how to meet the needs of the present, without creating difficulties or shortages in the future. Sustainable development encourages the conservation and preservation of natural resources.

■ Progress

In 1992, representatives from 172 states, including 108 heads of government, met in the Brazilian city of Rio de Janeiro, at the first of what are now termed the 'Earth Summits'. The conference was organised by the UN and produced a number of important international agreements.

Agenda 21 This is the name given to one of the plans for action, drawn up in Rio, designed to protect the environment *and* to support the development of economically less-developed countries in a way that provides for a sustainable future.

Agenda 21 (a strategy for the twenty-first century) requires all countries to work towards these aims at international, national and local levels.

❓ Questions

1. Water is a vital commodity that is required by everyone on the planet. Without fresh water crops, animals and people will die. However, in many countries, at various times, water can be:

   - in short supply
   - polluted
   - costly.

   Draw up a list of ways, using the principles of Agenda 21, each of these problems may be tackled at international, national and local levels.

CO₂ and Kyoto A second agreement reached at the Summit was the Framework Convention on Climate Change in which countries signed up to finding ways of reducing greenhouse gas emissions and, in particular, carbon dioxide.

After a great deal of preparation and negotiation, a point was reached in 1997 when most industrial countries were ready to sign a legally binding agreement promising to reduce their carbon emissions by a set amount. The venue for this was the Japanese city of Kyoto. By the end of the conference most industrialised countries had agreed to reduce their emissions by between five and seven per cent of 1990 levels between 2008 and 2012. Developing countries said that they too would reduce their emissions – in due course. The agreed rates of reduction were much lower than scientists had recommended – but, nevertheless, many people thought that the Kyoto agreement was an important step in dealing with climate change.

However, in March 2001, shortly after he became US President, George W. Bush announced that the United States had withdrawn its support for the Kyoto agreement. Explaining the reason for his decision, Mr Bush said that the agreement would harm the US economy and hurt American workers. It was unfair, he said, to expect industrialised countries to reduce their levels of greenhouse gases when developing countries were not expected to do so. Shortly before he came into

office, US President Barack Obama announced that he would overturn this decision and pledged America to cuts in greenhouse gas emissions.

No commitment Over the past 100 years, build-up of carbon emissions in the atmosphere has come largely from long-established industrialised countries, such as the USA, Germany and the UK. However, today, China and India are amongst the highest polluters, but both are reluctant to reduce carbon emissions at the same rate as more wealthy countries. China has said that its first priority must be its economy, and that rich countries must take more responsibility for tackling climate change.

? Questions

2. Do countries like the USA, Britain and Germany have more responsibility today to reduce their carbon emission than China and India? Explain your answer.

3. Who should be responsible for emissions from a factory making flat-screen televisions in China? Should it be the country where they are made, or the country (e.g. Britain) where they are bought and used?

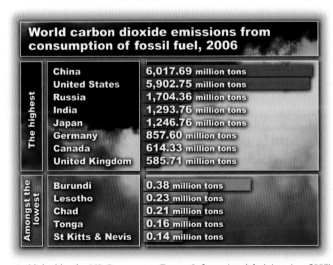

World carbon dioxide emissions from consumption of fossil fuel, 2006

The highest	China	6,017.69 million tons
	United States	5,902.75 million tons
	Russia	1,704.36 million tons
	India	1,293.76 million tons
	Japan	1,246.76 million tons
	Germany	857.60 million tons
	Canada	614.33 million tons
	United Kingdom	585.71 million tons
Amongst the lowest	Burundi	0.38 million tons
	Lesotho	0.23 million tons
	Chad	0.21 million tons
	Tonga	0.16 million tons
	St Kitts & Nevis	0.14 million tons

(published by the US Government Energy Information Administration, 2008)

Choices for the future

This unit examines the question of how Britain should obtain its energy supplies over the next 30–40 years.

Powering the nation

■ Blowing in the wind

In 2004, plans were announced to build 16 100-metre-high wind turbines along a ridge between the villages of Boxworth and Conington in Cambridgeshire.

Although the proposals, at first, received the support of the local council there were strong objections from many people living in the area. They formed a protest group and began campaigning to have the plans withdrawn.

Advantages   Its supporters say it has a number of advantages over other forms of energy. Wind power:
- provides clean energy
- is free
- is safe
- helps to conserve existing stocks of coal, oil and gas
- reduces dependency on fuel imports.

Disadvantages   Critics of wind farms say that wind power:
- works intermittently, producing only a limited amount of power
- can reduce CO_2 emissions by only a limited amount
- damages the local landscape – especially for those living nearby
- creates a noise hazard for local residents
- is of no benefit to the local community.

Time to change?   Most electricity in Britain is generated by burning fossil fuels – coal, gas and oil – producing significant amounts of carbon dioxide. Electricity generation produces 31 per cent of all UK emissions, making it the single largest source of CO_2 emissions in Britain. If the UK is to meet its targets of reducing CO_2 emissions by 60 per cent by 2050, cleaner ways of producing electricity need to be found.

? Questions

1. The Government plans to build 4,000 wind turbines in the UK by 2020. What is your immediate reaction? Do you broadly favour or oppose this move? Explain your answer.

2. In 2009, the Government Minister with responsibility for dealing with climate change in Britain said that 'it was socially unacceptable to be against wind turbines in your area – like not wearing your seatbelt or driving past a zebra crossing'. Why do you think he said this? Do you agree with him? Were the residents of Boxworth and Conington wrong to oppose the wind farm?

I ♥ WIND POWER

WIND OUT!

■ Thinking ahead

Today the Government faces a number of important questions about the way in which Britain will obtain its energy supplies over the next 30–40 years.

Problems Power stations, wind farms and energy-saving technology all take time to develop – so the Government needs to plan its energy policy at least ten or 15 years ahead.

The problem the Government faces is how to make sure that Britain can:

- produce enough energy to meet its needs.
- have secure and affordable energy supplies.
- produce the energy that it needs *and* keep its commitment to lower CO_2 emissions.

Where does our power come from today?

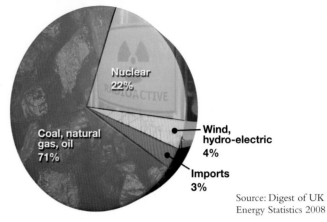

Nuclear 22%

Coal, natural gas, oil 71%

Wind, hydro-electric 4%

Imports 3%

Source: Digest of UK Energy Statistics 2008

Options Most experts agree that there is not just one single solution to these problems, but that the answer lies in choosing the right combination of measures. But what are they?

More coal and gas-fired power stations

Gas and coal-fired power stations can reliably provide Britain with much of its energy needs. **But** Britain now has to import increasingly large amounts of natural gas, making supplies possibly less reliable and more expensive. However, using more and gas will not cut CO_2 emissions, and may add to them.

New wind and tidal power plants

Wind and tidal power can provide safe, clean, low-cost energy, and help to reduce Britain's dependence on overseas fuel supplies. **But** there may be opposition to the siting of some plants, and wind power is not always able to provide a continuous source of power. Wind and tidal power projects tend to be located in remote areas well away from major cities, where the power is needed.

More nuclear power stations

Most of Britain's nuclear power stations are due to be decommissioned over the next 20 years, so new stations are needed to bridge the energy gap. Nuclear power stations provide an important low-carbon source of energy, and nuclear fuel supplies are assured. The nuclear industry says that modern reactors are safe and robust. **But** critics argue that a new generation of nuclear power reactors will provide

new targets for terrorists, increase the risk of serious accidents and create thousands of tons of dangerous radioactive waste, requiring expensive storage facilities.

Use less energy

More than 50 per cent of greenhouse gas emissions come directly or indirectly from buildings. The key to reducing these emissions lies in greater energy efficiency. **But** how can people be persuaded to use less energy without lowering their standard of living, and how can businesses stay competitive by using less energy?

Wait a little longer

The world economic downturn may lower the demand for energy, and give more time to develop and decide on the right option. **But** if the demand for energy does not decline Britain will not be able to generate all the electricity it needs and will fail to meet its commitment to cut emissions.

? Questions

3. Look again at the information above. Are there any options that you would immediately rule out? Give reasons for your answer.

4. In which order should the Government place the remaining options? What should be the Government's main priority? Explain why.

Civil law

This unit looks at the way in which a case of civil law may be dealt with.

Taking a case to court

■ On the bench

Mark plays five-a-side football every Monday night at the local leisure centre.

One evening the footballers were late getting into the sports hall because the trampoline club, which meets beforehand, had been slow to finish. One of the centre staff tried to clear everything away as quickly as possible, but failed to remove a bench that had been left by the wall on one side of the hall.

Mark noticed that the bench had been left out, but did nothing about it. He knew that everyone was keen to get started. Twenty minutes into the match, taking the ball down the wing, he sidestepped another player and ran straight into the bench. As he went down he fell badly on his right arm.

Mark spent the rest of the evening in casualty. He had a small cut above his eye, his shin was heavily bruised, and his right arm was broken just above the wrist.

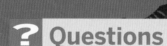 **Counting the cost** Mark is a self-employed builder and, because of his injuries, had to take a month off work – without pay. A week before the accident Mark had bought tickets for a music festival, costing £100 each, for himself and his girlfriend. With a broken arm, he was unable to drive and the tickets were not used.

? Questions

1. The actions of the leisure centre staff, the trampoline club, his team mates, the opposition and Mark himself all led in some way to the accident. Who do you think has the main responsibility? Explain why.

2. What do you think Mark should do next? You may find the information on the right helpful.

■ Next

Mark phoned Community Legal Advice who gave him the names of local solicitors specialising in cases of personal injury. He rang one of these and made an appointment, deliberately selecting a firm where the first half-hour consultation was free.

Advice The solicitor said she believed that Mark had a good case for claiming **damages** against the local authority, which ran the leisure centre, as the staff there had a legal duty to make sure that the sports facilities were safe for people to use.

However, the solicitor explained, taking action of this kind could be time consuming and stressful, particularly if the case went to court.

Costs The solicitor said that, under what is known as the 'no win, no fee' scheme, Mark would not be charged a fee if his case did not succeed – although he would face some expense in getting a doctor's report and travelling to court, if the case went to trial.

However, if he lost the court case, he would almost certainly have to pay the other side's costs. These could be at least £1,500. Insurance was available to cover this, but the cost of taking this out would be quite expensive.

If he won, as the solicitor believed he would, he could receive several thousand pounds in damages – but these

could be reduced, the solicitor pointed out, if the court decided that Mark had contributed to the accident himself. Under the 'no win, no fee' arrangement, his solicitor's costs would be deducted from his award of damages.

? Questions

3. What options does Mark face? Which one would you recommend that he took? Explain why.

Key words

Damages
Money awarded by a court to compensate someone for the loss or injury they have suffered.

Civil law

The county court

■ Seeking a settlement

Mark puts together evidence to support his claim. This includes his account of what happened, statements from two other players in the five-a-side team, a doctor's report, and details of his losses arising from the accident. These are sent to the solicitor acting for the local authority, which runs the leisure centre.

Special damages
Loss of earnings; 4 weeks @ £510 a week £2,040
Replacing glasses, damaged in the accident £180
Taxi fares, when unable to drive £70
Music festival tickets, unused £200

General damages
Pain and suffering from broken arm, a badly bruised shin, minor bruising to the head.

Shortly afterwards, Mark's solicitor receives copies of the evidence obtained by the local authority, indicating why they feel they should not be held responsible for Mark's accident.

■ Evidence in court

As both sides have been unable to settle their disagreement, the case now moves to court – about six months after the accident took place.

Mark's solicitor is claiming that Mark's injuries were caused by the **negligence** of the leisure centre staff.

Proof If Mark is to be successful his solicitor must show:
- that staff at the leisure centre had a responsibility to make sure that the sports hall was safe for playing football
- that they failed in this responsibility by not putting the bench away
- that this was the cause of Mark's injuries.

Inside a county court

County courts deal with a wide range of civil disputes. Most cases are brought by people trying to recover debts or money owed as part of a contract. However, county courts also handle cases involving personal injury, family matters, divorce and discrimination not connected with work.

Although the judge usually wears a wig and robes, other people in court are dressed in ordinary clothes.

Small claims track For personal injury claims up to £1,000 and for most other claims up to £5,000, there is a simpler procedure designed to save time and allow people to conduct their case without a solicitor. A typical case of this kind could be a holiday that did not live up to expectations.

The case is heard in an ordinary room, rather like an office. The hearing is quite informal – the judge does not wear a wig or a gown – and both sides are seated around a table. The judge will try to draw out the relevant information and having reached a verdict will explain the reasons for his or her decision.

? Questions

1. Put yourself in the position first of Mark's solicitor, and then the lawyer acting for the local authority. List the arguments that you think each side could make in support of their case.

? Questions

2. Now put yourself in the position of the judge. What verdict would you give in this case? Give the reasons for your judgement.

3. If you decide that the leisure centre staff were negligent, what would you award Mark in damages? Again give your reasons.

■ Verdict

The judge must decide, on the basis of the evidence, what happened in the sports hall that night – and who had responsibility in law for the injuries that Mark received.

In a civil matter such as this, the case must be proved 'on the balance of probabilities'. This is a lower level of proof than is required in a criminal court, where the jury must be sure that the defendant is guilty.

Guidelines for damages All judges use the same guide when awarding damages for injury. The current guide, in 2009, states that damages for a broken arm should be between £3,500 and £10,000.

However, if the judge decides that Mark should receive damages but that he contributed to the accident in some way himself, then the damages may be reduced. This is known as contributory negligence.

Key words

General damages
The name given to damages that cannot be precisely calculated – for example, the effect of pain and suffering.

Negligence
Careless action, or lack of action, causing someone loss or injury.

Special damages
Damages arising from an incident that can be specifically calculated – for example loss of earnings as a result of an accident.

Criminal law

This unit covers police powers, the work of the magistrates' court and the Crown Court, and asks whether offenders who are sent to prison should be required to serve their full sentence.

Arrest and charge

■ Confessions of guilt

On 22 April 1972, the emergency services were called to a house fire in Catford, south-east London. Once the fire was under control, police discovered the body of a 26-year-old man, named Maxwell Confait, who had rented a bed-sit in the house. An examination of Mr Confait's body indicated that he had died from strangulation before the fire had taken hold in his room.

Two days later, whilst the police were following up various leads, three small fires were reported nearby – one in a derelict house, one in a sports hut and the third on a railway line. The police soon picked up Colin, aged 18, for questioning. Colin, who had severe learning difficulties, immediately confessed to starting the three small fires, and went on to admit responsibility for the larger fire in Catford. He also told the police that a younger boy, Ronald, aged 15, had been with him at the time.

The police immediately went round to see Ronald, whom they arrested, along with his 14-year-old friend, Ahmet, who was with him at the time. All three boys were questioned separately and alone at the police station, and by the end of the day each had confessed to involvement in Maxwell Confait's murder. (Ahmet said that he had been present when Mr Confait had died, but claimed not to have taken part in his murder.)

All three boys said that they had been pushed around and assaulted during questioning by the police.

Colin and Ronald were both charged with murder and arson, and Ahmet was charged with the lesser crimes of burglary and arson.

? Questions

1. Look again at the information on the left. What comments do you have on the way in which the three suspects were questioned? How different is this from the way in which the same enquiry might be conducted today?

Trial   The trial took place almost six months after the murders, and each boy pleaded 'not guilty'. Each boy had a strong alibi for the time at which the deaths were believed to have taken place, and their defence lawyers claimed that their confessions were not reliable because of the physical pressure used by the police.

However, it took the jury three-and-a-half-hours to decide that the boys were guilty. Colin and Ronald were sentence to life imprisonment, and Ahmet to four years in youth custody.

Colin's father, however, was convinced of their innocence and led a campaign for the boys' release. Three years later, the Court of Appeal decided that all three convictions were unreliable, and the boys were released.

Enquiry   The Government also agreed to conduct an enquiry into the case, which recommended that changes should be made in the way in which suspects were treated by the police. Proposals for change included a recommendation for compulsory tape recording of police interviews with suspects.

The Confait case, together with a number of others in which the actions of the police were criticised, gave rise to major changes in the way in which police were allowed to carry out their enquiries. Today, many of the powers and duties of the police are set out in the *Police and Criminal Evidence Act 1984* known as PACE.

■ Rights on arrest

When someone is arrested and taken to a police station, the custody officer must give them written details of their rights. Under the *Police and Criminal Evidence Act 1984*, anyone who is arrested by the police is entitled to:

- know the reason for their arrest
- inform someone that they have been arrested
- be allowed to see a solicitor
- see the police **Codes of Practice**.

■ Questioning

Under 17   If the person arrested is under 17 years of age, the police must find a responsible person, known as an 'appropriate adult'. This is someone such as a parent, family member, carer or social worker, not involved with the case, who can advise and help the young person and do their best to make sure the interview is conducted fairly. The young person and adult can talk privately at any time.

THEN

Learning difficulties   The police should only interview someone with learning difficulties when an 'appropriate adult' is present, unless delay would result in a risk of injury or harm to property or people. This person could be a relative, a carer, or someone experienced in dealing with people with learning difficulties, who is not employed by the police.

The duty solicitor   In almost all circumstances, anyone who has been arrested, or goes to a police station voluntarily, is entitled to legal advice in private from either the duty solicitor or from a solicitor of their choice. The consultation with the duty solicitor is free. There are clear rules governing the ways in which the police can question a person, designed to prevent unfair pressure being placed on a suspect.

NOW

? Questions

2. Why do you think the law now requires an 'appropriate adult' to be present when a young person is questioned by the police?

3. 'Suspects only need the help of a solicitor when they have something to hide or have done something wrong.' What are the strengths and weaknesses of this statement?

Key words

Codes of practice
Official guidelines, issued by the Home Office, setting out the powers and duties of the police when collecting evidence.

Criminal law

Arrest and charge

■ The Crown Prosecution Service

In addition to changes in police procedures, cases like that of Maxwell Confait (page 176) also gave rise to changes in the way in which decisions were made over whether to charge a suspect and, if so, with what offence.

In 1981, a **Royal Commission** recommended to the Government that the police should no longer be responsible for both investigating a case and deciding who should be prosecuted. It suggested, instead, a system in which the police present their case to a second group of people who can look at the evidence and decide in a dispassionate and objective way whether there is enough evidence for the case to proceed.

In 1986, this gave rise to the Crown Prosecution Service, which is today responsible for charging and prosecuting most criminal case in England and Wales today. The Crown Prosecution Service (usually known as the CPS) deals with over a million cases each year in magistrates' courts, and more than 100,000 cases in the Crown Court.

In less serious cases, where the suspect admits the offence, the police may charge the suspect themselves. In all other cases, the evidence is passed to the CPS, who will decide whether to bring the case to court.

Prosecution The CPS is made up of trained lawyers who decide, in each case, whether there is a realistic chance of conviction and whether the seriousness of the crime merits a trial. If the answer to either of these questions is 'no', the case will be dropped. Lawyers in the CPS base their decision on whether:

a) they believe that there is more than a 50/50 chance that the case is likely to end in a conviction, and

b) going ahead with the case is likely to be in the public interest.

A prosecution usually goes ahead unless there are overwhelming reasons that this would not be in the public interest. Important factors here are the seriousness of the crime, the impact on the victim, and the mental state of the accused.

Crime scene?

Sophie, 19, and her friend Lauren, 17, are doing some shopping together. Lauren says that she wants to buy some make-up. Inside the store they spend about ten minutes in the cosmetics section talking to the shop assistant and looking at various products. Lauren chooses some lipstick, which she pays for, and tells Sophie that she has a few other things to buy. They agree to meet for coffee in 15 minutes.

Sophie looks around the store, picks up a chocolate bar and a bottle of water and goes to the checkout. She had just joined the queue when a security guard asks if she will come with him to the manager's office.

Sophie follows the guard into an office where Lauren is seated with two other people. The woman at the desk introduces herself as the store manager and explains that a few minutes ago Lauren was stopped outside the shop on suspicion of taking something without paying for it. She says that Lauren's bag and coat have been searched, and a small bottle of perfume found, valued at £49.16.

The manager then explains that the store's CCTV system shows them both examining the perfume and other beauty products in the cosmetics section. She says that Sophie can be seen talking to the sales' assistant just as Lauren slips something from the counter into her coat pocket, the same pocket in which the perfume was found.

Lauren says that the perfume was a present from a friend, which she hadn't got round to opening, and that it was probably her mobile phone that she had been seen putting in her pocket. Sophie denies all knowledge of the theft.

? Questions

1. At that moment, two police officers arrive. What do they need to know, who should they talk to, and what questions should they ask?

2. Lauren and Sophie are taken to the police station. What are their legal rights?

3. Both Lauren and Sophie claim not to have stolen the perfume. The police pass details of all evidence to the CPS. Using the information given in the case and details of the law, below, decide whether you feel the CPS should charge Sophie and/or Lauren with an offence. Give reasons for your answer.

4. Should the CPS support cases where the chances of a successful prosecution are rated as lower than 50/50? If they did, what are likely to be the implications?

The law

Under the *Theft Act 1968*, a person is guilty of theft if it is shown that they dishonestly took something that belonged to someone else, with the intention either of not giving it back or of keeping it permanently.

Anyone who helps someone commit a crime is normally guilty of the same crime themselves. A person who drives the getaway car in an armed robbery would be charged with the same offence as the man or woman who held the cashier at gunpoint.

The police refer the case to the Crown Prosecution Service to decide whether or not to charge them and if so, with what offence.

Key words
Royal Commission
An investigation and report into a particular area of law, often chaired by a senior judge. They often give rise to major changes in the law.

Criminal law

Inside a magistrates' court

Press

Reports of a trial may be given in the local or national media. In some circumstances, however, the press are not allowed to reveal the names of children involved in a case in order to prevent them from being identified. Victims of serious sexual assault are also protected in this way.

Witness stand

Legal adviser

A qualified lawyer, who advises magistrates on the law and on legal procedure.

Probation service

Probation officers provide magistrates with reports on the social circumstances of offenders, used to help magistrates decide on an appropriate sentence.

Public gallery

Magistrates

There are two kinds of magistrate, *lay justices* and *district judges*.

Lay justices are members of the local community, working as magistrates part-time, on average one day a fortnight, normally hearing cases in court in twos or threes. They are unpaid, except for expenses, and have no legal qualifications, but do receive training for their work as a magistrate. Lay justices are also known as *JPs*, or *justices of the peace*.

District judges do the same job as magistrates, but are trained and experienced lawyers and work in court alone.

Magistrates, clerks and solicitors wear ordinary clothes in court, and do not wear wigs.

Prosecution and defence

Lawyers for the prosecution and defence question each witness and each make opening and closing statements at the beginning and end of the trial.

If the accused has pleaded or been found guilty, the defence will probably suggest to the court why the defendant might be given a more lenient sentence – perhaps giving reasons why the defendant acted in a particular way or saying that the crime was totally out of character.

Defendant

Court usher

The usher escorts witnesses to and from the witness stand and helps with the smooth running of the court.

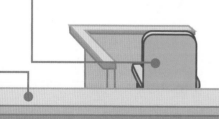

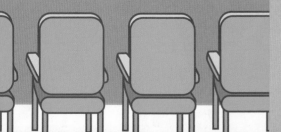

On trial

■ Criminal proceedings

Arrest   The police have the power to arrest anyone they reasonably suspect of committing a crime. That person can be held for up to 24 hours, 96 hours for a serious offence; longer for terrorist offences but must then normally be charged with an offence or cautioned or released.

Advice   In almost all circumstances, anyone who is arrested or goes to a police station voluntarily is entitled to see a solicitor. This consultation is free and in private.

Charge   If the police feel that they have enough evidence, they will charge the suspect with the offence.

The accused will then generally be released on bail and told when and where they are due to appear in court. If the offence is very serious, or the police have good reason to believe that the suspect will not attend court, they can apply to a magistrate to have the suspect held on remand in prison until the trial takes place.

Summons   This is an order issued by a court requiring someone to appear in court on a certain date. This procedure is used only in less serious cases.

Crown Prosecution Service   When the police have investigated an offence they pass the file to the Crown Prosecution Service who decides whether there is enough evidence for the case to proceed to court (see page 178).

Magistrates' court   All criminal cases are first brought to a magistrates' court – where most of them are dealt with. If the accused is aged 17 or under, the case will be heard in a youth court.

The more serious offences are passed on to the Crown Court if magistrates are satisfied that there is a reasonable case to be made out against the accused. In some cases, such as theft, defendants have the right to ask to be tried by a judge and jury, rather than magistrates. If the request is granted, these cases too are passed to the Crown Court.

Crown Court   A case in the Crown Court is heard by a judge, who presides over the trial and makes sure that it is run fairly. The verdict is reached by the jury and, if the defendant is found guilty, the judge will pass sentence.

Help with costs   The accused is entitled to help with the cost of legal advice and the presentation of their case in court. This is funded by the Criminal Defence Service.

Criminal law

In court

■ The magistrate's tale

Michael Marks is a magistrate in Wolverhampton. Until he retired a year ago, he was a primary school head teacher.

'I sit in court about 50 days a year. Last Thursday morning I had three cases of household burglary, three assaults, and cases of benefit fraud, driving under the influence of drink, and possessing Class A drugs. The drugs case and one of the assaults went on to the Crown Court.

'I also sit on the youth bench, dealing with young offenders, trying to help them not to re-offend and to again lead useful lives.

'I've lived in this area almost all my life – and I think the local knowledge that magistrates bring is invaluable.'

? Questions

1. Most magistrates are a) local b) unpaid and c) have no legal training. Write down what you feel are the advantages and disadvantages of at least one of these points.

■ Drink driving

This is one of the cases that Michael Marks had to deal with.

The defendant   Rhys Hughes, aged 34

The offence   Driving a motor vehicle while over the prescribed alcohol limit, contrary to Section 5(1) of the Road Traffic Act 1988.

Plea   Guilty

Prosecution evidence   At 2.00 p.m., on Thursday, 12 March 2009, the defendant drove his car into a stationary vehicle. No one was injured, but there was extensive damage to both cars.

Following a positive breath test at the scene of the accident, the defendant was breathalysed again at the police station. This result was twice the legal level.

Defence statement   Through his solicitor, Rhys Hughes explained that he had met his partner for lunch, and been told that she wished to end their three-year relationship. After his friend left, Rhys stayed in the restaurant and continued to drink. The accident occurred on his way back to work.

Mr Hughes has worked for his employer for 16 years and believes he will lose his job if he is sent to prison.

Sentencing

- The defendant must be disqualified from driving for at least one year, and up to a maximum of three years, unless there are special reasons not to do so.
- Magistrates will also impose one of the following sentences, depending on how much the defendant is over the prescribed limit:
  - a term of imprisonment of up to six months
  - a fine of up to £5,000, which is decided on the basis of the defendant's earnings. The average fine is £300–£400
  - a community penalty of up to 300 hours' unpaid work in the community
  - a Drink Driver's Rehabilitation Course, which, if undertaken successfully, will reduce the period of disqualification.

? Questions

2. Is there anything else you need to know about Rhys Hughes before passing sentence? Why would this information be useful?

3. Look at the punishment tariff above and decide how you feel Rhys Hughes should be dealt with. Now draft Michael Mark's statement to the court announcing the magistrate's decision.

Local justice

Strong efforts are now made to try to make sure that magistrates reflect, as far as possible, the community in which they serve.

However, although there is now an equal balance of male and female magistrates, people from ethnic minorities are under-represented, particularly in large towns and cities, as are those below the age of 40.

Magistrates' duties

Magistrates handle more than 95 per cent of all criminal cases, but also deal with some civil cases. (You can check the difference between civil and criminal law on page 11.)

Civil law cases include matters of family law, such as the care of children and problems people face after the break-up of their family.

Other parts of a magistrate's caseload include dealing with non-payment of council tax or fines, failure to have a TV licence, people who have broken a court order, and deciding whether a person who has been arrested should be remanded in custody or released on bail.

Youth courts

Specially trained magistrates also sit in youth courts, hearing cases involving young offenders below the age of 18. Youth courts are much less formal than adult courts, and members of the public are excluded from them.

Powers

Magistrates can impose a range of sentences. These include community sentences, fines of up to £5,000, and sentences up to six months in custody for cases tried in an adult court, and up to two years' detention and training for those heard in a youth court.

Qualifications

Magistrates must be between the ages of 18 and 65 when they are appointed and may continue to sit until they are 70. They must live close to the area served by the court to which they are appointed and must be of 'good character'.

? Questions

4. What kind of person do you think would make a good magistrate? List the sort of qualities you think that person should have.

5. Why do you think people give up time to work unpaid as a magistrate?

6. What measures can you suggest that might ensure that magistrates are more representative of the communities that they serve?

Criminal law
Crown Court

■ Trial by jury

Tessa, 27, received a letter summoning her for jury service. Her name had been chosen by computer at random from the local electoral roll. She is instructed to report to the local Crown Court in six weeks' time. Jury service, it explains, will last a minimum of two weeks.

Tessa is not very keen to go. She works as a midwife, and is always very busy. Two weeks away from her job will cause major problems.

She hopes the case won't be too serious, because she does not want to have to listen to details of violent offences, and is also worried about being responsible for sending someone to prison.

Excuse me Until relatively recently, two out of three people summoned for jury service either failed to attend or managed to have themselves excused. In 2004, the Government introduced a number of measures designed to change this, making it harder to get out of jury service and more likely that juries were typical of the population as a whole.

? Questions

1. What do you think Tessa should do? Does she have a duty to do jury service? Do you think pressure of work is a good reason for her to be excused?

2. Juries are supposed to reflect a cross-section of the general public. Does it matter if certain sections of the population are not represented?

3. Some people have argued that we should make it much harder for a person not to serve on a jury, with heavy penalties for those who fail to attend. What is your view?

4. Would you like to serve on a jury? Try to explain the reasons why, or why not. How would you respond to Tessa's point about her concern over sending someone to prison?

■ Juries

A jury sits in a Crown Court and has the job of deciding on the guilt or innocence of the accused, based on the evidence they hear in Court. A jury is made up of 12 adults, aged 18 to 70.

Ineligible　Certain people may not serve on a jury. These include anyone on bail, anyone who has served a prison sentence or detention order in the last ten years, anyone who has ever been sentenced to five or more years in prison, and anyone currently being regularly treated for mental illness.

Excused　It is now expected that everyone summoned for jury service will attend for the required period. (In the past MPs, ministers of religion, judges, magistrates, solicitors and police officers were all exempt.)
　Anyone called for jury service who finds that the time is inconvenient (e.g. by interfering with work or holiday plans) can ask for the date to be postponed. Government guidelines suggest that people will be excused from jury service only when they are likely to be completely unsuitable (e.g. insufficient understanding of English) or, as a result, will face severe financial hardship.

Finance　There is no requirement for employers to pay employees while they are on jury service, though many do. Jurors may claim travelling expenses and loss of earnings, but the maximum amount available is significantly below the national average wage. Some people, particularly those who are self-employed, can lose money when serving on a jury.

■ Six weeks later

Tessa knew that people are given the opportunity to do jury service usually just once in their life. She decided, therefore, that it would be a shame to miss this chance.
　Tessa arrived at the Crown Court, joining the 30 to 40 other people who had been called on that day. After a short introduction, they were shown a video, explaining what will happen in court.
　A court official then chose 15 people at random, including Tessa, and led them to the court, where a trial was about to begin.

Swearing in　Once inside the courtroom, another random selection was made. Twelve of the 15 people present were told to sit in the jury box. Again, Tessa was chosen. Each member of the jury was sworn in – but, just before this happened, both the prosecution and defence could challenge the choice of a person as a juror, if they had good reason.

I'M NOT *#@•%#* SWEARIN' IN!

? Questions

5. 'The state should pay a person on jury service their normal wage.' To what extent do you agree with this statement? Are there any problems associated with this view? What would you recommend to the Government?

Criminal law
Cause of death

During her two-week jury service, Tessa heard three cases. The first involved assault and the second, dangerous driving. The third was a charge of burglary and manslaughter.

■ Accused

The defendant
Graham Eden, aged 26

Charges
Burglary, contrary to Section 9(1) of the *Theft Act 1968* and manslaughter – that is, killing resulting from an unlawful and dangerous act.

Plea
Guilty to burglary. Not guilty to manslaughter.

■ The facts

On 16 January, Frank Bingham, aged 72, was alone in his house on Victoria Road. Around 3.45 p.m. a brick was pushed through a small pane of glass in the front door and a man entered the house. Mr Bingham walked into the hallway and asked the intruder what he was doing.

The man said that he was looking for cash. Shouting at Mr Bingham, he walked straight into the front room and started to search a small cupboard and then some shelves, pulling out the contents onto the floor. Mr Bingham said that he had no money in the house, other than £15 that he had in his pocket. The man took the money and left.

A witness later identified Graham Eden as the person she had seen running away from the house shortly before 4 p.m. His fingerprints were found on the front door and on several pieces of furniture. He was arrested two days later.

Immediately after the burglary Mr Bingham telephoned the police. Three officers were at his house in less than ten minutes. Two council workmen also arrived within an hour, called to repair the damage to Mr Bingham's front door.

Shortly after the police left his house, and about an hour and a half after the break in, Mr Bingham was taken ill. He had suffered a heart attack and was pronounced dead on arrival at hospital.

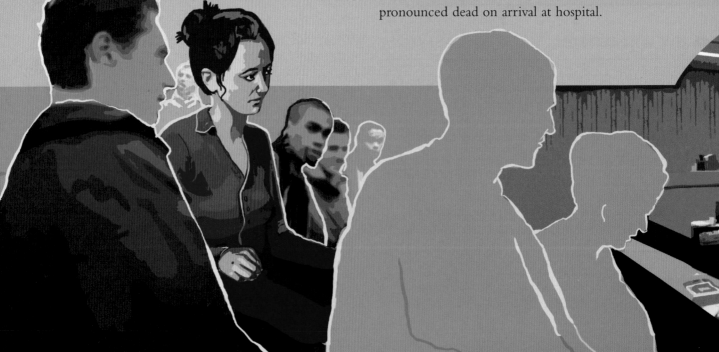

■ Evidence

Prosecution The chief witness called by the prosecution was Dr Geddes, who had examined Mr Bingham's body after he had died. He stated that, in his experience, the shock brought on by a stressful incident could last for at least an hour and a half, particularly for someone like Mr Bingham who suffered from a heart complaint.

Dr Geddes said that he believed that the shock and anxiety of the burglary undoubtedly brought on Mr Bingham's heart attack.

Defence Graham Eden did not give evidence, but lawyers for the defence called two witnesses – Dr Foster and Eileen Lewis, a neighbour.

Eileen Lewis stated that there was a considerable amount of noise outside Mr Bingham's house in the period immediately after the burglary. She heard several police sirens and loud banging at the front of the house as the door was being repaired.

Dr Foster, a heart specialist, said that stress brought on by the burglary would have subsided after 20 minutes,

■ Assessing the evidence

The job of the jury in a criminal trial is to listen to the evidence and to decide whether the defendant is guilty or not guilty.

Proof Criminal cases of law require a higher level of proof than civil cases. Members of the jury are told by the judge that they should reach a verdict of guilty only if they are really sure of the defendant's guilt.

Verdict A judge will ask the jury to reach a unanimous verdict. However, if they have been deliberating for more than two hours, the judge may call the jury back into court and tell them that a majority verdict of eleven or ten will be acceptable.

Secrecy Jurors are not allowed by law to discuss the case with anyone else either during or after the trial.

and could not be a cause of death one and a half hours later. If anything, it was likely to be the presence of the police or the workmen that triggered the attack.

■ Summing up

The judge told the jury that they must consider the opinions that they had heard in court very carefully. If they were certain that Mr Bingham died as a direct consequence of the burglary, they should find Graham Eden guilty of manslaughter. On the other hand, if they felt that Dr Foster was correct, or even that he may be correct, they should find the defendant not guilty.

❓ Questions

1. On the information that you have been given, would you find Graham Eden guilty or not guilty of manslaughter?

2. It has been suggested that juries should give reasons for their verdict. What do you think would be the advantages and disadvantages of this idea?

Criminal law
Prisons and sentencing

■ Serious crime

Until about four years ago, Richard, aged 42, had his own business selling second-hand cars. Everything was going well until the day he was suddenly taken ill.

In hospital, the doctor told Richard that he had a serious heart condition and needed a long period of rest. All plans for expansion were shelved, and the business was sold. After about six months Richard's condition started to improve, and he began to sell a few cars from home. Although this brought in some money, it did not make him a proper living.

One day, Richard's brother-in-law, Mark, called to ask if he would take a small package to Manchester – for a hundred pounds. Richard agreed. He didn't ask what was in the packet. A few days later, he was asked to make another delivery, and another a few days after that.

Mark worked as a security guard in a clothes shop, and Richard had always wondered how he managed to pay for the expensive car, the large house and the exotic holidays that he and his family enjoyed. Once he had started working for Mark, Richard knew the answer. Mark was part of a wide network that bought, prepared and stored drugs, in huge quantities, which were then sold in towns and cities across the UK. Richard had become one of Mark's couriers, carrying cocaine, amphetamines and cannabis to dealers.

The business came to a sudden end after a series of raids by the police. Ten people were charged with, and found guilty of, supplying illegal drugs. Their sentences ranged from 15 months to 17 years (in Mark's case). Richard was sentenced to four years' imprisonment.

■ Prison

Until the early the eighteenth century, prison was little-used in Britain as a form of punishment. Offenders might instead be required to pay a fine, to compensate their victims, or to face a public punishment in the stocks or the ducking stool – or face the death penalty.

By the mid-nineteenth century, prison had become widely used as a means of holding offenders, a trend that continues today.

Today   There are more people in prison today in Britain than in any other period in history. At the beginning of 2009, prisons in England and Wales held more than 83,000 people – the highest rate in Western Europe. France, with the same population as Britain, had 56,000 in prison, and for Germany, with 20 million more people, the figure was 73,000.

Between 1997 and 2007, the number of people in prison in Britain increased by 30 per cent, but the numbers found guilty by the courts remained largely

？ Questions

1. What is the purpose of sending Richard to prison? What do you think prison sentences are designed to achieve?

2. Are there any drawbacks in sending someone to prison? Explain your answer.

■ Release

Halfway through his sentence, Richard will be released from prison under licence. He will be able to return home and resume normal life, but will supervised by a **probation officer** for the remaining two years of his sentence. During this time he will be required to meet his supervisor and will have certain limits placed on what he can do. If Richard breaks the conditions of his licence or commits a further offence he may be recalled to prison immediately.

Dangerous offenders People who have been convicted of violent or sexual offences and who, the court believes, might reoffend in the same way are treated differently. Those convicted of an offence with a minimum penalty of two years' imprisonment, and a maximum of ten years or more, stay in custody until the **Parole Board** is satisfied that they may be safely released. This is known as an indeterminate sentence. It is designed to protect the public from someone who has been dangerous or violent in the past and might reoffend if released. Some prisoners in this category serve longer sentences than the set tariff for their offence.

constant. Although many new prisons have been built in recent years, overcrowding continues to be a problem.

In 2006, it cost an average of £40,992 each year to keep a person in prison in England and Wales.

Some 47 per cent of prisoners released from prison are reconvicted within one year of release. This figure rises to 59 per cent for those sentenced to less than twelve months.

? Questions

3. Richard will probably be released from prison in two years' time. Should he serve his full sentence? Explain your views.

4. In a recent speech David Cameron said that 'prison will not be a deterrent until all prisoners serve their sentence in full'. Do you agree? What might be some of the effects if his view became government policy?

5. Prisoners who have an indeterminate sentence have no idea when they will be released. Is it right to imprison someone under these conditions?

Key words

Parole Board
An independent body that decides whether a prisoner may be released from prison before the end of their sentence.

Probation officer
A court officer who can offer guidance to a court on the best way to deal with an offender, who ensures that offenders follow orders made by the court, and who works with prisoners both during and after their sentence.

Key words

Anti-Semitism Persecution and discrimination against Jewish people.

Asylum seeker A person seeking political asylum.

Backbenches Seats, towards the back of the House of Commons, occupied by MPs who do not hold office in government or opposition.

Bill The name given to a proposed new law as it passes through Parliament. If it is approved by both Houses, it receives the royal assent and becomes statute law, known as an Act of Parliament.

Cabinet The group of about 20 senior ministers responsible for final decisions about all the important areas of government policy.

Case law Law that has been established by the decision of a judge or judges that is applied in later cases to similar situations.

Civil liberties Freedoms or rights that are thought to be especially important, such as free speech.

Codes of practice Official guidelines, issued by the Home Office, setting out the powers and duties of the police when collecting evidence.

Community cohesion People sharing a sense of belonging and community identity.

Compensation A sum of money to make up for loss or damage a person suffers.

Constitution The powers, rights, rules and procedures of government. May be written or unwritten.

Council tax A tax paid to the council by most householders based on the value of their property.

Coup Sometimes called a coup d'état: a sudden and violent overthrow of a government, usually by the military.

Creditor A person or organisation to whom money is owed.

Damages Money awarded by a court to compensate someone for the loss or injury they have suffered.

Democracy Government by the people or by their elected representatives.

Democratic government A system of government in which decisions are taken, either by the population directly, or through representatives they have elected.

Electoral register A list of names and addresses of everyone in the area who is registered to vote in local, national or European elections.

Employment tribunal A court of law that decides on employment disputes, such as discrimination and unfair dismissal.

Equality and Human Rights Commission An organisation working to eliminate discrimination, reduce inequality and protect human rights. It is able to help people who feel they have been unlawfully discriminated against.

European Court of Human Rights A court that decides on cases in which it is claimed there has been a breach of the European Convention on Human Rights. It is situated in Strasbourg, in north-eastern France.

Exports Goods and services produced in one country and sold in another.

General damages The name given to damages that cannot be precisely calculated – for example, the effect of pain and suffering.

General election An election to choose the MPs who will form a new Parliament, held every five years or less.

Goods Items or possessions.

Home Office A government department with responsibilities that include law and order and immigration. The Home Secretary is the head of the Home Office.

Home Secretary The Government minister with chief responsibility for the maintenance of law and order in the UK.

House of Commons The section of Parliament made up of elected MPs.

House of Lords The section of Parliament that consists mainly of people who have been specially appointed as peers. At the moment, certain judges, senior bishops and people who have inherited a title are also members.

Inflation A continual increase in the prices of the things that people have to buy.

Interest rate The price charged to borrow money.

Internally displaced People who are forced to leave their homes, but remain within their own country.

Law centre Law centres provide free legal advice, on matters such as discrimination, housing or employment; they try especially to help people who would not otherwise be able to afford legal help.

Local elections Elections to choose councillors for the local council.

Migrant Someone moving from one place or country to another. Emigrant describes a person who leaves their region or country. Immigrant refers to a person arriving from another region or country.

Negligence Careless action, or lack of action, causing someone loss or injury.

The Opposition Political groups in Parliament who oppose the Government and its policies.

Parliament The main law-making body of the United Kingdom, consisting of the House of Commons, the House of Lords and the Crown.

Parole Board An independent body that decides whether a prisoner may be released from prison before the end of their sentence.

Political asylum Protection given to someone who is fleeing persecution in their own country.

Prejudice Disliking people from a particular group or category, based on their race, gender or sexuality, etc.

Prime Minister's Question Time A weekly opportunity for MPs to question the Prime Minister.

Probation officer A court officer who can offer guidance to a court on the best way to deal with an offender, who ensures that offenders follow orders made by the court, and who works with prisoners both during and after their sentence.

Public services Services needed by the community as a whole, e.g. street lighting, education, waste disposal.

Public spending Spending by government, at either local or national level.

Rates A tax on property, imposed by the local council.

Refugee A person who has been granted political asylum.

Royal Commission An investigation and report into a particular area of law, often chaired by a senior judge. They often give rise to major changes in the law.

Rule of law The idea that actions taken by the state (and those who work on its behalf) must be based on proper legal authority, as opposed to the whims or wishes of those in power.

Services Work that is done for payment, such as hairdressing, plumbing or repairs to a car.

Sex discrimination Treating someone less favourably because of their sex.

Shareholder Someone who invests in a company.

Special damages Damages arising from an incident that can be specifically calculated – for example, loss of earnings as a result of an accident.

Statute A law that has been passed by both Houses of Parliament and received royal assent; also known as an Act of Parliament.

Trading standards department People employed by the local authority to check that local shops and businesses are not breaking the law in the way that they trade. If they believe that an offence has been committed they can prosecute the trader.

Values Beliefs or principles that we hold to be important.

Young Offenders Institution Secure accommodation where young offenders between the ages 15 and 21 are held in custody.

Index